AIR FRYER

COOKBOOK FOR BEGINNERS

#2020

550 Simple & Easy Recipes
for Your Crispy Mood

Brian Orem

CONTENTS

MEAT RECIPES 72

BREAKFAST 159

SWEETS AND DESSERTS..182

INTRODUCTION

If air fryer is something you're completely new to - this book will be a great discovery for you. If you're an old bird, you'll enjoy it no less as the book is full of mouth-watering recipes for every opportunity.

Let's, however, start from the very beginning. What is an air fryer? An Air fryer is a kitchen appliance designed for cooking food without using too much of unhealthy processed oils that are so harmful to your body in many ways.

Even though there are many brands and different models of air fryers, the recipes in this book are ready to be prepared with just any model out there. Also, feel free to make little adjustments based on your taste, preference, or fantasy! You can adjust cooking temperate or time without worrying that it's not exactly the way this book tells you it should be.

Breakfasts, lunch, appetizers, desserts...no matter what you're up to reading this book - I've got you covered. Also, whether you're a carnivore, vegetarian, or vegan, you'll be able to find recipes you'll not want to put aside for months. And the best part is that you can choose between sticking to super healthy recipes and those that are...let's say a little bit more decadent. Don't be surprised when you salivate over the very recipe when reading it.

So let me tell you one thing upfront. This book isn't necessarily for those who watch every single bite they take. Many of my recipes are composed to be enjoyed with a hint of self-indulgence. That being said, it doesn't mean that if you're on a strict diet, you cannot take away anything from this book. You can maintain a balanced approach by establishing "cheat days," should your diet allow it. So let's now move on and see what is this Air Fryer craze all about...

AIR FRYER IN A NUTSHELL

The secret of Air Fryer is the unique cooking technology that uses hot-air that circulates inside the frier. It works no different than any other thermic-processing method, but without all the detrimental side-effects you get when you eat deep-fried foods, for example. Depending on the model, you may be able not only to fry but also to bake, broil, roast, rotisserie, and steam things as well. Air Fryer can also be a great substitute for your microwave, oven, or a stove. Except it's much healthier, easier, and faster to use.

On top of that, you can use an air fryer to prepare batters and marinades. The only thing that you should never put in there is generally speaking liquids. That means that things like broth or other soups are not coming at play here. Remember, safety comes first. But given the wide variety of other things you can do with it - it's a tiny con.

AIR FRYER BENEFITS

- *Almost no fat and oil involved*

Probably the biggest benefit of using Air Fryer is reducing the amount of oil or other fats you normally use to cook your meals. With the help of Air Fryer as much as one tablespoon is enough to gain the same effect as if you were cooking regular deep fried fries or spring rolls. As hot air circulates inside of the chamber, it makes the food crispy on the outside and tender on the inside.

- *Fewer calories*

Needless to say, as you reduce the amount of fat in your meals, their calorific value drops as well. So not only you eat overall healthier but even your "cheat meals" are less of a problem now. As you can see, using an air fryer can effectively help you drop some extra weight. Maybe it's time you reinstated your relationship with French fries?

- *It's compact, and it fits everywhere*

Because it takes so little space on the kitchen countertop, you don't have to worry about additional clutter. It also doesn't kill the aesthetics of your countertop. You can also put all the accessories inside the fryer, so you reduce unnecessary mess to a 0 level. See how you can start enjoying being in the kitchen again.

- *It's multifunctional*

If you have a proper Air Fryer, you don't need any other kitchen device. Depending on the model you have, it usually offers many different features and cooking modes.

HOW TO USE AN AIR FRYER?

- **Prepare the air fryer**

Some recipes will require using a basket, a rack, or a rotisserie. Some other recipes require cake or muffin pans. Before you pick the recipe and prepare your accessories, make sure they fit into your fryer.

-   Prepare the ingredients

Once you have all that's necessary to prepare your recipe, place the ingredients directly inside the appliance or use a basket, a rack, or a pan to do so. To prevent sticking use parchment baking paper or simply spray the food with a little bit of oil. A word of caution is necessary here. Never over-stuff the chamber with too much food. It will not cook to an equal measure, and you may find yourself getting frustrated chewing under-cooked bits. If you're planning on cooking more, multiple rounds of air-frying may be necessary.

-   Set the temperature and time

Most of Air Fryers use pre-set modes depending on the type of recipe. You can adjust settings such as time and temperature manually to make the best use of your recipes.

-   Check food during cooking

Many recipes will require you to control from time to time the content of your fryer while cooking. This is to make sure everything gets cooked evenly. Normally all it takes is to shake or flip the food to distribute it. For some recipes, however, you'll need to turn the food around some time halfway through the cooking.

Cleaning time

Before you start cleaning, plug the air fryer off and let it cool down. Once it's ready, stick to instructions you got from the manufacturer and never scrub or use any other abrasive material on the inner surface of the chamber.

AIR FRYER RECIPES

-   Which model to pick?

My recipes can go with any model you have. Whether you use an oven-styled type with horizontal racks, or perhaps one with a removable basket with a handle, it's just a matter of details. The recipes were tested on mine, which is a basic oven-type fryer with temperature and time setting functions only.

-   Keep an eye on timing

You may discover that different models cook at different temperatures depending on the model. Therefore, you should check the texture of the ingredients so that you don't burn or under-cook them. And remember, my tips are not written in stone so you shouldn't take them as gospel. Feel free to adjust and experiment with details according to your preference and common sense.

-   Using oil sprays

It doesn't matter what brand you go with, so you can choose your favorite one. I use PAM. You can also use olive oil and put it into a small spray bottle.

MEATLESS RECIPES

Potatoes, Spinach and Broccoli Croquettes

Prep + Cook Time: 1 hour 30 minutes | Serves: 3

Ingredients

1 lb red potatoes
2 cups water
1 ¼ cups milk
Salt to taste
2 tsp + 3 tsp butter
2 tsp olive oil
2 red peppers, chopped
½ cup baby spinach, chopped
3 mushrooms, chopped

1/6 broccoli florets, chopped
1/6 cup sliced green onion
½ red onion, chopped
2 cloves garlic, minced
1 medium carrot, grated
⅓ cup flour
2 tbsp cornstarch
1 ½ cups breadcrumbs

Directions

Place the potatoes in a pot, add the water, and bring it to boil over medium heat on a stove top. Boil until tender and mashable. Drain the potatoes through a sieve and place them in a bowl.

Add the 2 teaspoons of butter, 1 cup of milk, and salt. Use a potato masher to mash well; set aside.

Place a skillet over medium heat on a stove top and melt the remaining butter. Add the onion, garlic, red peppers, broccoli, and mushrooms; stir-fry for 2 minutes. Add green onion and spinach, and cook until the spinach wilts.

Season with salt and stir. Turn the heat off and pour the veggie mixture into the potato mash. Use the potato masher to mash the veggies into the potatoes; allow cooling. Using your hands, form oblong balls of the mixture and place them on a baking sheet in a single layer. Refrigerate for 30 minutes.

In 3 separate bowls, add breadcrumbs in one, flour in another, and cornstarch, remaining milk and salt in a third bowl. Mix cornstarch, salt and 1 tbsp of water. Remove the patties from the fridge. Preheat the fryer to 390 F.

Dredge each veggie mold in flour, then in the cornstarch mixture, and then in the breadcrumbs. Place the patties in batches in a single layer in the basket without overlapping. Spray with olive oil and cook for 2 minutes. Flip, spray them with cooking spray and cook for more 3 minutes. Remove to a wire rack and serve with tomato sauce.

Easy Roasted Balsamic Veggies

Prep + Cook Time: 30 minutes | Serves: 4

Ingredients

2 lb chopped veggies: potatoes, parsnips, zucchini, pumpkin, carrot, leeks
3 tbsp olive oil

1 tbsp balsamic vinegar
tbsp maple syrup
Salt and black pepper

Directions

In a bowl, add oil, balsamic vinegar, agave syrup, salt, and black pepper; mix well with a fork. Arrange the veggies into the fryer, drizzle with the dressing and massage with hands until well-coated. Cook for 25 minutes at 360 F, tossing halfway through.

Veggies & Halloumi Cheese

Prep + Cook Time: 15 minutes | Serves: 2

Ingredients

6 oz block of firm halloumi cheese, cubed
2 zucchinis, cut into even chunks
1 large carrot, cut into chunks
1 large eggplant, peeled, cut into chunks

2 tsp olive oil
1 tsp dried mixed herbs
Salt and black pepper

Directions

In a bowl, add halloumi, zucchini, carrot, eggplant, olive oil, herbs, salt and pepper. Sprinkle with oil, salt and pepper. Arrange halloumi and veggies in the Air fryer and cook for 14 minutes at 340 F. When ready, make sure the veggies are tender and the halloumi is golden. Sprinkle with olive oil and scatter with fresh arugula leaves.

Vegetable Mix with Dipping Sauce

Prep + Cook Time: 20 minutes | Serves: 4

Ingredients

2 lb chopped veggies: carrot, parsnip, green beans, zucchini, onion rings, asparagus, cauliflower
1 ½ cups plain flour

Salt and black pepper
1 ½ tbsp vegan cornstarch
¾ cup cold water

Dipping sauce:
4 tbsp soy sauce
Juice of 1 lemon
½ tsp sesame oil

½ tsp sugar
½ garlic clove, chopped
½ tsp sweet chili sauce

Directions

Line the Air fryer's basket with baking paper. In a bowl, mix flour, salt, pepper and cornstarch; whisk to combine.

Keep whisking as you add water into the dry ingredients to a smooth batter is formed. Dip each veggie piece into the batter and place into your Air Fryer. Cook for 12 minutes at 360 F, turning once halfway through; cook until crispy. For the dipping sauce, mix all ingredients in a bowl.

Parsley Corn Cakes with Green Onions

Prep + Cook Time: 25 minutes | Serves: 8

Ingredients

2 cups corn kernels, fresh or canned, drained
2 eggs, lightly beaten
⅓ cup finely chopped green onions
¼ cup roughly chopped parsley

½ cup self-raising flour
½ cup all-purpose flour
½ tsp baking powder
Salt and black pepper

Directions

In a bowl, add corn, eggs, parsley and onion, and season with salt and pepper; mix well to combine. Sift flour and baking powder into the bowl and stir. Line the air fryer's basket with baking paper and spoon batter dollops, making sure they are separated by at least an inch. Work in batches if needed.

Cook for 10 minutes at 400 F, turning once halfway through. Serve with sour cream and chopped scallions.

Friendly Crunchy Veggie Bites

Prep + Cook Time: 1 hour 30 minutes | Serves: 13 to 16 bites

Ingredients

1 medium cauliflower, cut in florets
6 medium carrots, diced
1 medium broccoli, cut in florets
1 onion, diced
½ cup garden peas
2 leeks, sliced thinly
1 small zucchini, chopped
⅓ cup flour
1 tbsp garlic paste

2 tbsp olive oil
1 tbsp curry paste
2 tsp mixed spice
1 tsp coriander
1 tsp cumin powder
1 ½ cups milk
1 tsp ginger paste
Salt and black pepper to taste

Directions

In a pot, steam all vegetables, except the leek and courgette, for 10 minutes; set aside. Place a wok over medium heat, and add the onion, ginger, garlic and olive oil. Stir-fry until onions turn transparent.

Add in leek, zucchini and curry paste. Stir and cook for 5 minutes. Add all spices and milk; stir and simmer for 10 minutes.

Once the sauce has reduced, add the steamed veggies; mix evenly. Transfer to a bowl and refrigerate for 1 hour. Remove the veggie base from the fridge and mold into bite sizes. Arrange the veggie bites in the fryer basket and cook at 350 F for 10 minutes. Once ready, serve warm with yogurt sauce.

Savory Brussels Sprouts with Spicy Aioli Salsa

Prep + Cook Time: 25 minutes | Serves: 4

Ingredients

1 lb brussels sprouts, trimmed and excess leaves removed
Salt and black pepper to taste
1 ½ tbsp olive oil
2 tsp lemon juice

1 tsp powdered chili
3 cloves garlic
. ¾ cup mayonnaise, whole egg
2 cups water

Directions

Place a skillet over medium heat on a stove top, add the garlic cloves with the peels on it and roast until lightly brown and fragrant. Remove the skillet and place a pot with water over the same heat; bring to a boil.

Using a knife, cut the brussels sprouts in halves lengthwise. Add to the boiling water to blanch for just 3 minutes. Drain through a sieve and set aside. Preheat the Air Fryer to 350 F.

Remove the garlic from the skillet to a plate; peel, crush and set aside. Add olive oil to the skillet and light the fire to medium heat on the stove top.

Stir in the brussels sprouts, season with pepper and salt; sauté for 2 minutes and turn off the heat. Pour the brussels sprouts in the fryer's basket and cook for 5 minutes.

Meanwhile, make the garlic aioli. In a bowl, add mayonnaise, crushed garlic, lemon juice, powdered chili, pepper and salt; mix well. Remove the brussels sprouts onto a serving bowl and serve with the garlic aioli.

Vegetarian Tacos with Guacamole

Prep + Cook Time: 30 minutes | Serves: 3

Ingredients

3 soft taco shells
1 cup kidney beans, drained
1 cup black beans, drained
½ cup tomato puree
1 fresh jalapeño pepper, chopped
1 cup fresh cilantro, chopped

1 cup corn kernels
½ tsp ground cumin
½ tsp cayenne pepper
Salt and black pepper
1 cup grated mozzarella cheese
Guacamole to serve

Directions

In a bowl, add beans, beans, tomato puree, chili, cilantro, corn, cumin, cayenne, salt and pepper; stir well. Spoon the mixture onto one half of the taco, sprinkle the cheese over the top and fold over. Spray the basket, and lay the tacos inside. Cook for 14 minutes at 360 F, until the cheese melts. Serve hot with guacamole.

Saturday Night Fried Cauliflower

Prep + Cook Time: 20 minutes | Serves: 4

Ingredients

1 head of cauliflower, cut into florets
2 tbsp olive oil

½ tsp salt
¼ tsp freshly ground black pepper

Directions

In a bowl, toss cauliflower, oil, salt, and black pepper, until the florets are well-coated. Arrange the florets in the air fryer and cook for 8 minutes at 360 F; work in batches if needed. Serve the crispy cauliflower in lettuce wraps with chicken, cheese or mushrooms.

Easy Vegan Falafels

Prep + Cook Time: 25 minutes | Serves: 6

Ingredients

2 cups cooked chickpeas
½ cup chickpea flour
1 cup fresh parsley, chopped
Juice of 1 lemon
4 garlic cloves, chopped

1 onion, chopped
2 tsp ground cumin
2 tsp ground coriander
1 tsp chili powder
Salt and black pepper

Directions

In a blender, add chickpeas, flour, parsley, lemon juice, garlic, onion, cumin, coriander, chili, turmeric, salt and pepper, and blend until well-combined but not too battery; there should be some lumps. Shape the mixture into 15 balls and press them with hands, making sure they are still around.

Spray them with oil and arrange them in a paper-lined air fryer basket; work in batches if needed. Cook at 360 F for 14 minutes, turning once halfway through. They should be crunchy and golden.

Fried Buttery Ham Wraps

Prep + Cook Time: 17 minutes | Serves: 3

Ingredients

1 lb chopped ham
3 packages pepperidge farm rolls
1 tbsp softened butter

1 tsp mustard seeds
1 tsp poppy seeds
1 small chopped onion

Directions

Mix butter, mustard, onion and poppy seeds. Spread the mixture on top of the rolls. Cover the bottom halves with the chopped ham. Arrange the rolls in the basket of the Air fryer and cook at 350 F for 15 minutes.

Roasted Vegetables with Penne

Prep + Cook Time: 25 minutes | Serves: 6

Ingredients

1 lb penne, cooked
1 zucchini, sliced
1 pepper, sliced
1 acorn squash , sliced
4 oz mushrooms, sliced
½ cup kalamata olives, pitted and halved

¼ cup olive oil
1 tsp Italian seasoning
1 cup grape tomatoes, halved
3 tbsp balsamic vinegar
2 tbsp chopped basil
Salt and black pepper to taste

Directions

Preheat the Air fryer to 380 F, and combine pepper, zucchini, squash, mushrooms, and olive oil, in a large bowl.

Season with salt and pepper. Air fry the veggies for 15 minutes. In a large bowl, combine penne, roasted vegetables, olives, tomatoes, Italian seasoning, and vinegar. Sprinkle basil and serve.

Southwest Quinoa Stuffed Peppers

Prep + Cook Time: 16 minutes | Serves: 1

Ingredients

¼ cup cooked quinoa
1 bell pepper
½ tbsp diced onion
½ diced tomato, plus one tomato slice

¼ tsp smoked paprika
Salt and black pepper to taste
1 tsp olive oil
¼ tsp dried basil

Directions

Preheat the Air fryer to 350 F, core and clean the bell pepper to prepare it for stuffing. Brush the pepper with half of the olive oil on the outside. In a small bowl, combine all of the other ingredients, except the tomato slice and reserved half-teaspoon of olive oil.

Stuff the pepper with the filling and top with the tomato slice. Brush the tomato slice with the remaining half-teaspoon of olive oil and sprinkle with basil. Air fry for 10 minutes, until thoroughly cooked.

Best Stuffed Butternut Squash

Prep + Cook Time: 50 minutes | Serves: 3

Ingredients

½ butternut squash
6 grape tomatoes, halved
1 poblano pepper, cut into strips

¼ cup grated mozzarella, optional
2 tsp olive oil divided
Salt and black pepper to taste

Directions

Preheat the Air fryer to 350 F, trim the ends and cut the squash lengthwise. You will only need one half for this recipe Scoop the flash out, so you make room for the filling. Brush 1 tsp. oil over the squash.

Place in the Air fryer and roast for 30 minutes. Combine the other teaspoon of olive oil with the tomatoes and poblanos; season with salt and pepper, to taste. Place the peppers and tomatoes into the squash. Cook for 15 more minutes. If using mozzarella, add it on top of the squash, two minutes before the end.

Parsley & Garlic Mushrooms

Ready in about: 15 minutes | Serves: 2

Ingredients

2 cups small mushrooms
2 slices white bread
1 garlic clove, crushed

2 tsp olive oil
2 tbsp parsley, finely chopped
Salt and black pepper

Directions

Preheat the Air fryer to 360 F, and in a food processor, grind the bread into very fine crumbs. Add garlic, parsley and pepper; mix and stir in the olive oil. Cut off the mushroom stalks and fill the caps with the breadcrumbs.

Pat the crumbs inside the caps to ensure there are no loose crumbs. Place the mushroom caps, one by one, inside the cooking basket and carefully slide them in the air fryer. Cook for 10 minutes or until golden and crispy.

Easy Stuffed Mushrooms with Vegetables

Prep + Cook Time: 15 minutes | Serves: 3

Ingredients

3 portobello mushrooms
1 tomato, diced
1 small red onion, diced
1 green bell pepper, diced

½ cup grated mozzarella cheese
½ tsp garlic powder
¼ tsp pepper
¼ tsp salt

Directions

Preheat the Air fryer to 330 F, wash the mushrooms, remove the stems, and pat them dry. Coat with the olive oil.

Combine all remaining ingredients, except mozzarella, in a small bowl. Divide the filling between the mushrooms. Top the mushrooms with mozzarella. Place in the Air fryer and cook for 8 minutes.

Cilantro Bell Pepper & Tomatoes

Prep + Cook Time: 25 minutes | Serves: 6

Ingredients

¾ lb green bell pepper
¾ lb tomatoes
1 medium onion
1 tbsp lemon juice

1 tbsp olive oil
½ tbsp salt
1 tbsp cilantro powder

Directions

Preheat the Air fryer to 360 F, and line the peppers, the tomatoes and the onion in the basket. Cook for 5 minutes, then flip and cook for 5 more minutes. Remove them from the fryer and peel the skin. Place the vegetables in a blender and sprinkle with the salt and coriander powder. Blend to smooth and season with salt and olive oil.

Festive Bell Pepper & Potato Skewers

Prep + Cook Time: 20 minutes | Serves: 1

Ingredients

1 large sweet potato
1 beetroot
1 red bell pepper
1 tsp chili flakes
¼ tsp black pepper

½ tsp turmeric
¼ tsp garlic powder
¼ tsp paprika
1 tbsp olive oil

Directions

Soak 3 to 4 skewers until ready to use. Preheat the Air fryer to 350 F, peel the veggies and cut into bite-sized chunks. Place the chunks in a bowl, along with the remaining ingredients; mix until fully coated.

Thread the veggies in this order: potato, pepper, beetroot. Place in the Air fryer and cook for 15 minutes.

Cabbage & Tofu Sandwich

Prep + Cook Time: 20 minutes | Serves: 1

Ingredients

2 slices of bread
1 1-inch thick Tofu slice
¼ cup red cabbage, shredded

2 tsp olive oil divided
¼ tsp vinegar
Salt and black pepper to taste

Directions

Preheat the Air fryer to 350 F, add in the bread slices and toast for 3 minutes; set aside. Brush the tofu with 1 tsp. oil and place in the Air fryer; grill for 5 minutes on each side. Combine the cabbage, remaining oil, and vinegar, and season with salt and pepper. Place the tofu on top of one bread slice, place the cabbage over, and top with the other bread slice. Serve and enjoy.

Effortless Avocado Rolls

Prep + Cook Time: 15 minutes | Serves: 5

Ingredients

3 ripe avocados, pitted and peeled
10 egg roll wrappers
1 tomato, diced

¼ tsp pepper
½ tsp salt

Directions

Place all filling ingredients in a bowl; mash with a fork until somewhat smooth. There should be chunks left.

Divide the feeling between the egg wrappers. Wet your finger and brush along the edges, so the wrappers can seal well. Roll and seal the wrappers. Arrange them on a baking sheet lined dish, and place in the Air fryer.

Cook at 350 F, for 5 minutes. Serve with sweet chili dipping and enjoy.

Speedy Vegetable Pizza

Prep + Cook Time: 15 minutes | Serves: 1

Ingredients

1 ½ tbsp tomato paste
¼ cup grated cheddar cheese
¼ cup grated mozzarella cheese
1 tbsp cooked sweet corn
4 zucchini slices
4 eggplant slices

4 red onion rings
½ green bell pepper, chopped
3 cherry tomatoes, quartered
1 tortilla
¼ tsp basil
¼ tsp oregano

Directions

Preheat the Air fryer to 350 F, and spread the tomato paste on the tortilla. Arrange the zucchini and eggplant slices first, then green peppers, and onion rings. Arrange the cherry tomatoes and sprinkle the sweet corn over.

Sprinkle with oregano and basil and top with cheddar and mozzarella. Place in the fryer and cook for 10 minutes.

Homemade Cheese Ravioli

Prep + Cook Time: 15 minutes | Serves: 6

Ingredients

1 package cheese ravioli
2 cup Italian breadcrumbs
¼ cup Parmesan cheese, grated

1 cup buttermilk
1 tsp olive oil
¼ tsp garlic powder

Directions

Preheat the Air fryer to 390 F, and in a small bowl, combine the breadcrumbs, Parmesan cheese, garlic powder, and olive oil. Dip the ravioli in the buttermilk and then coat them with the breadcrumb mixture.

Line a baking sheet with parchment paper and arrange the ravioli on it. Place in the Air fryer and cook for 5 minutes. Serve the air-fried ravioli with marinara jar sauce.

Chili Veggie Skewers

Prep + Cook Time: 20 minutes | Serves: 4

Ingredients

2 tbsp cornflour
1 cup canned beans
⅓ cup grated carrots
2 boiled and mashed potatoes
¼ cup chopped fresh mint leaves
½ tsp garam masala powder

½ cup paneer
1 green chili
1-inch piece of fresh ginger
3 garlic cloves
Salt, to taste

Directions

Soak 12 skewers until ready to use. Preheat the Air fryer to 390 F, and place the beans, carrots, garlic, ginger, chili, paneer, and mint, in a food processor; process until smooth, then transfer to a bowl.

Add the mashed potatoes, corn flour, some salt, and garam masala powder to the bowl; mix until fully incorporated. Divide the mixture into 12 equal pieces. Shape each of the pieces around a skewer. Cook skewers for 10 minutes.

Oregano Paneer Cutlet

Prep + Cook Time: 15 minutes | Serves: 1

Ingredients

2 cup grated paneer
1 cup grated cheese
½ tsp chai masala
1 tsp butter

½ tsp garlic powder
1 small onion, finely chopped
½ tsp oregano
½ tsp salt

Directions

Preheat the Air fryer to 350 F, and grease a baking dish. Mix all ingredients in a bowl, until well incorporated.

Make cutlets out of the mixture and place them on the greased baking dish. Place the baking dish in the Air fryer and cook the cutlets for 10 minutes, until crispy.

Crispy Chili Nachos

Prep + Cook Time: 20 minutes | Serves: 2

Ingredients

1 cup sweet corn
1 cup all-purpose flour
1 tbsp butter

½ tsp chili powder
3 tbsp water
Salt to taste

Directions

Add a small amount of water to the sweet corn and grind until you obtain a very fine paste. In a large bowl, add the flour, salt, chili powder, butter and mix very well; add corn and stir well. Start to knead with your palm until you obtain a stiff dough. Preheat the Air fryer to 350 F.

Dust a little bit of flour and spread the dough with a rolling pin. Make it around ½ inch thick. Cut it in any shape you want and fry the shapes in the Air fryer for around 10 minutes. Serve with guacamole salsa.

Cheddar Cheese English Muffins

Prep + Cook Time: 8 minutes | Serves: 3

Ingredients

3 split English muffins, toasted
1 cup cheddar cheese , smoked and shredded
1 mashed avocado
¼ cup ranch-style salad dressing

1 cup alfalfa sprouts
1 tomato, chopped
1 sweet onion, chopped
¼ cup sesame seeds, toasted

Directions

Arrange the muffins open-faced in the Air fryer's basket. Spread the mashed avocado on each half of the muffin. Place the halves close to each other. Cover the muffins with the sprouts, tomatoes, onion, dressing, sesame seeds and the cheese. Cook for 7-8 minutes at 350 F.

Vegetable Salad

Prep + Cook Time: 25 minutes | Serves: 1

Ingredients

1 potato, peeled and chopped
¼ onion, sliced
1 carrot, sliced diagonally
½ small beetroot, sliced
1 cup cherry tomatoes
Juice of 1 lemon
A handful of rocket salad

A handful of baby spinach
3 tbsp canned chickpeas
½ tsp cumin
½ tsp turmeric
¼ tsp sea salt
2 tbsp olive oil
Parmesan shavings

Directions

Preheat the Air fryer to 370 F, and combine the onion, potato, cherry tomatoes, carrot, beetroot, cumin, sea salt, turmeric, and 1 tbsp. olive oil, in a bowl. Place in the fryer and cook for 20 minutes; let cool for 2 minutes.

Place the rocket, salad, spinach, lemon juice, and 1 tbsp. olive oil, into a serving bowl; mix to combine. Stir in the roasted veggies. Top with chickpeas and Parmesan shavings.

Spicy Cheese Lings

Prep + Cook Time: 15 minutes | Serves: 4

Ingredients

4 cups grated cheese , any
1 cup all-purpose flour
1 tbsp butter
1 tbsp baking powder

¼ tsp chili powder
¼ tsp salt, to taste
2 tbsp water

Directions

In a bowl, mix the flour and the baking powder. Add the chili powder, salt, butter, cheese and 1-2 tbsp. of water to the mixture. Make a stiff dough. Knead the dough for a while and sprinkle about a tbsp. of flour on the table.

With a rolling pin, roll the dough into ½-inch thickness. Cut into any shape and cook for 6 minutes at 370 F.

Green Chili Paneer Ginger Cheese Balls

Prep + Cook Time: 12 minutes | Serves: 2

Ingredients

2 oz paneer cheese
2 tbsp flour
2 medium onions, chopped
1 tbsp corn flour
1 green chili, chopped

1-inch ginger piece, chopped
1 tsp red chili powder
A few leaves of cilantro, chopped
Salt to taste

Directions

Mix all ingredients, except the oil and cheese. Take a small part of the mixture, roll it up and slowly press it to flatten. Stuff in 1 cube of cheese and seal the edges. Repeat with the rest of the mixture. Fry the balls in the fryer for 12 minutes and at 370 F. Serve hot with ketchup!

Mustard Seed Potato Filled Bread Rolls

Prep + Cook Time: 25 minutes | Serves: 4

Ingredients

8 bread slices
5 large potatoes, boiled and mashed
½ tsp turmeric
2 green chilies, deseeded and chopped
1 medium onion, finely chopped

½ tsp mustard seeds
1 tbsp olive oil
2 sprigs curry leaf
Salt to taste

Directions

Preheat the Air fryer to 350 F, and combine the olive oil, onion, curry leaves, and mustard seed, in a baking dish. Air fry for 5 minutes. Mix the onion mixture with the mashed potatoes, chilies, turmeric, and some salt.

Divide the mixture into 8 equal pieces. Trim the sides of the bread, and wet with some water. Make sure to get rid of the excess water. Take one wet bread slice in your palm and place one of the potato pieces in the center. Roll the bread over the filling, sealing the edges. Place the rolls in a baking dish, and fry for 12 minutes.

Potato Pancakes

Prep + Cook Time: 15 minutes | Serves: 4

Ingredients

4 medium potatoes, shredded
1 medium onion, chopped
1 beaten egg
¼ cup milk
2 tbsp unsalted butter

½ tsp garlic powder
¼ tsp salt
3 tbsp flour
Black pepper to taste

Directions

Preheat your Air fryer to 390 F, and in a medium bowl, mix egg, potatoes, onion, milk, butter, pepper, garlic powder and salt; add flour and form batter. Forms cakes about ¼ cup of batter. Place the cakes in the fryer's cooking basket and cook for 12 minutes. Serve and enjoy!

Paprika Blooming Onion

Prep + Cook Time: 20 minutes | Serves: 4

Ingredients

2 pounds cipollini onions, cut into flowers
Olive oil as needed
1 tsp cayenne pepper
1 tsp garlic powder
2 cups flour
1 tbsp pepper

1 tbsp paprika
1 tbsp salt
¼ cup mayonnaise
1 tbsp ketchup
¼ cup mayonnaise
¼ cup sour cream

Directions

In a bowl, mix salt, pepper, paprika, flour, garlic powder, and cayenne pepper. Add mayonnaise, ketchup, sour cream to the mixture and stir. Coat the onions with the prepared mixture and spray with oil. Preheat your Air fryer to 360 F. Add the coated onions to the basket and cook for 15 minutes.

Hot Coconut & Spinach Chickpeas

Prep + Cook Time: 20 minutes | Serves: 4

Ingredients

2 tbsp olive oil
1 tbsp pepper
1 onion, chopped
1 tsp salt
4 garlic cloves, minced
1 can coconut milk

1 tbsp ginger, minced
1 pound spinach
½ cup dried tomatoes, chopped
1 can chickpeas
1 lemon, juiced
1 hot pepper

Directions

Preheat your Air fryer to 370 F, and in a bowl, mix lemon juice, tomatoes, pepper, ginger, coconut milk, garlic, salt, hot pepper and onion. Rinse chickpeas under running water to get rid of all the gunk. Put them in a large bowl.

Cover with spinach. Pour the sauce over, and stir in oil. Cook in the Air fryer for 15 minutes. Serve warm.

Rosemary Balsamic Beet Dish

Prep + Cook Time: 20 minutes | Serves: 2

Ingredients

4 beets, cubed
⅓ cup balsamic vinegar
1 tbsp olive oil

1 tbsp honey
Salt and black pepper to taste
2 springs rosemary

Directions

In a bowl, mix rosemary, pepper, salt, vinegar and honey. Cover beets with the prepared sauce and then coat with oil. Preheat your Air fryer to 400 F, and cook the beets in the Air Fryer for 10 minutes. Meanwhile, pour the balsamic vinegar in a pan over medium heat; bring to a boil and cook until reduced by half. Drizzle the beets with balsamic glaze, to serve.

Parsnip & Potato Bake with Parmesan

Prep + Cook Time: 30 minutes | Serves: 8

Ingredients

28 oz potato, cubed
3 tbsp pine nuts
28 oz parsnips, chopped
1 ¾ oz Parmesan cheese, shredded
6 ¾ oz crème fraiche

1 slice bread
2 tbsp sage
4 tbsp butter
4 tsp mustard

Directions

Preheat the Air fryer to 360 F, and boil salted water in a pot over medium heat. Add potatoes and parsnips. Bring to a boil. In a bowl, mix mustard, crème fraiche, sage, salt and pepper. Drain the potatoes and parsnips and mash them with butter using a potato masher. Add mustard mixture, bread, cheese, and nuts to the mash and mix.

Add the batter to your Air fryer's basket and cook for 25 minutes. Serve and enjoy!

Dilled Zucchini with Feta

Prep + Cook Time: 25 minutes | Serves: 4

Ingredients

12 oz thawed puff pastry
4 large eggs, beaten
1 medium zucchini, sliced

4 ounces feta cheese, drained and crumbled
2 tbsp fresh dill, chopped
Salt and black pepper to taste

Directions

Preheat the Air fryer to 360 F, and in a bowl, add the beaten eggs and season with salt and pepper.

Stir in zucchini, dill and feta cheese. Grease 8 muffin tins with cooking spray. Roll pastry and arrange them to cover the sides of the muffin tins. Divide the egg mixture evenly between the holes. Place the prepared tins in your Air fryer and cook for 15 minutes. Serve and enjoy!

Brussels Sprouts & Pine Nuts

Prep + Cook Time: 20 minutes | Serves: 6

Ingredients

15 oz brussels sprouts, stems cut off and cut in half
1 tbsp olive oil
1 ¾ oz raisins, drained

Juice of 1 orange
Salt to taste
1 ¾ oz toasted pine nuts

Directions

Take raisins and soak in orange juice for 20 minutes. Meanwhile, in a bowl, pop the sprouts with oil and salt and stir to combine well. Preheat your Air Fryer to 392 degrees F.

Add the sprouts to the Air Fryer and roast for 15 minutes. Check often and remove Brussel sprouts from the air fryer. Mix with toasted pine nuts and soaked raisins. Drizzle with remaining orange juice, to serve.

Savory Mediterranean Veggies

Prep + Cook Time: 10 minutes | Serves: 8

Ingredients

4 tbsp olive oil
18 oz eggplant, cubed
4 garlic cloves, minced
18 oz zucchini, sliced
A bunch of thyme sprig

18 oz bell pepper, sliced and deseeded
Salt and black pepper to taste
4 whole onions, chopped
18 oz tomatoes, sliced
Breadcrumb as needed

Directions

Preheat your Air fryer to 380 F and in a bowl, mix eggplant, garlic, oil, spices, and transfer the mix to the cooking basket; cook for 4 minutes. Add zucchini, tomatoes, bell pepper, onion, and bake for 6 minutes. Serve and enjoy!

Cilantro Indian Potatoes with Bell Pepper

Prep + Cook Time: 20 minutes | Serves: 2

Ingredients

4 potatoes, cubed
3 tbsp lemon juice
1 bell pepper, sliced
Salt and black pepper to taste
2 onions, chopped

4 tbsp fennel
5 tbsp flour
2 tbsp ginger-garlic paste
½ cup mint leaves, chopped
2 cups cilantro, chopped

Directions

Preheat your Air fryer to 360 F, and in a bowl, mix coriander, mint, fennel, ginger garlic paste, flour, salt and lemon juice. Blend to form a paste and add potato cubes. In another bowl, mix capsicum, onions and fennel mixture. Blend the mixture until you have a thick mix. Divide the mixture evenly into 5-6 cakes.

Add the prepared potato cakes into your Air Fryer and cook for 15 minutes. Serve with ketchup and enjoy.

Simple Zucchini Fries

Prep + Cook Time: 25 minutes | Serves: 4

Ingredients

3 medium zucchini, sliced
2 egg whites
½ cup seasoned breadcrumbs

2 tbsp grated Parmesan cheese
¼ tsp garlic powder
Salt and black pepper to taste

Directions

Preheat your Air fryer to 420 F, and coat cooling rack with cooking spray; place it in the fryer's basket. In a bowl, beat the egg whites and season with salt and pepper. In another bowl, mix garlic powder, cheese and breadcrumbs.

Take zucchini slices and dredge them in eggs, followed by breadcrumbs. Add zucchini to the rack (in the cooking basket) and spray more oil. cook for 20 minutes. Serve and enjoy!

Creole Fried Tomatoes

Prep + Cook Time: 15 minutes | Serves: 3

Ingredients

1 green tomato, sliced
¼ tbsp creole seasoning
Salt and black pepper to taste

¼ cup flour
½ cup buttermilk
Breadcrumbs as needed

Directions

Add flour to one bowl and buttermilk to another. Season the tomatoes with salt and pepper. Make a mix of creole seasoning and breadcrumbs. Cover tomato slices with flour, dip in buttermilk and then into the breadcrumbs.

Do the same for all the slices. Cook the tomato slices in your air fryer for 5 minutes at 400 F. Serve and enjoy!

Basil Bell Pepper Bites

Prep + Cook Time: 20 minutes | Serves: 4

Ingredients

1 medium red bell pepper, cut into small portions
1 medium yellow pepper, cut into small portions
1 medium green bell pepper, cut into small portions
3 tbsp balsamic vinegar
2 tbsp olive oil

1 tbsp garlic, minced
½ tsp dried basil
½ tsp dried parsley
Salt and black pepper to taste
½ cup garlic mayo to serve

Directions

In a bowl, mix peppers, oil, garlic, balsamic vinegar, basil, and parsley; season with salt and black pepper. Preheat your Air fryer to 390 F and place the pepper mixture inside; cook for 10-15 minutes, tossing once or twice. Serve with garlic mayo and enjoy.

Crispy Basil Tofu

Prep + Cook Time: 25 minutes | Serves: 4

Ingredients

1 block firm tofu, cubed
1 tbsp potato starch
Salt and black pepper to taste
2 tsp rice vinegar

2 tsp soy sauce
2 tsp sesame oil
1 green onion, chopped
A bunch of basil, chopped

Directions

Preheat your Air fryer to 370 F, open your tofu pack and transfer to a plate. In a bowl, make a marinade of sesame oil, soy sauce and rice vinegar. Add spices to the marinade and pour the marinade over the tofu block. Set aside for 10 minutes to get tasty.

Toss the marinated tofu with the potato starch; place into the fryer's basket and cook for 20 minutes shaking after 10 minutes. Serve with a topping of chopped onion and basil.

Avocado, Carrot and Wasabi Sushi

Prep + Cook Time: 60 minutes | Serves: 4

Ingredients

2 cups cooked sushi rice
4 nori sheets
1 carrot, sliced lengthways
1 red bell pepper, seeds removed, sliced
1 avocado, sliced

1 tbsp olive oil mixed with
1 tbsp rice wine vinegar
1 cup panko crumbs
2 tbsp sesame seeds
soy sauce, wasabi and pickled ginger to serve

Directions

Prepare a clean working board, a small bowl of lukewarm water and a sushi mat. Wet hands, and lay a nori sheet onto sushi mat and spread half cup sushi rice, leaving a half inch of nori clear, so you can seal the roll. Place carrot, pepper and avocado sideways to the rice. Roll sushi tightly and rub warm water along the clean nori strip to seal.

In a bowl, mix olive oil and rice vinegar. In another bowl, mix the crumbs with the sesame seeds. Roll each sushi log in the vinegar mixture and then straight to the sesame bowl to coat. Arrange the coated sushi into the Air fryer and cook for 14 minutes at 360 F, turning once halfway through. When ready, check if the sushi is golden and crispy on the outside. Slice and serve with soy sauce, pickled ginger and wasabi.

Potatoes with Cottage Cheese

Prep + Cook Time: 30 minutes | Serves: 5

Ingredients

4 medium potatoes, cubed, skin shells reserved
1 bunch asparagus, trimmed
¼ cup fresh cream

¼ cup cottage cheese , cubed
1 tbsp whole grain mustard

Directions

Preheat the Air fryer to 400 F and place the potatoes in the basket; cook for 25 minutes. Boil salted water in a pot over medium heat. Add asparagus and cook for 3 minutes until tender.

In a bowl, mix cooked potatoes, cottage cheese, cream, asparagus and mustard. Toss well and season with salt and black pepper. Transfer the mixture to the potato skin shells and serve.

Hot Paprika Potato Wedges

Prep + Cook Time: 30 minutes | Serves: 6

Ingredients

26 oz large waxy potatoes, cut into wedges
2 tbsp olive oil
2 tsp smoked paprika

2 tbsp sriracha hot chili sauce
½ cup Greek yogurt

Directions

Soak potatoes under cold water for 30 minutes; pat dry with a towel. Preheat your Air Fryer to 340 F, and coat potatoes with oil and paprika. Cook them for 20 minutes, shaking once halfway through. Remove to a paper to let them dry; season with salt and pepper. Serve with the yogurt and chili sauce on the side.

Grana Padano Cheese Balls with Mushrooms

Prep + Cook Time: 50 minutes | Serves: 4

Ingredients

½ lb mushrooms, diced
3 tbsp olive oil
1 small red onion, chopped
3 cloves garlic, minced
3 cups cauliflower, chopped
2 tbsp chicken stock

1 cup breadcrumbs
1 cup Grana Padano cheese
¼ cup coconut oil
2 sprigs chopped fresh thyme
Salt and black pepper to taste

Directions

Place a skillet over medium heat on a stove top. Add olive oil, once heated, sauté garlic and onion, until translucent.

Add the mushrooms, stir-fry for 4 minutes; add the cauliflower and stir-fry for 5 minutes. Pour in the stock, thyme, and simmer until the cauliflower has absorbed the stock. Add Grana Padano cheese, pepper, and salt.

Stir and turn off the heat. Allow the mixture cool and make bite-size balls of the mixture. Place them in a plate and refrigerate for 30 minutes to harden. Preheat the Air Fryer to 350 F.

In a bowl, add the breadcrumbs and coconut oil and mix well. Remove the mushroom balls from the refrigerator, stir the breadcrumb mixture again, and roll the balls in the breadcrumb mixture. Place the balls in the Air fryer's basket without overcrowding, and cook for 15 minutes, tossing every 5 minutes for an even cook. Repeat until all the mushroom balls are fried. Serve with sautéed zoodles and tomato sauce.

Soy Chorizo & Spring Onion Toast

Prep + Cook Time: 12 minutes | Serves: 2

Ingredients

1 cup soy chorizo, chopped
1 large spring onion, finely sliced
3 white bread slices

½ cup sweet corn
1 egg white, whisked
1 tbsp black sesame seeds

Directions

In a bowl, place the chopped soy chorizo, sliced, corn, spring onion and the black sesame seeds. Add the whisked egg and mix the ingredients. Spread the mixture over the bread slices. Place in the Air fryer's basket and sprinkle oil. Fry until golden, for 8-10 minutes at 370 F. Serve with ketchup or chili sauce.

Parmesan Broccoli Dish

Prep + Cook Time: 25 minutes | Serves: 4

Ingredients

1 head broccoli, cut into florets
1 tbsp olive oil
1 lemon, Juiced

Salt and black pepper to taste
1 ounce Parmesan cheese , grated

Directions

In a bowl, mix all ingredients. Add the mixture to your Air fryer and cook for 20 minutes at 360 F. Serve warm.

Sweet and Spicy Cauliflower Appetizer

Prep + Cook Time: 20 minutes | Serves: 4

Ingredients

1 big cauliflower head, cut into florets
½ cup soy sauce
3 tbsp brown sugar
1 tsp sesame oil

⅓ cup water
½ chili powder
2 cloves garlic, chopped
1 tsp cornstarch

Directions

In a measuring cup, whisk soy sauce, sugar, sesame oil, water, chili powder, garlic and cornstarch, until smooth. In a bowl, add cauliflower, and pour teriyaki sauce over the top; toss with hands until well-coated.

Take the cauliflower to the Air fryer's basket and cook for 14 minutes at 340 F, turning once halfway through. When ready, check if the cauliflower is cooked but not too soft. Serve with rice and edamame beans!

Eggplant Rolls with Quinoa

Prep + Cook Time: 15 minutes | Serves: 3

Ingredients

1 whole eggplant, sliced
Marinara sauce for dipping
½ cup cheese , grated

2 tbsp milk
1 whole egg, beaten
2 cups breadcrumbs

Directions

Preheat your Air fryer to 400 F, and in a bowl, mix beaten egg and milk. In another bowl, mix crumbs and cheese until crumbly. Place eggplant slices in the egg mixture, followed by a dip in the crumb mixture. Place the eggplant slices in the cooking basket and cook for 5 minutes. Serve with marinara sauce.

Golden Cauliflower Florets

Prep + Cook Time: 34 minutes | Serves: 4

Ingredients

1 large cauliflower head
Salt to taste
1 ½ tbsp curry powder

½ cup olive oil
⅓ cup fried pine nuts

Directions

Preheat the Air Fryer to 390 F, and mix the pine nuts and 1 tsp of olive oil, in a medium bowl. Pour them in the air fryer's basket and cook for 2 minutes; remove to cool.

Place the cauliflower on a cutting board. Use a knife to cut them into 1-inch florets. Place them in a large mixing bowl. Add the curry powder, salt, and the remaining olive oil; mix well. Place the cauliflower florets in the fryer's basket in 2 batches, and cook each batch for 10 minutes.

Remove the curried florets onto a serving platter, sprinkle with the pine nuts, and toss. Serve the florets with tomato sauce or as a side to a meat dish.

Best Crispy Tofu

Prep + Cook Time: 25 minutes | Serves: 4

Ingredients

3 blocks of firm tofu, cut into ½-inch thick
2 tbsp olive oil
½ cup flour

½ cup crushed cornflakes
Salt and black pepper to taste

Directions

Sprinkle oil over tofu and massage gently until well-coated. In a plate, mix flour, cornflakes, salt, and black pepper.

Dip each strip into the mixture to coat, spray with oil and arrange the strips in your air fryer lined with baking paper. Cook for 14 minutes at 360 F, turning once halfway through.

Easy Avocado Fries

Prep + Cook Time: 20 minutes | Serves: 2

Ingredients

½ cup breadcrumbs
Salt as needed

1 avocado, cubed
¼ cup aquafaba

Directions

In a bowl, mix crumbs, aquafaba and salt. Preheat your Air Fryer to 390 F, and roll the avocado cubes in the crumbs mixture to coat evenly. Place the prepared cubes in your air fryer's cooking basket and cook for 10 minutes.

Stuffed Green Peppers with Cauliflower & Parmesan

Prep + Cook Time: 40 minutes | Serves: 4

Ingredients

4 green peppers
Salt and black pepper to taste
½ cup olive oil
1 red onion, chopped
1 large tomato, chopped

½ cup crumbled Goat cheese
3 cups cauliflower, chopped
2 tbsp grated Parmesan cheese
2 tbsp chopped basil
1 tbsp lemon zest

Directions

Preheat the Air Fryer to 350 F, and cut the peppers a quarter way from the head down and lengthwise. Remove the membrane and seeds. Season the peppers with pepper, salt, and drizzle olive oil over.

Place the pepper bottoms in the fryer's basket and cook them for 5 minutes at 350 F to soften a little bit.

In a mixing bowl, add the tomatoes, goat cheese, lemon zest, basil, and cauliflower; season with salt and pepper, and mix well. Remove the bottoms from the Air fryer to a flat surface and spoon the cheese mixture into them.

Sprinkle Parmesan cheese on top of each and gently place in the basket; cook for 15 minutes. Serve warm.

Parsley Hearty Carrots

Prep + Cook Time: 25 minutes | Serves: 4

Ingredients

2 tsp olive oil
2 shallots, chopped
3 carrots, sliced
Salt to taste

¼ cup yogurt
2 garlic cloves, minced
3 tbsp parsley , chopped

Directions

Preheat your Air fryer to 370 F, and in a bowl, mix sliced carrots, salt, garlic, shallots, parsley and yogurt. Sprinkle with oil. Place the veggies in your Air fryer basket and cook for 15 minutes. Serve with basil and garlic mayo.

Beetroot Chips

Prep + Cook Time: 9 minutes | Serves: 2

Ingredients

4 cups golden beetroot, sliced
2 tbsp olive oil
1 tbsp yeast flakes

1 tsp vegan seasoning
Salt to taste

Directions

In a bowl, add the oil, beetroot, the vegan seasoning, and the yeast and mix well. Dump the coated chips in the basket. Set the heat to 370 F and fry for a total of 6 minutes, shaking once halfway through cooking.

Coconut Vegan Fries

Prep + Cook Time: 20 minutes | Serves: 2

Ingredients

2 potatoes
1 tbsp tomato ketchup
2 tbsp olive oil

Salt and black pepper to taste
2 tbsp coconut oil

Directions

Preheat your Air Fryer to 360 F and use a spiralizer to spiralize the potatoes. In a bowl, mix oil, coconut oil, salt and pepper. Cover the potatoes with the oil mixture. Place the potatoes in the cooking basket and cook for 15 minutes. Serve with ketchup and enjoy!

Garlicky Vermouth Mushrooms

Prep + Cook Time: 20 minutes | Serves: 3

Ingredients

2 pounds portobello mushrooms, sliced
2 tbsp vermouth
½ tsp garlic powder

1 tbsp olive oil
2 tsp herbs
1 tbsp duck fat

Directions

Preheat your Air fryer to 350 F, add duck fat, garlic powder and herbs in a blender, and process. Pour the mixture over the mushrooms and cover with vermouth.

Place the mushrooms in the cooking basket and cook for 10 minutes. Top with more vermouth and cook for 5 more minutes.

Vegetable Au Gratin

Prep + Cook Time: 30 minutes | Serves: 2 to 3

Ingredients

1 cup cubed eggplant
¼ cup chopped red pepper
¼ cup chopped green pepper
¼ cup chopped onion
⅓ cup chopped tomatoes
1 clove garlic, minced
1 tbsp sliced pimiento-stuffed olives

1 tsp capers
¼ tsp dried basil
¼ tsp dried marjoram
Salt and black pepper to taste
¼ cup grated mozzarella cheese
1 tbsp breadcrumbs

Directions

Preheat the Air Fryer to 300 F, and in a bowl, add the eggplant, green pepper, red pepper, onion, tomatoes, olives, garlic, basil marjoram, capers, salt, and pepper. Lightly grease a baking dish with the olive oil cooking spray.

Ladle the eggplant mixture into the baking dish and level it using the vessel. Sprinkle the mozzarella cheese on top and cover with the breadcrumbs. Place the dish in the Air Fryer and cook for 20 minutes. Serve with rice.

Sandwiches with Tomato, Nuts and Cheese

Prep + Cook Time: 60 minutes | Serves: 2

Ingredients

1 heirloom tomato
1 (4- oz) block Feta cheese
1 small red onion, thinly sliced
1 clove garlic
Salt to taste

2 tsp + ¼ cup olive oil
1 ½ tbsp toasted pine nuts
¼ cup chopped parsley
¼ cup grated Parmesan cheese
¼ cup chopped basil

Directions

Add basil, pine nuts, garlic and salt to a food processor. Process while adding the ¼ cup of olive oil slowly. Once the oil is finished, pour the basil pesto into a bowl and refrigerate for 30 minutes. Preheat the Air fryer to 390 F.

Slice the feta cheese and tomato into ½ inch circular slices. Use a kitchen towel to pat the tomatoes dry. Remove the pesto from the fridge and use a tablespoon to spread some pesto on each slice of tomato.

Top with a slice of feta cheese. Add the onion and remaining olive oil in a bowl and toss. Spoon on top of feta cheese.

Place the tomato in the fryer's basket and cook for 12 minutes. Remove to a serving platter, sprinkle lightly with salt and top with the remaining pesto. Serve with a side of rice or lean meat.

Cheesy Cabbage Wedges

Prep + Cook Time: 25 minutes | Serves: 4

Ingredients

½ head cabbage, cut into wedges
2 cups Parmesan cheese, chopped
4 tbsp melted butter

Salt and black pepper to taste
½ cup blue cheese sauce

Directions

Preheat your Air fryer to 380 F, and cover cabbage wedges with melted butter; coat with mozzarella. Place the coated cabbage in the cooking basket and cook for 20 minutes. Serve with blue cheese.

Roasted Carrots

Prep + Cook Time: 15 minutes | Serves: 6

Ingredients

20 oz carrots, julienned
1 tbsp olive oil

1 tsp cumin seeds
A handful of fresh cilantro

Directions

Preheat the fryer to 350 F, and in a bowl, mix oil, carrots, and cumin seeds. Gently stir to coat the carrots well. Place the carrots in your Air fryer basket and cook for 12 minutes. Scatter fresh coriander over the carrots.

Cayenne Spicy Green Beans

Prep + Cook Time: 20 minutes | Serves: 6

Ingredients

1 cup panko
2 whole eggs, beaten
½ cup Parmesan cheese , grated
½ cup flour

1 tsp cayenne pepper
1 ½ pounds green beans
Salt to taste

Directions

Preheat your Air fryer to 400 F, and in a bowl, mix panko, Parmesan cheese, cayenne pepper; season with salt and pepper. Cover the green beans in flour and dip in eggs. Dredge beans in the parmesan-panko mix. Place the prepared beans in your Air Fryer's cooking basket and cook for 15 minutes. Serve and enjoy!

Garlicky Veggie Bake

Prep + Cook Time: 30 minutes | Serves: 3

Ingredients

3 turnips, sliced
1 large red onion, cut into rings
1 large zucchini, sliced
Salt and black pepper to taste

2 cloves garlic, crushed
1 bay leaf, cut in 6 pieces
1 tbsp olive oil

Directions

Place the turnips, onion, and zucchini in a bowl. Toss with olive oil and season with salt and pepper.

Preheat the Air Fryer to 330 F, and place the veggies into a baking pan that fits in the Air fryer. Slip the bay leaves in the different parts of the slices and tuck the garlic cloves in between the slices. Insert the pan in the Air fryer's basket and cook for 15 minutes. Serve warm with as a side to a meat dish or salad.

Sweet Baby Carrots

Prep + Cook Time: 20 minutes | Serves: 4

Ingredients

1 pound baby carrots
1 tsp dried dill
1 tbsp olive oil

1 tbsp honey
Salt and black pepper to taste

Directions

Preheat your Air fryer to 350 F, and in a bowl, mix oil, carrots and honey; gently stir to coat the carrots. Season with dill, pepper and salt. Place the prepared carrots in your Air Fryer's cooking basket and cook for 12 minutes.

Traditional Jacket Potatoes

Prep + Cook Time: 30 minutes | Serves: 4

Ingredients

17 oz potatoes
2 garlic cloves, minced
Salt and black pepper to taste

1 tsp rosemary
1 tsp butter

Directions

Wash the potatoes thoroughly under water. Preheat your Air fryer to 360 F, and prick the potatoes with a fork. Place them into your Air Fryer's cooking basket and cook for 25 minutes. Cut the potatoes in half and top with butter and rosemary; season with salt and pepper. Serve immediately.

Tasty Polenta Crisps

Prep + Cook Time: 80 minutes | Serves: 4

Ingredients

2 cups water
2 cups milk
1 cup instant polenta

Salt and black pepper

fresh thyme, chopped

Directions

Line a tray with paper. Pour water and milk into a saucepan and let it simmer. Keep whisking as you pour in the polenta. Continue to whisk until polenta thickens and bubbles; season to taste. Add polenta into the lined tray and spread out. Refrigerate for 45 minutes. Slice the cold, set polenta into batons and spray with oil. Arrange polenta chips into the air fryer basket and cook for 16 minutes at 380 F, turning once halfway through. Make sure the fries are golden and crispy.

Awesome Sweet Potato Fries

Prep + Cook Time: 30 minutes | Serves: 4

Ingredients

½ tsp salt
½ tsp garlic powder
½ tsp chili powder

¼ tsp cumin
3 tbsp olive oil
3 sweet potatoes, cut into thick strips

Directions

In a bowl, mix salt, garlic powder, chili powder, and cumin, and whisk in oil. Coat the strips well in this mixture and arrange them in the Air fryer's basket, without overcrowding. Cook for 20 minutes at 380 F, or until crispy.

Rosemary Butternut Squash Roast

Prep + Cook Time: 30 minutes | Serves: 2

Ingredients

1 butternut squash
1 tbsp dried rosemary

Salt to season

Directions

Place the butternut squash on a cutting board and peel it; cut it in half and remove the seeds. Cut the pulp into wedges and season with salt.

Preheat the Air Fryer to 350 F, spray the squash wedges with cooking spray and sprinkle with rosemary. Grease the fryer's basket with cooking spray and place the wedges inside it without overlapping. Slide the fryer basket back in and cook for 20 minutes, flipping once halfway through. Serve with maple syrup and goat cheese.

Herby Tofu

Prep + Cook Time: 30 minutes | Serves: 2

Ingredients

6 oz extra firm tofu
Black pepper to taste
1 tbsp vegetable broth
1 tbsp soy sauce

⅓ tsp dried oregano
⅓ tsp garlic powder
⅓ tsp dried basil
⅓ tsp onion powder

Directions

Place the tofu on a cutting board, and cut it into 3 lengthwise slices with a knife. Line a side of the cutting board with paper towels, place the tofu on it and cover with a paper towel. Use your hands to press the tofu gently until as much liquid has been extracted from it.

Remove the paper towels and use a knife to chop the tofu into 8 cubes; set aside. In another bowl, add the soy sauce, vegetable broth, oregano, basil, garlic powder, onion powder, and black pepper; mix well with a spoon.

Pour the spice mixture on the tofu, stir the tofu until well coated; set aside to marinate for 10 minutes. Preheat the Air Fryer to 390 F, and arrange the tofu in the fryer's basket, in a single layer; cook for 10 minutes, flipping it at the 6-minute mark. Remove to a plate and serve with green salad.

Colourful Vegetarian Delight

Prep + Cook Time: 30 minutes | Serves: 2

Ingredients

1 parsnip, peeled and sliced in a 2-inch thickness
1 cup chopped butternut squash
2 small red onions, cut in wedges
1 cup chopped celery

1 tbsp chopped fresh thyme
Salt and black pepper to taste
2 tsp olive oil

Directions

Preheat the Air Fryer to 200 F, and in a bowl, add turnip, squash, red onions, celery, thyme, pepper, salt, and olive oil; mix well. Pour the vegetables into the fryer's basket and cook for 16 minutes, tossing once halfway through.

Vegetable Fried Mix Chips

Prep + Cook Time: 45 minutes | Serves: 4

Ingredients

1 large eggplant
5 potatoes
3 zucchinis
½ cup cornstarch

½ cup water
½ cup olive oil
Salt to season

Directions

Preheat the Air Fryer to 390 F, and cut the eggplant and zucchini in long 3-inch strips. Peel and cut the potatoes into 3-inch strips; set aside. In a bowl, stir in cornstarch, water, salt, pepper, oil, eggplants, zucchini, and potatoes.

Place one-third of the veggie strips in the fryer's basket and cook them for 12 minutes. Once ready, transfer them to a serving platter. Repeat the cooking process for the remaining veggie strips. Serve warm.

Chickpea and Carrot Balls

Prep + Cook Time: 30 minutes | Serves: 3

Ingredients

2 tbsp olive oil
2 tbsp soy sauce
1 tbsp flax meal
2 cups cooked chickpeas
½ cup sweet onion, diced
½ cup grated carrots

½ cup roasted cashews
Juice of 1 lemon
½ tsp turmeric
1 tsp cumin
1 tsp garlic powder
1 cup rolled oats

Directions

Combine the oil, onions, and carrots into a baking dish and cook them in the air fryer for 6 minutes at 350 F.

Meanwhile, ground the oats and cashews in a food processor. Place them in a large bowl. Process the chickpeas with the lemon juice and soy sauce, until smooth. Add them to the bowl as well.

Add onions and carrots to the bowl with chickpeas. Stir in the remaining ingredients; mix until fully incorporated. Make meatballs out of the mixture. Increase the temperature to 370 degrees F and cook for 12 minutes.

Cheesy Frittata with Vegetables

Prep + Cook Time: 35 minutes | Serves: 2

Ingredients

1 cup baby spinach
⅓ cup sliced mushrooms
1 large zucchini, sliced with a 1-inch thickness
1 small red onion, sliced
¼ cup chopped chives
¼ lb asparagus, trimmed and sliced thinly

2 tsp olive oil
4 eggs, cracked into a bowl
⅓ cup milk
Salt and black pepper to taste
⅓ cup grated Cheddar cheese
⅓ cup crumbled Feta cheese

Directions

Preheat the Air Fryer to 320 F and line a 6 x 6 inches baking dish with parchment paper; set aside. In the egg bowl, add milk, salt, and pepper; beat evenly. Place a skillet over medium heat on a stove top, and heat olive oil.

Add the asparagus, zucchini, onion, mushrooms, and baby spinach; stir-fry for 5 minutes. Pour the veggies into the baking dish and top with the egg mixture. Sprinkle feta and cheddar cheese over and place in the Air Fryer.

Cook for 15 minutes. Remove the baking dish and garnish with fresh chives.

Baby Spinach & Pumpkin with Nuts & Cheese

Prep + Cook Time: 30 minutes | Serves: 1

Ingredients

½ small pumpkin
2 oz blue cheese , cubed
2 tbsp pine nuts
1 tbsp olive oil

½ cup baby spinach, packed
1 spring onion, sliced
1 radish, thinly sliced
1 tsp vinegar

Directions

Preheat the Air fryer to 330 F, and place the pine nuts in a baking dish to toast them for 5 minutes; set aside. Peel the pumpkin and chop it into small pieces. Place in the baking dish and toss with the olive oil. Increase the temperature to 390 F and cook the pumpkin for 20 minutes.

Place the pumpkin in a serving bowl. Add baby spinach, radish and spring onion; toss with the vinegar. Stir in the cubed blue cheese and top with the toasted pine nuts, to serve.

Yummy Chili Bean Burritos

Prep + Cook Time: 30 minutes | Serves: 6

Ingredients

6 tortillas
1 cup grated cheddar cheese

1 can (8 oz) beans
1 tsp seasoning, any kind

Directions

Preheat the Air fryer to 350 F, and mix the beans with the seasoning. Divide the bean mixture between the tortillas and top with cheddar cheese. Roll the burritos and arrange them on a lined baking dish.

Place in the Air fryer and cook for 5 minutes, or to your liking.

Mozzarella Eggplant Patties

Prep + Cook Time: 10 minutes | Serves: 1

Ingredients

1 hamburger bun
2-inch eggplant slice, cut along the round axis
1 mozzarella slice
1 red onion cut into 3 rings

1 lettuce leaf
½ tbsp tomato sauce
1 pickle, sliced

Directions

Preheat the air fryer to 330 F, and place the eggplant slice to roast for 6 minutes. Place the mozzarella slice on top of the eggplant and cook for 30 more seconds. Spread the tomato sauce on one half of the bun.

Place the lettuce leaf on top of the sauce. Place the cheesy eggplant on top of the lettuce. Top with onion rings and pickles, and then with the other bun half and enjoy.

Broccoli & Eggs with Cheddar Cheese

Prep + Cook Time: 15 minutes | Serves: 4

Ingredients

1 lb broccoli
4 eggs
1 cup cheddar cheese, shredded
1 cup cream

1 pinch nutmeg
1 tsp ginger powder
Salt and black pepper to taste

Directions

Steam the broccoli for 5 minutes. Then drain them and add 1 egg, cream, nutmeg, ginger, salt and pepper. Butter small ramekins and spread the mixture. Sprinkle the shredded cheese on top. Cook for 10 minutes at 280 F.

Parsley Feta Triangles

Prep + Cook Time: 20 minutes | Serves: 4

Ingredients

4 oz feta cheese
2 sheets filo pastry
1 egg yolk
2 tbsp parsley, finely chopped

1 scallion, finely chopped
2 tbsp olive oil
salt and black pepper

Directions

In a large bowl, beat the yolk and mix with the cheese, the chopped parsley and scallion. Season with salt and black pepper. Cut each filo sheet in three parts or strips. Put a teaspoon of the feta mixture on the bottom.

Roll the strip in a spinning spiral way until the filling of the inside mixture is completely wrapped in a triangle. Preheat the Air Fryer to 360 F, and brush the surface of the filo with oil. Place up to 5 triangles in the Air frier's basket and cook for 5 minutes. Lower the temperature to 330 F, cook for 3 more minutes or until golden brown.

Cumin and Cayenne Spicy Sweet Potatoes

Prep + Cook Time: 30minutes | Serves: 4

Ingredients

½ tsp salt
½ tsp garlic powder
½ tsp cayenne pepper
¼ tsp cumin

3 tbsp olive oil
3 sweet potatoes, cut into ½-inch thick wedges
A handful of chopped fresh parsley
Sea salt to taste

Directions

In a bowl, mix salt, garlic powder, chili powder, and cumin. Whisk in oil, and coat the potatoes. Arrange in the Air fryer, without overcrowding, and cook for 20 minutes at 380 F; toss regularly to get the crispy on all sides. Sprinkle with parsley and sea salt, and serve!

Zucchini Parmesan Crisps

Prep + Cook Time: 40 minutes | Serves: 4

Ingredients

4 small zucchini cut lengthwise
½ cup grated Parmesan cheese
½ cup breadcrumbs
¼ cup melted butter

¼ cup chopped parsley
4 garlic cloves, minced
Salt and black pepper to taste

Directions

Preheat the Air fryer to 350 F, and in a bowl, mix the breadcrumbs, Parmesan cheese, garlic, and parsley. Season with salt and pepper, to taste; stir in the melted butter. Arrange the zucchinis with the cut side up.

Spread the mixture onto the zucchini evenly. Place half of the zucchinis in the air fryer and cook for 13 minutes.

Increase the temperature to 370 F, and cook for 3 more minutes for extra crunchiness. Repeat, and serve hot.

Simple Ricotta & Spinach Balls

Prep + Cook Time: 20 minutes | Serves: 4

Ingredients

14 oz store-bought crescent dough
1 cup steamed spinach
1 cup crumbled ricotta cheese

¼ tsp garlic powder
1 tsp chopped oregano
¼ tsp salt

Directions

Preheat the Air fryer to 350 F, and roll the dough onto a lightly floured flat surface. Combine the ricotta, spinach, oregano, salt, and garlic powder together in a bowl. Cut the dough into 4 equal pieces.

Divide the spinach/feta mixture between the dough pieces. Make sure to place the filling in the center. Fold the dough and secure with a fork. Place onto a lined baking dish, and then in the Air fryer. Cook for 12 minutes, until lightly browned.

Mom's Blooming Buttery Onion

Prep + Cook Time: 40 minutes | Serves: 4

INGREDIENTS

4 onions
4 butter dollops

1 tbsp olive oil

DIRECTIONS

Peel the onions and slice off the root bottom so it can sit well. Cut slices into the onion to make it look like a blooming flower, make sure not to go all the way through; four cuts will do. Preheat the Air fryer to 350 F and place the onions in the Air fryer.

Drizzle with olive oil, place a dollop of butter on top of each onion and cook for about 30 minutes. Serve with garlic mayo dip.

Stuffed Green Chilies with Cheese in Tomato Sauce

Prep + Cook Time: 35 minutes | Serves: 4

Ingredients

2 cans green chili peppers
1 cup cheddar cheese , shredded
1 cup Monterey Jack cheese.
2 tbsp all-purpose flour

2 large eggs, beaten
½ cup milk
1 can tomato sauce

Directions

Preheat the Air fryer to 380 F, and spray a baking dish with cooking spray. Take half of the chilies and arrange them in the baking dish. Top with half of the cheese and cover with the other half of the chilies.

In a medium bowl, combine the eggs, the milk, the flour and pour the mixture over the chillies. Cook for 20 minutes. Remove the chilies from the Air Fryer and pour the tomato sauce over them; cook for more 15 minutes.

Remove from the Air fryer and top with the remaining cheese.

Russian-Style Eggplant Caviar

Prep + Cook Time: 20 minutes | Serves: 3

Ingredients

3 medium eggplants
½ red onion, chopped and blended
2 tbsp balsamic vinegar

1 tbsp olive oil
Salt

Directions

Arrange the eggplants in the basket and cook them for 15 minutes at 380 F. Remove them and let them cool. Then cut the eggplants in half, lengthwise, and empty their insides with a spoon.

Blend the onion in a blender. Put the inside of the eggplants in the blender and process everything. Add the vinegar, olive oil and salt, then blend again. Serve cool with bread and tomato sauce or ketchup.

Cauliflower Rice with Tofu and Peas

Prep + Cook Time: 30 minutes | Serves: 4

Ingredients

Tofu:
½ block tofu
½ cup diced onion
2 tbsp soy sauce

1 tsp turmeric
1 cup diced carrot

Cauliflower:
3 cups cauliflower rice (pulsed in a food processor)
2 tbsp soy sauce
½ cup chopped broccoli
2 garlic cloves, minced

1 ½ tsp toasted sesame oil
1 tbsp minced ginger
½ cup frozen peas
1 tbsp rice vinegar

Directions

Preheat the Air fryer to 370 F, crumble the tofu and combine it with all tofu ingredients. Place in a baking dish and air fry for 10 minutes. Meanwhile, place all cauliflower ingredients in a large bowl; mix to combine well.

Add the cauliflower mixture to the tofu and stir to combine; cook for 12 minutes. Serve and enjoy.

Cheese with Spinach Enchiladas

Prep + Cook Time: 20 minutes | Serves: 4

Ingredients

8 corn tortillas
2 cups mozzarella cheese, shredded
1 cup ricotta cheese
1 package frozen spinach
1 garlic clove, minced

½ cup sliced onions
½ cup sour cream
1 tbsp butter
1 can enchilada sauce

Directions

In a saucepan, heat oil and sauté garlic and onion, until brown. Stir in the frozen spinach and cook for 5 more minutes. Remove from the heat and stir in the ricotta cheese, sour cream and the shredded cheese.

Warm the tortillas on low heat for 15 seconds in the Air fryer. Spoon ¼ cup of spinach mixture in the middle of a tortilla. Roll up and place seam side down in the Air fryer's basket. Pour the enchilada sauce over the tortillas and sprinkle with the remaining cheese. Cook for 15 minutes at 380 F.

Classic Ratatouille

Prep + Cook Time: 30 minutes | Serves: 2

Ingredients

1 tbsp olive oil
3 roma tomatoes, thinly sliced
2 garlic cloves, minced
1 zucchini, thinly sliced
2 yellow bell peppers, sliced

1 tbsp vinegar
2 tbsp herbs de Provence
Salt and black pepper to taste

Directions

Preheat the Air fryer to 390 F, and place all ingredients in a bowl. Season with salt and pepper, and stir until the veggies are well coated. Arrange the vegetable in a round baking dish and place in the Air fryer. Cook for 15 minutes, shaking occasionally. Let sit for 5 more minutes after the timer goes off.

Garlicky Fennel Cabbage Steaks

Prep + Cook Time: 25 minutes | Serves: 3

Ingredients

1 cabbage head
1 tbsp garlic paste
1 tsp salt

2 tbsp olive oil
½ tsp black pepper
2 tsp fennel seeds

Directions

Preheat the Air fryer to 350 F, and slice the cabbage into 1 ½-inch slice. In a small bowl, combine all the other ingredients; brush cabbage with the mixture. Arrange the cabbage steaks in the Air fryer and cook for 15 minutes.

Vegetable Spring Rolls

Prep + Cook Time: 15 minutes | Serves: 4

Ingredients

½ cabbage, grated
2 carrots, grated
1 tsp minced ginger
1 tsp minced garlic
1 tsp sesame oil

1 tsp soy sauce
1 tsp sesame seeds
½ tsp salt
1 tsp olive oil
1 package spring roll wrappers

Directions

Preheat the Air fryer to 370 F, and combine all ingredients in a large bowl. Divide the mixture between the spring roll sheets, and roll them up; arrange on the baking mat. Cook in the air fryer for 5 minutes.

Cheddar & Tempeh Stuffed Mushrooms

Prep + Cook Time: 20 minutes | Serves: 3 to 4

Ingredients

14 small button mushrooms
1 clove garlic, minced
Salt and pepper to taste
4 slices tempeh, chopped

¼ cup grated Cheddar cheese
1 tbsp olive oil
1 tbsp chopped parsley

Directions

Preheat the Air Fryer to 390 F, and in a bowl, add the oil, tempeh, cheddar cheese, parsley, salt, pepper, and garlic. Mix well with a spoon. Cut the stalks of the mushrooms off and fill each cap with the tempeh mixture.

Press the tempeh mixture into the caps to avoid from falling off. Place the stuffed mushrooms in the fryer's basket and cook at 390 F for 8 minutes. Once golden and crispy, plate them and serve with a green salad.

POULTRY RECIPES

Spicy Chicken Tenders with Aioli Sauce

Prep + Cook Time: 15 minutes | Serves: 4

Ingredients

3 chicken breasts, skinless, cut into strips
4 tbsp olive oil
1 cup breadcrumbs
Salt and black pepper to taste
½ tbsp garlic powder

½ tbsp ground chili
Prep + Cook Time½ cup mayonnaise
2 tbsp olive oil
½ tbsp ground chili

Directions

Mix breadcrumbs, salt, pepper, garlic powder and chili, and spread onto a plate. Spray the chicken with oil. Roll the strips in the breadcrumb mixture until well coated. Spray with a little bit of oil.

Arrange an even layer of strips into your air fryer and cook for 6 minutes at 360 F, turning once halfway through. To prepare the hot aioli: combine mayo with oil and ground chili. Serve hot.

Marinara Sauce Cheese Chicken

Prep + Cook Time: 25 minutes | Serves: 2

Ingredients

2 chicken breasts, skinless, beaten, ½-inch thick
1 egg, beaten
½ cup breadcrumbs
A pinch of salt and black pepper

2 tbsp marinara sauce
2 tbsp Grana Padano cheese, grated
2 slices mozzarella cheese

Directions

Dip the breasts into the egg, then into the crumbs and arrange in the fryer; cook for 5 minutes at 400 F. Then, turn over and drizzle with marinara sauce, Grana Padano and mozzarella. Cook for 5 more minutes at 400 F.

Honey Thighs with Garlic

Prep + Cook Time: 30 minutes | Serves: 4

Ingredients

4 thighs, skin-on
3 tbsp honey
2 tbsp Dijon mustard

½ tbsp garlic powder
Salt and black pepper to taste

Directions

In a bowl, mix honey, mustard, garlic, salt, and black pepper. Coat the thighs in the mixture and arrange them in your air fryer. Cook for 16 minutes at 400 F, turning once halfway through.

Buttery Chicken with Monterrey Jack Cheese

Prep + Cook Time: 30 minutes | Serves: 4

Ingredients

½ cup Italian breadcrumbs
2 tbsp grated Parmesan cheese
1 tbsp butter, melted

4 chicken thighs
½ cup marinara sauce
½ cup shredded Monterrey Jack cheese

Directions

Spray the air fryer basket with cooking spray. In a bowl, mix the crumbs and Parmesan cheese. Pour the butter into another bowl. Brush the thighs with butter. Dip each one into the crumbs mixture, until well-coated.

Arrange two chicken thighs in the air fryer, and lightly spray with cooking oil. Cook for 5 minutes at 380 F. Flip over, top with a few tbsp marinara sauce and shredded Monterrey Jack cheese. Cook until no longer pink in the center, for 4 minutes. Repeat with the remaining thighs.

Chicken Breasts with Rosemary

Prep + Cook Time: 30minutes | Serves: 2

Ingredients

2 tbsp Dijon mustard
1 tbsp maple syrup
2 tsp minced fresh rosemary
¼ tsp salt

⅛ tsp black pepper
2 chicken breasts, boneless, skinless

Directions

In a bowl, mix mustard, maple syrup, rosemary, salt, and pepper. Rub mixture onto chicken breasts. Spray generously the air fryer basket generously with cooking spray. Arrange the breasts inside and cook for 20 minutes, turning once halfway through.

Thyme Whole Chicken with Pancetta and Lemon

Prep + Cook Time: 60 minutes | Serves: 4

Ingredients

1 small whole chicken
1 lemon
4 slices pancetta, roughly chopped
1 onion, chopped

1 sprig fresh thyme
Olive oil
Salt and black pepper

Directions

In a bowl, mix pancetta, onion, thyme, salt, and black pepper. Pat dry the chicken with a dry paper towel. Insert the pancetta mixture into chicken's cavity and press tight.

Put in the whole lemon, and rub the top and sides of the chicken with salt and black pepper. Spray the air fryer's basket with olive oil and arrange the chicken inside. Cook for 30 minutes on 400 F, turning once halfway through.

Green Chicken Drumsticks with Coconut Cream

Prep + Cook Time: 25 minutes | Serves: 4

Ingredients

4 chicken drumsticks, boneless, skinless
2 tbsp green curry paste
3 tbsp coconut cream

Salt and black pepper
½ fresh jalapeno chili, finely chopped
A handful of fresh parsley, roughly chopped

Directions

In a bowl, add drumsticks, paste, cream, salt, black pepper and jalapeno; coat the chicken well. Arrange the drumsticks in the air fryer and cook for 6 minutes at 400 F, flipping once halfway through. Serve with fresh cilantro.

Creamy Chicken Nuggets

Prep + Cook Time: 15 minutes | Serves: 4

Ingredients

2 chicken breasts, skinless, boneless, cut into nuggets
4 tbsp sour cream
½ cup breadcrumbs
½ tbsp garlic powder

½ tsp cayenne pepper
Salt and black pepper to taste

Directions

In a bowl, add sour cream and place the chicken. Stir well. Mix the breadcrumbs, garlic, cayenne, salt, and black pepper and scatter onto a plate. Roll up the chicken in the breadcrumbs to coat well. Grease the air with oil. Arrange the nuggets in an even layer and cook for 10 minutes on 360 F, turning once halfway through cooking.

Herby Stuffed Chicken

Prep + Cook Time: 50 minutes | Serves: 2

Ingredients

1 small chicken
1 ½ tbsp olive oil
Salt and black pepper to taste to season
1 cup breadcrumbs
⅓ cup chopped sage

⅓ cup chopped thyme
2 cloves garlic, crushed
1 brown onion, chopped
3 tbsp butter
2 eggs, beaten

Directions

Rinse the chicken gently, pat dry with a paper towel and remove any excess fat with a knife; set aside. On a stove top, place a pan. Add the butter, garlic and onion and sauté to brown. Add the eggs, sage, thyme, pepper, and salt.

Mix well. Cook for 20 seconds and turn the heat off. Stuff the chicken with the mixture into the cavity. Then, tie the legs of the spatchcock with a butcher's twine and brush with olive oil. Rub the top and sides of the chicken generously with salt and pepper. Preheat the Air Fryer to 390 F.

Place the spatchcock into the fryer basket and roast for 25 minutes. Turn the chicken over and continue cooking for 10-15 minutes more; check throughout the cooking time to ensure it doesn't dry or overcooks. Remove onto a chopping board and wrap it with aluminum foil; let rest for 10 minutes. Serve with a side of steamed broccoli.

Chili Chicken Wings

Prep + Cook Time: 16 hrs 40 minutes | Serves: 4

Ingredients

2 lb chicken wings
1 tbsp olive oil
3 cloves garlic, minced
1 tbsp chili powder
½ tbsp cinnamon powder
½ tsp allspice
1 habanero pepper, seeded
1 tbsp soy sauce

½ tbsp white pepper
¼ cup red wine vinegar
3 tbsp lime juice
2 Scallions, chopped
½ tbsp grated ginger
½ tbsp chopped fresh thyme
⅓ tbsp sugar
½ tbsp salt

Directions

In a bowl, add the olive oil, soy sauce, garlic, habanero pepper, allspice, cinnamon powder, cayenne pepper, white pepper, salt, sugar, thyme, ginger, scallions, lime juice, and red wine vinegar; mix well.

Add the chicken wings to the marinade mixture and coat it well with the mixture. Cover the bowl with cling film and refrigerate the chicken to marinate for 16 hours. Preheat the Air Fryer to 400 F. Remove the chicken from the fridge, drain all the liquid, and pat each wing dry using a paper towel.

Place half of the wings in the basket and cook for 16 minutes. Shake halfway through. Remove onto a serving platter and repeat the cooking process for the remaining wings. Serve with blue cheese dip or ranch dressing.

Spice and Juicy Chicken Breasts

Prep + Cook Time: 35 minutes | Serves: 3

Ingredients

2 chicken breasts
Salt and black pepper to taste
1 cup flour
3 eggs
½ cup apple cider vinegar
½ tbsp ginger paste
½ tbsp garlic paste
1 tbsp sugar

2 red chilies, minced
2 tbsp tomato puree
1 red pepper
1 green pepper
1 tbsp paprika
4 tbsp water

Directions

Preheat the Air Fryer to 350 F. Put the chicken breasts on a clean flat surface. Cut them in cubes. Pour the flour in a bowl, crack the eggs in, add the salt and pepper; whisk. Put the chicken in the flour mixture; mix to coat.

Place the chicken in the fryer's basket, spray with cooking spray, and fry for 8 minutes. Pull out the fryer basket, shake to toss, and spray again with cooking spray. Keep cooking for 7 minutes or until golden and crispy.

Remove the chicken to a plate. Put the red, yellow, and green peppers on a chopping board. Using a knife, cut open and deseed them; cut the flesh in long strips. In a bowl, add the water, apple cider vinegar, sugar, ginger and garlic puree, red chili, tomato puree, and smoked paprika; mix with a fork.

Place a skillet over medium heat on a stovetop and spray with cooking spray. Add the chicken and pepper strips. Stir and cook until the peppers are sweaty but still crunchy. Pour the chili mixture on the chicken, stir, and bring to simmer for 10 minutes; turn off the heat. Dish the chicken chili sauce into a serving bowl and serve.

Chicken Kabobs with Garlic Sauce

Prep + Cook Time: 35 minutes | Serves: 3

Ingredients

3 chicken breasts
Salt to season
1 tbsp chili powder
¼ cup maple syrup
½ cup soy sauce

2 red peppers
1 green pepper
7 mushrooms
2 tbsp sesame seeds

Prep + Cook Time1 garlic clove

2 tbsp olive oil
Zest and juice from 1 lime

A pinch of salt
¼ cup fresh parsley, chopped

Directions

Put the chicken breasts on a clean flat surface and cut them in 2-inch cubes with a knife. Add them to a bowl, along with the chili powder, salt, maple syrup, soy sauce, sesame seeds, and spray them with cooking spray. Toss to coat and set aside. Place the peppers on the chopping board. Use a knife to open, deseed and cut in cubes.

Likewise, cut the mushrooms in halves. Start stacking up the ingredients - stick 1 red pepper, then green, a chicken cube, and a mushroom half. Repeat the arrangement until the skewer is full. Repeat the process until all the ingredients are used. Preheat the Air Fryer to 330 F.

Brush the kabobs with soy sauce mixture and place them into the fryer basket. Grease with cooking spray and grill for 20 minutes; flip halfway through. Meanwhile, mix all salsa verde ingredients in your food processor and blend until you obtain a chunky paste. Remove the kabobs when ready and serve with a side of salsa verde.

Zucchini Stuffed Lemony Chicken

Prep + Cook Time: 100 minutes | Serves: 6

Ingredients

Prep + Cook Time1 whole chicken, 3 lb
2 red and peeled onions
2 tbsp olive oil
2 apricots
1 zucchini

1 apple
2 cloves finely chopped garlic
Fresh chopped thyme
Salt and black pepper to taste

Prep + Cook TimePrep + Cook Time5 oz honey

juice from 1 lemon
2 tbsp olive oil

Salt and black pepper to taste

Directions

For the stuffing, chop all ingredients into tiny pieces. Transfer to a large bowl and add the olive oil. Season with salt and black pepper. Fill the cavity of the chicken with the stuffing, without packing it tightly.

Place the chicken in the Air Fryer and cook for 35 minutes at 340 F. Warm the honey and the lemon juice in a large pan; season with salt and pepper. Reduce the temperature of the Air Fryer to 320 F.

Brush the chicken with some of the honey-lemon marinade and return it to the fryer. Cook for another 70 minutes; brush the chicken every 20-25 minutes with the marinade. Garnish with parsley, and serve with potatoes.

Drumsticks with Blue Cheese Sauce

Prep + Cook Time: 2 hrs 25 minutes | Serves: 4

Ingredients

Prep + Cook Time1 lb mini drumsticks
3 tbsp butter
3 tbsp paprika
2 tbsp powdered cumin

Prep + Cook Time½ cup mayonnaise
1 cup crumbled blue cheese
1 cup sour cream
1 ½ tbsp garlic powder
1 ½ tbsp onion powder
Salt and black pepper to taste

¼ cup hot sauce
1 tbsp maple syrup
2 tbsp onion powder
2 tbsp garlic powder

1 ½ tbsp cayenne pepper
1 ½ tbsp white wine vinegar
2 tbsp buttermilk
1 ½ worcestershire sauce

Directions

Start with the drumstick sauce; place a pan over medium heat on a stove top. Melt the butter, and add the hot sauce, paprika, garlic, onion, maple syrup, and cumin; mix well. Cook the mixture for 5 minutes or until the sauce reduces. Turn off the heat and let cool. Put the drumsticks in a bowl, pour half of the sauce over, and mix it.

Save the remaining sauce for serving. Refrigerate the drumsticks for 2 hours. Meanwhile, make the blue cheese sauce: in a jug, add the sour cream, blue cheese, mayonnaise, garlic powder, onion powder, buttermilk, cayenne pepper, vinegar, Worcestershire sauce, pepper, and salt. Using a stick blender, blend the ingredients until they are well mixed with no large lumps. Adjust the salt and pepper taste as desired. Preheat the Air Fryer to 350 F.

Remove the drumsticks from the fridge and place them in the fryer basket; cook for 15 minutes. Turn the drumsticks with tongs every 5 minutes to ensure that they are evenly cooked. Remove the drumsticks to a serving bowl and pour the remaining sauce over. Serve with the blue cheese sauce and a side of celery sticks.

Chili Lime Chicken Lollipop

Prep + Cook Time: 50 minutes | Serves: 3

Ingredients

1 lb mini chicken drumsticks
½ tbsp soy sauce
1 tbsp lime juice
Salt and black pepper to taste
1 tbsp cornstarch
½ tbsp minced garlic
½ tbsp chili powder
½ tbsp chopped cilantro

½ tbsp garlic- ginger paste
1 tbsp vinegar
1 tbsp chili paste
½ tbsp beaten egg
1 tbsp paprika
1 tbsp flour
2 tbsp maple syrup

Directions

Mix garlic ginger paste, chili powder, maple syrup, paprika powder, chopped coriander, plain vinegar, egg, garlic, and salt, in a bowl. Add the chicken drumsticks and toss to coat; Stir in cornstarch, flour, and lime juice.

Preheat the Air Fryer to 350 F. Remove each drumstick, shake off the excess marinade, and place in a single layer in the basket; cook for 5 minutes. Slide out the basket, spray the chicken with cooking spray and continue to cook for 5 minutes. Remove onto a serving platter and serve with tomato dip and a side of steamed asparagus.

Almond Turkey with Lemon and Eggs

Prep + Cook Time: 50 minutes | Serves: 3

Ingredients

1 lb turkey breasts
Salt and black pepper to taste to season
¼ cup chicken soup cream
¼ cup mayonnaise
2 tbsp lemon juice
¼ cup slivered almonds, chopped

¼ cup breadcrumbs
2 tbsp chopped green onion
2 tbsp chopped pimentos
2 Boiled eggs, chopped
½ cup diced celery

Directions

Preheat the Air Fryer to 390 F. Place the turkey breasts on a clean flat surface and season with salt and pepper.

Grease with cooking spray and place them in the fryer's basket; cook for 13 minutes. Remove turkey back onto the chopping board, let cool, and cut into dices. In a bowl, add the celery, chopped eggs, pimentos, green onions, slivered almonds, lemon juice, mayonnaise, diced turkey, and chicken soup cream and mix well.

Grease a 5 X 5 inches casserole dish with cooking spray, scoop the turkey mixture into the bowl, sprinkle the breadcrumbs on it, and spray with cooking spray. Put the dish in the fryer basket, and bake the ingredients at 390 F for 20 minutes. Remove and serve with a side of steamed asparagus.

Party Chicken Wings with Sesame

Prep + Cook Time: 25 minutes | Serves: 4

Ingredients

1 lb chicken wings
2 tbsp sesame oil
2 tbsp maple syrup

Salt and black pepper
3 tbsp sesame seeds

Directions

In a bowl, add wings, oil, maple syrup, salt and pepper, and stir to coat well. In another bowl, add the sesame seeds and roll the wings in the seeds to coat thoroughly. Arrange the wings in an even layer inside your air fryer and cook for 12 minutes on 360 F, turning once halfway through.

Buttermilk Chicken Bites

Prep + Cook Time: 25 minutes | Serves: 4

Ingredients

2 chicken breasts, skinless, cut into 2 pieces each
1 egg, beaten
¼ cup buttermilk

1 cup corn flakes, crushed
Salt and black pepper to taste

Directions

In a bowl, whisk egg and buttermilk. Add in chicken pieces and stir to coat. In a plate, spread the cornflakes out and mix with salt and pepper. Coat the chicken pieces in the cornflakes. Spray the air fryer with cooking spray.

Arrange the chicken in an even layer in the air fryer; cook for 12 minutes at 360 F, turning once halfway through.

Savory Chicken Burgers

Prep + Cook Time: 25 minutes | Serves: 4

Ingredients

1 lb ground chicken
½ onion, chopped
2 garlic cloves, chopped
1 egg, beaten
½ cup breadcrumbs

½ tbsp ground cumin
½ tbsp paprika
½ tbsp cilantro seeds, crushed
Salt and black pepper to taste

Directions

In a bowl, mix chicken, onion, garlic, egg, breadcrumbs, cumin, paprika, cilantro, salt, and black pepper, with hands; shape into 4 patties. Grease the air fryer with oil, and arrange the patties inside. Do not layer them. Cook in batches if needed. Cook for 10 minutes at 380 F, turning once halfway through.

Creamy Chicken With Prosciutto

Prep + Cook Time: 25 minutes | Serves: 2

Ingredients

2 chicken breasts
1 tbsp olive oil
Salt and black pepper to taste to season

1 cup semi-dried tomatoes, sliced
½ cup brie cheese, halved
4 slices thin prosciutto

Directions

Preheat the Air Fryer to 365 F. Put the chicken on a chopping board, and cut a small incision deep enough to make stuffing on both. Insert one slice of cheese and 4 to 5 tomato slices into each chicken.

Lay the prosciutto on the chopping board. Put the chicken on one side and roll the prosciutto over the chicken making sure that both ends of the prosciutto meet under the chicken.

Drizzle olive oil and sprinkle with salt and pepper. Place the chicken in the basket and cook for 10 minutes. Turn the breasts over and cook for another 5 minutes. Slice each chicken breast in half and serve with tomato salad.

Chicken Tenders with Tarragon

Prep + Cook Time: 15minutes | Serves: 2

Ingredients

2 chicken tenders
Salt and black pepper to taste

½ cup dried tarragon
1 tbsp butter

Directions

Preheat the Air Fryer to 390 F. Lay out a 12 X 12 inch cut of foil on a flat surface. Place the chicken breasts on the foil, sprinkle the tarragon on both, and share the butter onto both breasts. Sprinkle with salt and pepper.

Loosely wrap the foil around the breasts to enable air flow. Place the wrapped chicken in the basket and cook for 12 minutes. Remove the chicken and carefully unwrap the foil. Serve with the sauce extract and steamed veggies.

Herby Chicken with Lime

Prep + Cook Time: 50 minutes | Serves: 4

Ingredients

1 (2½ lb) whole chicken, on the bone
Salt and black pepper to taste to season
1 tbsp chili powder
1 tbsp garlic powder
4 tbsp oregano

2 tbsp cilantro powder
2 tbsp cumin powder
2 tbsp olive oil
4 tbsp paprika
1 lime, juiced

Directions

In a bowl, pour the oregano, garlic powder, chili powder, ground cilantro, paprika, cumin powder, pepper, salt, and olive oil. Mix well to create a rub for the chicken, and rub onto it. Refrigerate for 20 minutes.

Preheat the Air Fryer to 350 F. Remove the chicken from the refrigerator; place in the fryer basket and cook for 20 minutes. Use a skewer to poke the chicken to ensure that it is clear of juices. If not, cook the chicken further for 5 to 10 minutes; let to rest for 10 minutes. After, drizzle the lime juice over and serve with green salad.

Chicken Wrapped In Bacon

Prep + Cook Time: 20 minutes | Serves: 2 to 4

Ingredients

2 chicken breasts
8 oz onion and chive cream cheese
1 tbsp butter
6 turkey bacon

Salt to taste
1 tbsp fresh parsley, chopped
 juice from ½ lemon

Directions

Preheat the Air Fryer to 390 F. Stretch out the bacon slightly and lay them on in 2 sets; 3 bacon strips together on each side. Place the chicken breast on each bacon set and use a knife to smear the cream cheese on both. Share the butter on top and sprinkle with salt. Wrap the bacon around the chicken and secure the ends into the wrap.

Place the wrapped chicken in the fryer's basket and cook for 14 minutes. Turn the chicken halfway through. Remove the chicken onto a serving platter and top with parsley and lemon juice. Serve with steamed greens.

Fruity Chicken Breasts with BBQ Sauce

Prep + Cook Time: 20 minutes | Serves: 2

Ingredients

2 large chicken breasts, cubed
2 green bell peppers, sliced
½ onion, sliced

1 can drain pineapple chunks
½ cup barbecue sauce

Directions

Preheat the Air Fryer to 370 F. Thread the green bell peppers, the chicken, the onions and the pineapple chunks on the skewers. Brush with barbecue sauce and fry for 20 minutes, until thoroughly cooked and slightly crispy.

Broccoli Chicken Casserole

Prep + Cook Time: 45 minutes | Serves: 3

Ingredients

3 chicken breasts
Salt and black pepper to taste
1 cup shredded Cheddar cheese
1 broccoli head

½ cup mushroom soup cream
½ cup croutons

Directions

Preheat the Air Fryer to 390 F. Place the chicken breasts on a clean flat surface and season with salt and pepper. Grease with cooking spray and place them in the fryer basket. Close the Air Fryer and cook for 13 minutes. Meanwhile, place the broccoli on the chopping board and use a knife to chop.

Remove them onto the chopping board, let cool, and cut into bite-size pieces. In a bowl, add the chicken, broccoli, cheddar cheese, and mushroom soup cream; mix well. Scoop the mixture into a 3 X 3cm casserole dish, add the croutons on top and spray with cooking spray. Put the dish in the basket and cook for 10 minutes. Serve with a side of steamed greens.

Jalapeño Chicken Thighs

Prep + Cook Time: 25 minutes | Serves: 4

Ingredients

4 chicken thighs, boneless
2 garlic cloves, crushed
1 jalapeno pepper, finely chopped

4 tbsp chili sauce
Salt and black pepper

Directions

In a bowl, add thighs, garlic, jalapeno, chili sauce, salt, and black pepper, and stir to coat. Arrange the thighs in an even layer inside your air fryer and cook for 12 minutes at 360 F, turning once halfway through.

Easy Chicken Fingers with Parmesan

Prep + Cook Time: 1 hour 30 minutes | Serves: 2

Ingredients

2 skinless and boneless chicken breasts, cut strips
1 tbsp salt
1 tbsp black pepper
2 cloves garlic, crushed
3 tbsp cornstarch

4 tbsp breadcrumbs, like flour bread
4 tbsp grated Parmesan cheese
2 eggs, beaten

Directions

Mix salt, garlic, and pepper in a bowl. Add the chicken and stir to coat. Marinate for an hour in the fridge.

Meanwhile, mix the breadcrumbs with cheese evenly; set aside. Remove the chicken from the fridge, lightly toss in cornstarch, dip in egg and coat them gently in the cheese mixture. Preheat the Air Fryer to 350 F.

Lightly spray the air fryer basket with cooking spray and place the chicken inside; cook for 15 minutes, until nice and crispy. Serve the chicken with a side of vegetable fries and cheese dip.

Chicken with Soy Sauce

Prep + Cook Time: 1 hour 35 minutes | Serves: 3

Ingredients

2 chicken breasts
1 tbsp mayonnaise
2 eggs
1 tbsp chili pepper

1 tbsp curry powder
1 tbsp sugar
1 tbsp soy sauce

Directions

Put the chicken breasts on a clean flat surface and use a knife to slice in diagonal pieces. Gently pound them to become thinner using a rolling pin. Place in a bowl and add soy sauce, sugar, curry powder, and chili pepper.

Mix well and refrigerate for an hour; preheat the Air Fryer to 350 F. Remove the chicken and crack the eggs on. Add the mayonnaise and mix. Remove each chicken piece and shake well to remove as much liquid as possible.

Place them in the fryer basket and cook for 8 minutes. Flip and cook further for 6 minutes. Remove onto a serving platter and continue to cook with the remaining chicken. Serve with a side of steam greens.

Holiday Lemony Cornish Hen

Prep + Cook Time: 14 hrs 20 minutes | Serves: 4

Ingredients

2 lb cornish hen
1 lemon, zested
¼ tbsp sugar
¼ tsp salt

1 tbsp chopped fresh rosemary
1 tbsp chopped fresh thyme
¼ tsp red pepper flakes
½ cup olive oil

Directions

Place the hen on a chopping board with its back facing you, and use a knife to cut through from the top of the backbone to the bottom of the backbone, making 2 cuts; remove the backbone. Divide the hen into two lengthwise while cutting through the breastplate; set aside.

In a bowl, add the lemon zest, sugar, salt, rosemary, thyme, red pepper flakes, and olive oil; mix well. Add the hen pieces, coat all around with the spoon, and place in the refrigerator to marinate for 14 hours.

Preheat the Air Fryer to 390 F. After the marinating time, remove the hen pieces from the marinade and pat dry with a paper towel. Place in the fryer basket and roast for 16 minutes. Remove to a platter and serve with veggies.

Italian Chicken Schnitzel with Herbs

Prep + Cook Time: 25 minutes | Serves: 2

Ingredients

2 chicken breasts, skinless and boneless
2 eggs, cracked into a bowl
2 cups milk
4 tbsp tomato sauce
2 tbsp mixed herbs

2 cups mozzarella cheese
1 cup flour
¾ cup shaved ham
1 cup breadcrumbs

Directions

Place the chicken breast between to plastic wraps and use a rolling pin to pound them to flatten out. Whisk the milk and eggs together, in a bowl. Pour the flour in a plate, the breadcrumbs in another dish, and start coating the chicken. Toss the chicken in flour, then in the egg mixture, and then in the breadcrumbs.

Preheat the Air Fryer to 350 F. Put the chicken in the fryer basket and cook for 10 minutes. Remove them onto a plate and top the chicken with the ham, tomato sauce, mozzarella cheese, and mixed herbs. Return the chicken to the fryer's basket and cook further for 5 minutes or until the mozzarella cheese melts. Serve with vegetable fries.

Chicken with Honey and Orange

Prep + Cook Time: 20 minutes | Serves: 4

Ingredients

1 ½ pounds chicken breast, washed and sliced
Parsley to taste
1 cup coconut, shredded
¾ cup breadcrumbs
2 whole eggs, beaten
½ cup flour

½ tsp pepper
Salt to taste
½ cup orange marmalade
1 tbsp red pepper flakes
¼ cup honey
3 tbsp Dijon mustard

Directions

Preheat your Air Fryer to 400 F. In a mixing bowl, combine coconut, flour, salt, parsley and pepper. In another bowl, add the beaten eggs. Place breadcrumbs in a third bowl. Dredge chicken in egg mix, flour and finally in the breadcrumbs. Place the chicken in the Air Fryer cooking basket and bake for 15 minutes.

In a separate bowl, mix honey, orange marmalade, mustard and pepper flakes. Cover chicken with marmalade mixture and fry for 5 more minutes. Enjoy!

Maple Turkey Breast with Sage

Prep + Cook Time: 1 hour | Serves: 6

Ingredients

5 lb turkey breasts
¼ cup maple syrup
2 tbsp Dijon mustard
½ tbsp smoked paprika
1 tbsp thyme

2 tbsp olive oil
½ tbsp sage
½ tbsp salt and black pepper
1 tbsp butter, melted

Directions

Preheat the Air fryer to 350 F and brush the turkey with the olive oil. Combine all herbs and seasoning, in a small bowl, and rub the turkey with the mixture. Air fry the turkey for 25 minutes. Flip the turkey on its side and continue to cook for 12 more minutes.

Now, turn on the opposite side, and again, cook for an additional 12 minutes. Whisk the butter, maple and mustard together in a small bowl. When done, brush the glaze all over the turkey. Return to the air fryer and cook for 5 more minutes, until nice and crispy.

Parmesan Turkey Meatballs

Prep + Cook Time: 40 minutes | Serves: 3 to 4

Ingredients

1 lb ground turkey
1 egg
½ cup breadcrumbs
1 tbsp garlic powder
1 tbsp Italian seasoning

1 tbsp onion powder
¼ cup Parmesan cheese, grated
Salt and black pepper to taste

Directions

Preheat the Air Fryer to 400 F. In a bowl, add the ground turkey, crack the egg onto it, add the breadcrumbs, garlic powder, onion powder, Italian seasoning, parmesan cheese, salt, and pepper. Use your hands to mix them well. Spoon out portions and make bite-size balls out of the mixture.

Grease the fryer basket with cooking spray and add 10 turkey balls to the fryer's basket; cook for 12 minutes. Slide out the fryer basket halfway through and shake. When ready, remove onto a serving platter and continue the cooking process for the remaining balls. Serve the turkey balls with marinara sauce and a side of noodles.

Chicken Wings with Parmesan and Oregano

Prep + Cook Time: 35 minutes | Serves: 2

Ingredients

1 lb chicken wings
¼ cup butter
¼ cup grated Parmesan cheese
2 cloves garlic, minced

½ tbsp dried oregano
½ tbsp dried rosemary
Salt and black pepper to taste to season
¼ tsp paprika

Directions

Preheat the Air Fryer to 370 F. Place the chicken in a plate and season with salt and pepper. Put the chicken in the fryer basket, close the Air Fryer, and fry for 5 minutes. Meanwhile, place a skillet over medium heat on a stove top, add the butter, once melted add the garlic, stir and cook it for 1 minute.

Add the paprika, oregano, and rosemary to a bowl and mix them using a spoon. Add the mixture to the butter sauce. Stir and turn off the heat. Once the chicken breasts are ready, top them with the sauce, sprinkle with Parmesan cheese and cook in the Air Fryer for 5 minutes at 360 F.

Savory Chicken Breasts with Turmeric

Prep + Cook Time: 20 minutes | Serves: 3

Ingredients

3 chicken breasts
Salt to season

¼ cup sweet chili sauce
3 tbsp turmeric

Directions

Preheat the Air Fryer to 390 F. In a bowl, add the salt, sweet chili sauce, and turmeric; mix evenly with a spoon. Place the chicken breasts on a clean flat surface and with a brush, apply the turmeric sauce lightly on the chicken. Place in the fryer basket and grill for 18 minutes; turn them halfway through.

Buttery Chicken Legs with Rice

Prep + Cook Time: 40 minutes | Serves: 4

Ingredients

4 chicken legs
1 cup rice
2 cups water
2 tomatoes, cubed
3 tbsp butter

1 tbsp tomato paste
Salt and black pepper
1 onion
3 minced cloves garlic

Directions

Rub the chicken legs with butter. Sprinkle with salt and pepper and fry in a preheated Air Fryer for 30 minutes at 380 F. Then, add small onion and a little bit of oil; keep stirring. Add the tomatoes, the tomato paste, and the garlic, and cook for 5 more minutes.

Meanwhile, in a pan, boil the rice in 2 cups of water for around 20 minutes. In a baking tray, place the rice and top it with the air fried chicken and cook in the Air Fryer for 5 minutes. Serve and enjoy!

Chicken Thighs with Tomatoes

Prep + Cook Time: 20 minutes | Serves: 2

Ingredients

2 chicken thighs
1 cup tomatoes, quartered
4 cloves garlic, minced
½ tbsp dried tarragon

½ tbsp olive oil
¼ tsp red pepper flakes
Salt and black pepper to taste

Directions

Preheat the Air Fryer to 390 F. Add the tomatoes, red pepper flakes, tarragon, garlic, and olive oil to a medium bowl. Use a spoon to mix well. In a large ramekin, add the chicken and top with the tomato mixture.

Place the ramekin in the fryer basket and roast for 10 minutes. After baking, carefully remove the ramekin. Plate the chicken thighs, spoon the cooking juice over and serve.

Spicy Black Beans with Chicken and Corn

Prep + Cook Time: 18 minutes | Serves: 4

Ingredients

4 boneless and skinless chicken breasts, cubed
1 can sweet corn
1 can black beans, rinsed and drained

1 cup red and green peppers, stripes, cooked
1 tbsp vegetable oil
2 tbsp chili powder

Directions

Coat the chicken with salt, black pepper and a sprinkle of oil; cook for 15 minutes at 380 F. Meanwhile, in a deep skillet, pour 1 tbsp. of oil and stir in the chili powder, the corn and the beans. Add a little bit of hot water and keep stirring for 3 more minutes. Transfer the corn, the beans and the chicken to a serving platter. Enjoy.

Spicy Yogurt Chicken Strips

Prep + Cook Time: 25 minutes | Serves: 4

Ingredients

1 cup breadcrumbs
½ cup yogurt
1 lb chicken breasts cut into strips
1 tbsp ground cayenne

1 tbsp hot sauce
2 beaten eggs
1 tbsp sweet paprika
1 tbsp garlic powder

Directions

Preheat the air fryer to 390 degrees F. Whisk the eggs along with the hot sauce and yogurt. In a shallow bowl, combine the breadcrumbs, paprika, pepper, and garlic powder. Line a baking dish with parchment paper.

Dip the chicken in the egg/yogurt mixture first, and then coat with breadcrumbs. Arrange on the sheet and bake in the air fryer for 8 minutes. Flip the chicken over and bake for 8 more minutes on the other side.

Crispy Cajun Chicken Tenders

Prep + Cook Time: 25 minutes | Serves: 4

Ingredients

3 lb chicken breast cut into slices
3 eggs
2 ¼ cup flour, divided
1 tbsp olive oil
½ tbsp plus

½ tbsp garlic powder, divided
1 tbsp salt
3 tbsp cajun seasoning, divided
¼ cup milk

Directions

Season the chicken with salt, pepper, ½ tbsp garlic powder and 2 tbsp Cajun seasoning.

Combine 2 cups flour, the rest of the Cajun seasoning and the rest of the garlic powder, in a bowl. In another bowl, whisk the eggs, milk, olive oil, and quarter cup flour. Preheat the Air fryer to 370 F.

Line a baking sheet with parchment paper. Dip the chicken into the egg mixture first, and then into the flour mixture. Arrange on the sheet. If there isn't enough room, work in two batches. Cook for 12 to 15 minutes.

Fried Chicken Tenderloins

Prep + Cook Time: 15 minutes | Serves: 4

Ingredients

8 chicken tenderloins
2 tbsp butter

2 oz breadcrumbs
1 large egg, whisked

Directions

Preheat the Air fryer to 380 F. Combine the butter and the breadcrumbs, in a bowl. Keep mixing and stirring until the mixture gets crumbly. Dip the chicken in the egg wash. Then dip the chicken in the crumbs mix.

Making sure it is evenly and fully covered; cook for 10 minutes. Serve the dish and enjoy its crispy taste!

Parmesan Chicken Fingers with Fresh Chives

Prep + Cook Time: 8 minutes | Serves: 2

Ingredients

2 medium-sized chicken breasts, cut in stripes
3 tbsp Parmesan cheese, grated
¼ tbsp fresh chives, chopped
⅓ cup breadcrumbs
1 egg white

2 tbsp plum sauce, optional
½ tbsp fresh thyme, chopped
½ tbsp black pepper
1 tbsp water

Directions

Preheat the Air Fryer to 360 F. Mix the chives, Parmesan cheese, thyme, pepper and breadcrumbs. In another bowl, whisk the egg white and mix with the water. Dip the chicken strips into the egg mixture and the breadcrumb mixture. Place the strips in the air fryer basket and cook for 10 minutes. Serve with plum sauce.

Mom's Tarragon Chicken Breasts

Prep + Cook Time: 15 minutes | Serves: 3

Ingredients

1 boneless and skinless chicken breast
½ tbsp butter
¼ tbsp kosher salt

¼ cup dried tarragon
¼ tbsp black and fresh ground pepper

Directions

Preheat the Air Fryer to 380 F and place each chicken breast on a 12x12 inches foil wrap. Top the chicken with tarragon and butter; season with salt and pepper to taste. Wrap the foil around the chicken breast in a loose way to create a flow of air. Cook the in the Air Fryer for 15 minutes. Carefully unwrap the chicken and serve.

Creamy Chicken and Ham

Prep + Cook Time: 40 minutes | Serves: 4

Ingredients

4 skinless and boneless chicken breasts
4 slices ham
4 slices Swiss cheese
3 tbsp all-purpose flour
4 tbsp butter

1 tbsp paprika
1 tbsp chicken bouillon granules
½ cup dry white wine
1 cup heavy whipping cream
1 tbsp cornstarch

Directions

Preheat the Air Fryer to 380 F. Pound the chicken breasts and put a slice of ham on each of the chicken breasts. Fold the edges of the chicken over the filling and secure the edges with toothpicks. In a medium bowl, combine the paprika and the flour, and coat the chicken pieces. Fry the chicken for 20 minutes.

In a large skillet, heat the butter and add the bouillon and wine; reduce the heat to low. Remove the chicken from the Air Fryer and place it in the skillet. Let simmer for around 20-25 minutes.

Stuffed Turkey Brestas with Ham, Cheese and Herbs

Prep + Cook Time: 35 minutes | Serves: 4

Ingredients

2 turkey breasts
1 ham slice
1 slice cheddar cheese
2 oz breadcrumbs
1 tbsp cream cheese

1 tbsp garlic powder
1 tbsp thyme
1 tbsp tarragon
1 egg, beaten
Salt and black pepper to taste

Directions

Preheat the air fryer to 350 F. Cut the turkey in the middle, that way so you can add ingredients in the center. Season with salt, pepper, thyme and tarragon. Combine the cream cheese and garlic powder, in a small bowl.

Spread the mixture on the inside of the breasts. Place half cheddar slice and half ham slice in the center of each breast. Dip the cordon bleu in egg first, then sprinkle with breadcrumbs. Cook on a baking mat for 30 minutes.

Cayenne Cauliflower Florets with Chicken Drumsticks

Prep + Cook Time: 50 minutes | Serves: 4

Ingredients

8 chicken drumsticks
2 tbsp oregano
2 tbsp thyme
2 oz oats
¼ cup milk

¼ steamed cauliflower florets
1 egg
1 tbsp ground cayenne
Salt and black pepper to taste

Directions

Preheat the Air fryer to 350 F and season the drumsticks with salt and pepper; rub them with the milk. Place all the other ingredients, except the egg, in a food processor. Process until smooth. Dip each drumstick in the egg first, and then in the oat mixture. Arrange half of them on a baking mat inside the air fryer. Cook for 20 minutes. Repeat with the other batch.

Party Hot Chicken Wings

Prep + Cook Time: 4 hrs 20 minutes | Serves: 2

Ingredients

8 chicken wings
1 tbsp water
2 tbsp potato starch

2 tbsp cornstarch
2 tbsp hot curry paste
½ tbsp baking powder

Directions

Combine the hot curry paste and water, in a small bowl. Place the wings in a large bowl, add the tom yum mixture and coat well. Cover the bowl and refrigerate for 4 hours. Preheat the air fryer to 370 degrees.

Combine the baking powder, cornstarch and potato starch. Dip each wing in the starch mixture. Place on a lined baking dish in the air fryer and cook for 7 minutes. Flip over and cook for 5 to 7 minutes more.

Oregano Chicken Legs with Lemon

Prep + Cook Time: 50 minutes | Serves: 5

Ingredients

5 quarters chicken legs
2 lemons, halved
5 tbsp garlic powder
5 tbsp dried basil

5 tbsp oregano, dried
⅓ cup olive oil
Salt and black pepper

Directions

Set the Air Fryer to 350 F. Place the chicken in a large deep bowl. Brush the chicken legs with a tbsp of olive oil.

Sprinkle with the lemon juice and arrange in the Air Fryer. In another bowl, combine basil, oregano, garlic powder, salt and pepper. Sprinkle the seasoning mixture on the chicken. Cook in the preheated Air Fryer for 50 minutes, shaking every 10-15 minutes.

Chicken with Cashew Nuts and Bell Pepper

Prep + Cook Time: 30 minutes | Serves: 4

Ingredients

1 lb chicken cubes
2 tbsp soy sauce
1 tbsp corn flour
2 ½ onion cubes
1 carrot, chopped

⅓ cup cashew nuts, fried
1 bell pepper, cut
2 tbsp garlic, crushed
Salt and white pepper

Directions

Marinate the chicken cubes with ½ tbsp of white pepper, ½ tsp salt, 2 tbsp soya sauce, and add 1 tbsp corn flour.

Set aside for 25 minutes. Preheat the Air Fryer to 380 F and transfer the marinated chicken. Add the garlic, the onion, the bell pepper, and the carrot; fry for 5-6 minutes. Roll it in the cashew nuts before serving.

Oyster Chicken Breasts

Prep + Cook Time: 60 minutes | Serves: 2

Ingredients

2 chicken breasts
1 tbsp minced ginger
2 rosemary sprigs
½ lemon, cut into wedges

1 tbsp soy sauce
½ tbsp olive oil
1 tbsp oyster sauce
3 tbsp brown sugar

Directions

Add the ginger, soy sauce, and olive oil, in a bowl; add the chicken and coat well. Cover the bowl and refrigerate for 30 minutes. Preheat the air fryer to 370 F. Transfer the marinated chicken to a baking dish; cook for 6 minutes.

Meanwhile, mix the oyster sauce, rosemary and brown sugar, in a small bowl. Pour the sauce over the chicken. Arrange the lemon wedges in the dish. Return to the air fryer and cook for 13 more minutes.

Whole Chicken with Prunes and Capers

Prep + Cook Time: 55 minutes | Serves: 6

Ingredients

1 whole chicken, 3 lb
½ cup pitted prunes
3 minced cloves of garlic
2 tbsp capers
2 bay leaves
2 tbsp red wine vinegar

2 tbsp olive oil
1 tbsp dried oregano
¼ cup packed brown sugar
1 tbsp chopped and fresh parsley
Salt and black pepper

Directions

In a big and deep bowl, mix the prunes, the olives, capers, garlic, olive oil, bay leaves, oregano, vinegar, salt and pepper. Spread the mixture on the bottom of a baking tray, and place the chicken.

Preheat the Air Fryer to 360 F. Sprinkle a little bit of brown sugar on top of the chicken; cook for 55 minutes.

White Wine Chicken with Herbs

Prep + Cook Time: 45 minutes | Serves: 6

Ingredients

1 whole chicken, around 3 lb, cut in pieces
3 chopped cloves of garlic
½ cup olive oil
½ cup white wine
1 tbsp fresh rosemary

1 tbsp chopped fresh oregano
1 tbsp fresh thyme
Juice from 1 lemon
Salt and black pepper, to taste

Directions

In a large bowl, combine cloves of garlic, rosemary, thyme, olive oil, lemon juice, oregano, salt and pepper. Mix all ingredients very well and spread the mixture into a baking dish. Add the chicken and stir.

Preheat the Air Fryer to 380 F, and transfer in the chicken mixture. Sprinkle with wine and cook for 45 minutes.

Tasty Chicken Quarters with Broccoli & Rice

Prep + Cook Time: 60 minutes | Serves: 3

Ingredients

3 chicken leg quarters
1 package instant long grain rice
1 cup chopped broccoli

2 cups water
1 can condensed cream chicken soup
1 tbsp minced garlic

Directions

Preheat the Air Fryer to 390 F, and place the chicken quarters in the Air Fryer. Season with salt, pepper and one tbsp of oil; cook for 30 minutes. Meanwhile, in a large deep bowl, mix the rice, water, minced garlic, soup and broccoli. Combine the mixture very well.

Remove the chicken from the Air fryer and place it on a platter to drain. Spread the rice mixture on the bottom of the dish and place the chicken on top of the rice. Cook again for 30 minutes.

Asian-style Chicken with Vegetables

Prep + Cook Time: 35 minutes | Serves: 4

Ingredients

1 lb chicken, cut in stripes
2 tomatoes, cubed
3 green peppers, cut in stripes
1 tbsp cumin powder
1 large onion

2 tbsp oil
1 tbsp mustard
A pinch of ginger
A pinch of fresh and chopped coriander
Salt and black pepper

Directions

Heat the oil in a deep pan. Add the mustard, the onion, the ginger, the cumin and the green chili peppers. Sauté the mixture for 2-3 minutes. Then, add the tomatoes, the coriander and salt and keep stirring.

Preheat the Air Fryer to 380 F. Coat the chicken with oil, salt and pepper and cook it for 25 minutes. Remove from the Air Fryer and pour the sauce over and around.

Southwest-Style Buttermilk Chicken Thighs

Prep + Cook Time: 4 hrs 40 minutes | Serves: 6

Ingredients

1 ½ lb chicken thighs
1 tbsp cayenne pepper
3 tbsp salt divided
2 cups flour

2 tbsp black pepper
1 tbsp paprika
1 tbsp baking powder
2 cups buttermilk

Directions

Rinse and pat dry the chicken thighs. Place the chicken thighs in a bowl. Add cayenne pepper, 2 tbsp of salt, black pepper and buttermilk, and stir to coat well. Refrigerate for 4 hours. Preheat the air fryer to 350 F.

In another bowl, mix the flour, paprika, 1 tbsp of salt, and baking powder. Dredge half of the chicken thighs, one at a time, in the flour, and then place on a lined dish. Cook for 10 minutes, flip over and cook for 8 more minutes. Repeat with the other batch.

Coconut Crunch Chicken Strips

Prep + Cook Time: 22 minutes | Serves: 4

Ingredients

3 ½ cups coconut flakes
4 chicken breasts cut into strips
½ cup cornstarch

¼ tsp pepper
¼ tsp salt
3 eggs, beaten

Directions

Preheat the Air fryer to 350 F. Mix salt, pepper, and cornstarch in a small bowl. Line a baking sheet with parchment paper. Dip the chicken first in the cornstarch, then into the eggs, and finally, coat with coconut flakes. Arrange on the sheet and cook for 8 minutes. Flip the chicken over, and cook for 8 more minutes, until crispy.

American-Style Buttermilk Fried Chicken

Prep + Cook Time: 30 minutes | Serves: 4

Ingredients

6 chicken drumsticks, skin on and bone in
2 cups buttermilk
2 tbsp salt
2 tbsp black pepper
1 tbsp cayenne pepper

2 cups all-purpose flour
1 tbsp baking powder
1 tbsp garlic powder
1 tbsp paprika
1 tbsp salt

Directions

Rinse chicken thoroughly underwater and pat them dry; remove any fat residue. In a large bowl, mix paprika, black pepper and chicken. Toss well to coat the chicken evenly. Pour buttermilk over chicken and toss to coat.

Let the chicken chill overnight. Preheat your Air Fryer to 400 F. In another bowl, mix flour, paprika, pepper and salt. Roll the chicken in the seasoned flour. Place the chicken in the cooking basket in a single layer and cook for 10 minutes. Repeat the same steps for the other pieces.

Chicken With Parmesan and Sage

Prep + Cook Time: 12 minutes | Serves: 4

Ingredients

4 chicken breasts, skinless and boneless
3 oz breadcrumbs
2 tbsp grated Parmesan cheese
2 oz flour

2 eggs, beaten
1 tbsp fresh, chopped sage

Directions

Preheat the air fryer to 370 F. Place some plastic wrap underneath and on top of the chicken breasts. Using a rolling pin, beat the meat until it becomes really thin. In a bowl, combine the Parmesan cheese, sage and breadcrumbs.

Dip the chicken in the egg first, and then in the sage mixture. Spray with cooking oil and arrange the meat in the air fryer. Cook for 7 minutes.

Party Chicken Tenders

Prep + Cook Time: 25 minutes | Serves: 4

Ingredients

¾ pound chicken tenders
Prep + Cook Time2 whole eggs, beaten
½ cup seasoned breadcrumbs

½ cup all-purpose flour
1 tbsp black pepper
2 tbsp olive oil

Directions

Preheat your air fryer to 330 F. Add breadcrumbs, eggs and flour in three separate bowls (individually). Mix breadcrumbs with oil and season with salt and pepper. Dredge the tenders into flour, eggs and into the crumbs.

Add chicken tenders in the Air Fryer and cook for 10 minutes. Increase to 390 F, and cook for 5 more minutes.

Chicken Tenders with Pineapple Juice

Prep + Cook Time: 4h 15 minutes | Serves: 4

Ingredients

1 lb boneless and skinless chicken tenders
4 cloves garlic, chopped
4 scallions, chopped
2 tbsp sesame seeds, toasted
1 tbsp fresh ginger, grated

½ cup pineapple juice
½ cup soy sauce
⅓ cup sesame oil
A pinch of black pepper

Directions

Skew each tender and trim any excess fat. Mix the other ingredients in one large bowl. Add the skewered chicken and place in the fridge for 4 to 24 hours. Preheat the Air Fryer to 375°F.

Using a paper towel, pat the chicken until it is completely dry. Fry for 10 minutes.

Crispy Panko Turkey Breasts

Prep + Cook Time: 25 minutes | Serves: 6

Ingredients

3 turkey breasts, boneless and skinless
2 cups panko1 tbsp salt
½ tsp cayenne pepper

½ tbsp black pepper
1 stick butter, melted

Directions

In a bowl, combine the panko, half of the black pepper, cayenne pepper, and half of the salt. In another small bowl, combine the melted butter with salt and pepper. Don't add salt if you use salted butter.

Brush the butter mixture over the turkey breasts. Coat the turkey with the panko mixture. Arrange them on a lined baking dish. Air fry for 15 minutes at 390 degrees F. If the turkey breasts are thinner, cook only for 8 minutes.

Avocado-Mango Chicken Breasts

Prep + Cook Time: 3 hrs 20 minutes | Serves: 2

Ingredients

2 chicken breasts, cubed
1 large mango, cubed
1 medium avocado, sliced
1 red pepper, chopped
5 tbsp balsamic vinegar
15 tbsp olive oil

4 garlic cloves, minced
1 tbsp oregano
1 tbsp parsley, chopped
A pinch of mustard powder
Salt and black pepper to taste

Directions

In a bowl, mix whole mango, garlic, oil, and balsamic vinegar. Add the mixture to a blender and blend well. Pour the liquid over chicken cubes and soak for 3 hours. Take a pastry brush and rub the mixture over breasts as well.

Preheat your Air Fryer to 360 F. Place the chicken cubes in the cooking basket, and cook for 12 minutes. Add avocado, mango and pepper and toss well. Drizzle balsamic vinegar and garnish with chopped parsley.

Turkey Nuggets with Parsley & Thyme

Prep + Cook Time: 20 minutes | Serves: 2

Ingredients

8 oz turkey breast, boneless and skinless
1 egg, beaten
1 cup breadcrumbs

1 tbsp dried thyme
½ tbsp dried parsley
Salt and black pepper to taste

Directions

Preheat the air fryer to 350 F. Mince the turkey in a food processor; transfer to a bowl. Stir in the thyme and parsley, and season with salt and pepper.

Take a nugget-sized piece of the turkey mixture and shape it into a ball, or another form. Dip in the breadcrumbs, then egg, then in the breadcrumbs again. Place the nuggets onto a prepared baking dish, and cook for 10 minutes.

Korean-Style Honey Chicken Wings

Prep + Cook Time: 15 minutes | Serves: 5

Ingredients

1 pound chicken wings
8 oz flour
8 oz breadcrumbs
3 beaten eggs
4 tbsp Canola oil
Salt and black pepper to taste

2 tbsp sesame seeds
2 tbsp Korean red pepper paste
1 tbsp apple cider vinegar
2 tbsp honey
1 tbsp soy sauce
Sesame seeds, to serve

Directions

Separate the chicken wings into winglets and drumettes. In a bowl, mix salt, oil and pepper. Preheat your Air Fryer to a temperature of 350 F. Coat the chicken with beaten eggs followed by breadcrumbs and flour.

Place the chicken in your Air Fryer's cooking basket. Spray with a bit of oil and cook for 15 minutes.

Mix red pepper paste, apple cider vinegar, soy sauce, honey and ¼ cup of water in a saucepan and bring to a boil over medium heat. Transfer the chicken to sauce mixture and toss to coat. Garnish with sesame to enjoy!

Savory Chicken Drumsticks with Honey and Garlic

Prep + Cook Time: 20 minutes | Serves: 3

Ingredients

2 chicken drumsticks, skin removed
2 tbsp olive oil

2 tbsp honey
½ tbsp garlic, minced

Directions

Preheat your Air Fryer to 400 F. Add garlic, oil and honey to a sealable zip bag. Add chicken and toss to coat; set aside for 30 minutes. Add the coated chicken to the Air Fryer basket, and cook for 15 minutes. Serve and enjoy!

Garlic-Buttery Chicken Wings

Prep + Cook Time: 20 minutes | Serves: 4

Ingredients

16 chicken wings
¼ cup butter
¼ cup honey

½ tbsp salt
4 garlic cloves, minced
¾ cup potato starch

Directions

Preheat the air fryer to 370 F. Rinse and pat dry the wings, and place them in a bowl. Add the starch to the bowl, and mix to coat the chicken. Place the chicken in a baking dish that has been previously coated with cooking oil.

Cook for 5 minutes in the air fryer. Whisk the rest of the ingredients together in a bowl. Pour the sauce over the wings and cook for another 10 minutes.

Pineapple & Ginger Chicken Kabobs

Prep + Cook Time: 20 minutes | Serves: 4

Ingredients

¾ oz boneless and skinless chicken tenders
½ cup soy sauce
½ cup pineapple juice
¼ cup sesame oil
4 cloves garlic, chopped

1 tbsp fresh ginger, grated
4 scallions, chopped
2 tbsp toasted sesame seeds
1 A pinch of black pepper

Directions

Skewer the chicken pieces into the skewers and trim any fat. In a large sized bowl, mix the remaining ingredients.

Dip the skewered chicken into the seasoning bowl. Preheat your Air Fryer to 390 F. Pat the chicken to dry using a towel and place in the Air Fryer cooking basket. Cook for 5-7 minutes.

Worcestershire Chicken Breasts

Prep + Cook Time: 20 minutes | Serves: 6

Ingredients

¼ cup flour
½ tbsp flour
5 chicken breasts, sliced
1 tbsp Worcestershire sauce
3 tbsp olive oil

¼ cup onions, chopped
1 ½ cups brown sugar
¼ cup yellow mustard
¾ cup water
½ cup ketchup

Directions

Preheat your Fryer to 360 F. In a bowl, mix in flour, salt and pepper. Cover the chicken slices with flour mixture and drizzle oil over the chicken. In another bowl, mix brown sugar, water, ketchup, chopped onion, mustard, Worcestershire sauce and salt. Transfer chicken to marinade mixture; set aside for 10 minutes. Place the chicken in your Air Fryer's cooking basket and cook for 15 minutes.

Sherry Grilled Chicken

Prep + Cook Time: 25 minutes | Serves: 2

Ingredients

4 chicken breasts, cubed
2 garlic clove, minced
½ cup ketchup
½ tbsp ginger, minced
½ cup soy sauce

2 tbsp sherry
½ cup pineapple juice
2 tbsp apple cider vinegar
½ cup brown sugar

Directions

Preheat your Air Fryer to 360 F. In a bowl, mix in ketchup, pineapple Juice, sugar, cider vinegar, ginger. Heat the sauce in a frying pan over low heat. Cover chicken with the soy sauce and sherry; pour the hot sauce on top. Set aside for 15 minutes to marinate. Place the chicken in the Air Fryer cooking basket and cook for 15 minutes.

Mustard Chicken with Thyme

Prep + Cook Time: 20 minutes | Serves: 4

Ingredients

4 garlic cloves, minced
8 chicken slices
1 tbsp thyme leaves
½ cup dry wine
Salt as needed

½ cup Dijon mustard
2 cups breadcrumbs
2 tbsp melted butter
1 tbsp lemon zest
2 tbsp olive oil

Directions

Preheat your Air Fryer to 350 F. In a bowl, mix garlic, salt, cloves, breadcrumbs, pepper, oil, butter and lemon zest. In another bowl, mix mustard and wine. Place chicken slices in the wine mixture and then in the crumb mixture. Place the prepared chicken in the Air Fryer cooking basket and cook for 15 minutes.

Shrimp Paste Chicken

Prep + Cook Time: 30 minutes | Serves: 2

Ingredients

8 chicken wings, washed and cut into small portions
½ tbsp sugar
2 tbsp corn flour
½ tbsp wine

1 tbsp shrimp paste
1 tbsp ginger
½ tbsp olive oil

Directions

Preheat your Air Fryer to 360 F. In a bowl, mix oil, ginger, wine and sugar. Cover the chicken wings with the prepared marinade and top with flour. Add the floured chicken to shrimp paste and coat it.

Place the prepared chicken in your Air Fryer's cooking basket and cook for 20 minutes, until crispy on the outside.

Delicious Coconut Chicken Casserole

Prep + Cook Time: 20 minutes | Serves: 6

Ingredients

2 large eggs, beaten
2 tbsp garlic powder
1 tbsp salt
½ tbsp ground black pepper

¾ cup breadcrumbs
¾ cup shredded coconut
1 pound chicken tenders

Directions

Preheat your fryer to 400 F. Spray a baking sheet with cooking spray. In a wide dish, whisk in garlic powder, eggs, pepper and salt. In another bowl, mix the breadcrumbs and coconut.

Dip your chicken tenders in egg, then in the coconut mix; shake off any excess. Place the prepared chicken tenders in your Air Fryer's cooking basket and cook for 12-14 minutes until golden brown.

Sticky Chinese-Style Chicken

Prep + Cook Time: 25 minutes | Serves: 3

Ingredients

1 pound chicken wingettes
1 tbsp cilantro leaves, chopped
Salt and black pepper, to taste
1 tbsp roasted peanuts, chopped
½ tbsp apple cider vinegar

1 garlic clove, minced
½ tbsp chili sauce
1 ginger, minced
1 ½ tbsp soy sauce
2 ½ tbsp honey

Directions

Preheat your Air Fryer to 360 F. Wash chicken wingettes thoroughly; season with salt and pepper. In a bowl, mix ginger, garlic, chili sauce, honey, soy sauce, cilantro, and vinegar. Cover chicken with honey sauce. Place the prepared chicken to your Air Fryer's cooking basket and cook for 20 minutes. Serve sprinkled with peanuts.

Chicken with Peppercorns and Lemon

Prep + Cook Time: 20 minutes | Serves: 2

Ingredients

1 chicken breast
2 lemon, juiced and rind reserved
1 tbsp chicken seasoning

1 tbsp garlic puree
A handful of peppercorns
Salt and black pepper to taste

Directions

Preheat your fryer to 350 F. Place a silver foil sheet on a flat surface. Add all seasonings alongside the lemon rind.

Lay out the chicken breast onto a chopping board and trim any fat and little bones. Season each side with the pepper and salt. Rub the chicken seasoning on both sides well. Place on your silver foil sheet and rub.

Seal tightly and flatten with a rolling pin. Place the breast in the basket and cook for 15 minutes. Serve hot.

Cheesy Chicken Escallops

Prep + Cook Time: 10 minutes | Serves: 6

Ingredients

4 skinless chicken breast
2 ½ oz panko breadcrumbs
1 ounce Parmesan cheese, grated

6 sage leaves, chopped
1 ¼ ounce flour
2 beaten eggs

Directions

Place the chicken breasts between a cling film, beat well using a rolling pin until a ½ cm thickness is achieved.

In a bowl, add Parmesan cheese, sage and breadcrumbs. Dredge the chicken into the seasoned flour and dredge into the egg. Finally, dredge into the breadcrumbs. Preheat your Air Fryer to 390 F. Spray both sides of chicken breasts with cooking spray and cook in the Air Fryer for 4 minutes, until golden.

Lime-Chili Chicken Wings

Prep + Cook Time: 25 minutes | Serves: 2

Ingredients

10 chicken wings
2 tbsp hot chili sauce
½ tbsp lime juice

½ tbsp honey
½ tbsp kosher salt
½ tbsp black pepper

Directions

Preheat the Air Fryer to 350 F. Mix the lime juice, honey and chili sauce. Toss the mixture over the chicken wings. Put the chicken wings in the Air Fryer basket and cook for 25 minutes. Shake the basket every 5 minutes.

Sweet Chicken Drumsticks

Prep + Cook Time: 20 minutes | Serves: 2

Ingredients

2 chicken drumsticks, skin removed
2 tbsp olive oil

2 tbsp honey
½ tbsp garlic, minced

Directions

Add the ingredients to a resealable bag; massage until well-coated. Allow the chicken to marinate for 30 minutes. Preheat your Air Fryer to 400 F. Add the chicken to the cooking basket and cook for 15 minutes, shaking once.

Chicken with Avocado & Radish Bowl

Prep + Cook Time: 20 minutes | Serves: 2

INGREDIENTS

12 oz chicken breasts
1 avocado, sliced
4 radishes, sliced

1 tbsp chopped parsley
Salt and black pepper to taste

DIRECTIONS

Preheat the Air fryer to 300 degrees F, and cut the chicken into small cubes. Combine all ingredients in a bowl and transfer to a baking dish. Cook for 14 minutes. Serve with cooked rice or fried red kidney beans.

Savory Chicken with Onion

Prep + Cook Time: 20 minutes | Serves: 4

Ingredients

4 chicken breasts, cubed
1 ½ cup onion soup mix

1 cup mushroom soup
½ cup cream

Directions

Preheat your Fryer to 400 F. Add mushrooms, onion mix and cream in a frying pan. Heat on low heat for 1 minute. Pour the warm mixture over chicken slices and allow to sit for 25 minutes. Place the marinated chicken in the Air Fryer cooking basket and cook for 15 minutes. Serve with remaining cream and enjoy!

Savory Buffalo Chicken

Prep + Cook Time: 35 minutes | Serves: 4

Ingredients

4 pounds chicken wing
½ cup cayenne pepper sauce
½ cup coconut oil

1 tbsp worcestershire sauce
1 tbsp kosher salt

Directions

In a mixing cup, combine cayenne pepper sauce, coconut oil, Worcestershire sauce and salt; set aside. Pat the chicken dry and place in the Air Fryer cooking basket. Cook for 25 minutes at 380 F.

Increase the temperature to 400 F and cook for 5 more minutes. Transfer into a large sized mixing bowl and toss in the prepared sauce. Serve with celery sticks and enjoy!

Basil Cheese Chicken

Prep + Cook Time: 20 minutes | Serves: 4

Ingredients

4 chicken breasts, cubed
1 tbsp garlic powder
1 cup mayonnaise
½ tsp pepper

½ cup soft cheese
½ tbsp salt
Chopped basil for garnish

Directions

Preheat your Air Fryer to 380 F. In a bowl, mix cheese, mayonnaise, garlic powder and salt to form a marinade. Cover your chicken with the marinade. Place the marinated chicken in your Air Fryer's cooking basket and cook for 15 minutes. Serve with a garnish of chopped basil.

Cayenne Chicken with Coconut Flakes

Prep + Cook Time: 25 minutes | Serves: 4

Ingredients

3 chicken breasts, cubed
Oil as needed
3 cups coconut flakes
3 whole eggs, beaten

½ cup cornstarch
Salt to taste
1 tbsp cayenne pepper
Pepper to taste

Directions

Preheat your Air Fryer to 350 F. In a bowl, mix salt, cornstarch, cayenne pepper, pepper. In another bowl, add beaten eggs and coconut flakes. Cover chicken with pepper mix. Dredge chicken in the egg mix. Cover chicken with oil. Place the prepared chicken in your Air Fryer's cooking basket and cook for 20 minutes.

Honey Chicken Wings

Prep + Cook Time: 25 minutes | Serves: 4

Ingredients

8 chicken drumsticks
1 tbsp olive oil
1 tbsp sesame oil
4 tbsp honey
3 tbsp light soy sauce

2 crushed garlic clove
1 small knob fresh ginger, grated
1 small bunch coriander, chopped
2 tbsp sesame seeds, toasted

Directions

Add all ingredients in a freezer bag, except sesame and coriander. Seal up and massage until the drumsticks are coated well. Preheat your Air Fryer to 400 F. Place the drumsticks in the cooking basket and cook for 10 minutes. Lower the temperature to 325 F and cook for 10 more minutes. Sprinkle with some sesame and coriander seeds.

Ginger Chicken Wings

Prep + Cook Time: 25 minutes | Serves: 3

Ingredients

1 pound chicken wings
1 tbsp cilantro
Salt and black pepper to taste
1 tbsp cashews cream
1 garlic clove, minced

1 tbsp yogurt
2 tbsp honey
½ tbsp vinegar
½ tbsp ginger, minced
½ tbsp garlic chili sauce

Directions

Preheat the air fryer to 360 F. Season the wings with salt and pepper, and place them in the Air Fryer, and cook for 15 minutes. In a bowl, mix the remaining ingredients. Top the chicken with sauce and cook for 5 more minutes.

Enchilada Cheese Chicken

Prep + Cook Time: 65 minutes | Serves: 6

Ingredients

3 cups chicken breast, chopped
2 cups cheese, grated
½ cup salsa

1 can green chilies, chopped
12 flour tortillas
2 cans enchilada sauce

Directions

Preheat your Fryer to 400 F. In a bowl, mix salsa and enchilada sauce. Toss in the chopped chicken to coat. Place the chicken on the tortillas and roll; top with cheese. Place the prepared tortillas in the Air Fryer cooking basket and cook for 60 minutes. Serve with guacamole and Mexican dips!

Basil Mozzarella Chicken

Prep + Cook Time: 25 minutes | Serves: 6

Ingredients

6 chicken breasts, cubed
6 basil leaves
¼ cup balsamic vinegar

6 slices tomato
1 tbsp butter
6 slices mozzarella cheese

Directions

Preheat your Fryer to 400 F and heat butter and balsamic vinegar in a frying pan over medium heat. Cover the chicken meat with the marinade. Place the chicken in the cooking basket and cook for 20 minutes. Cover the chicken with basil, tomato slices and cheese. Serve and enjoy!

Parmesan Chicken Cutlets

Prep + Cook Time: 20 minutes | Serves: 4

Ingredients

¼ cup Parmesan cheese, grated
4 chicken cutlets
⅛ tbsp paprika
¼ tsp pepper

2 tbsp panko breadcrumbs
1 tbsp parsley
½ tbsp garlic powder
2 large eggs, beaten

Directions

Preheat your Air Fryer to 400 F. In a bowl, mix Parmesan cheese, breadcrumbs, garlic powder, pepper, paprika and mash the mixture. Add eggs in a bowl. Dip the chicken cutlets in eggs, dredge them in cheese and panko mixture. Place the prepared cutlets in the cooking basket and cook for 15 minutes.

MEAT RECIPES

Beef Burgers with Parsley & Oregano

Prep + Cook Time: 20 minutes | Serves: 4

Ingredients

1 lb ground beef
½ tsp onion powder
½ tsp salt
½ tsp oregano
1 tbsp worcestershire sauce

½ tsp garlic powder
½ tsp pepper
1 tsp parsley
1 tsp maggi seasoning sauce
1 tsp olive oil

Directions

Preheat the air fryer to 350 F. Combine all of the sauces and seasonings, except oil, in a small bowl. Place the beef in a bowl and stir in the seasonings. Mix until the mixture is well incorporated.

Divide the meat mixture into four equal pieces and form patties. Spread the olive oil in the air fryer. Arrange the 4 burgers inside and cook for 10 to 15 minutes, until thoroughly cooked.

Beef with Cauliflower and Green Peas

Prep + Cook Time: 25 minutes | Serves: 4

Ingredients

2 beef steaks, sliced into thin strips
2 garlic cloves, chopped
2 tsp maple syrup
1 tsp oyster sauce
1 tsp cayenne pepper
½ tsp olive oil

Juice of 1 lime
Salt and black pepper
1 cauliflower, cut into florets
2 carrots, cut into chunks
1 cup green peas

Directions

In a bowl, add beef, garlic, maple syrup, oyster sauce, cayenne, oil, lime juice, salt, and black pepper, and stir to combine. Place the beef along with the garlic and some of the juices into your air fryer and top with the veggies. Cook at 400 F for 8 minutes, turning once halfway through.

Awesome Rib Eye Steak

Prep + Cook Time: 20 minutes | Serves: 6

Ingredients

2 lb rib eye steak
1 tbsp. steak rub

1 tbsp. olive oil

Directions

Preheat the fryer to 400 F. Combine the steak rub and olive oil. Rub the steak with the seasoning. Place in the air fryer and cook for 10 minutes. Flip the steak over and cook for 7 more minutes. Serve hot with potatoes.

Delicious Hot Steaks

Prep + Cook Time: 15 minutes | Serves: 2

Ingredients

2 steaks, 1-inch thick
½ tsp black pepper
½ tsp cayenne pepper

1 tbsp olive oil
½ tsp ground paprika
Salt and black pepper to taste

Directions

Preheat the air fryer to 390 F. Mix olive oil, black pepper, cayenne, paprika, salt and pepper and rub onto steaks. Spread evenly. Put the steaks in the fryer, and cook for 6 minutes, turning them halfway through.

Herby-Tomato Meatloaf

Prep + Cook Time: 30 minutes | Serves: 4

Ingredients

1 lb ground beef
2 eggs, lightly beaten
½ cup breadcrumbs
2 garlic cloves, crushed

1 onion, finely chopped
2 tbsp tomato puree
1 tsp mixed dried herbs

Directions

Line a loaf pan that fits in your fryer with baking paper. In a bowl, mix beef, eggs, breadcrumbs, garlic, onion, puree, and herbs. Gently press the mixture into the pan and slide in the air fryer. Cook for 25 minutes on 380 F. If undercooked, and slightly moist, cook for 5 more minutes. Wait 15 minutes before slicing it.

Pork Ribs with BBQ Sauce

Prep + Cook Time: 4 h 35 minutes | Serves: 2

INGREDIENTS

1 lb. pork ribs
½ tsp five spice powder
1 tsp salt
3 garlic cloves, chopped
1 tsp black pepper

1 tsp sesame oil
1 tbsp honey, plus some more for brushing
4 tbsp barbecue sauce
1 tsp soy sauce

DIRECTIONS

Chop the ribs into smaller pieces and place them in a large bowl. In a smaller bowl, whisk together all of the other ingredients.

Add them to the bowl with the pork, and mix until the pork is fully coated. Cover the bowl, place it in the fridge, and let it marinate for about 4 hours. Preheat the Air fryer to 350 degrees F and cook the ribs in Air fryer for 15 minutes.

Brush the ribs with some honey and cook for another 15 minutes.

Creamy Beef Liver Cakes

Prep + Cook Time: 25 minutes | Serves: 2

Ingredients

1 lb beef liver, sliced
2 large eggs
1 tbsp butter

½ tbsp black truffle oil
1 tbsp cream
Salt and black pepper

Directions

Preheat the Air Fryer to 320 F. Cut the liver into thin slices and refrigerate for 10 minutes. Separate the whites from the yolks and put each yolk in a cup. In another bowl, add the cream, truffle oil, salt and pepper and mix with a fork. Arrange half of the mixture in a small ramekin.

Pour the white of the egg and divide it equally between ramekins. Top with the egg yolks. Surround each yolk with a liver. Cook for 15 minutes and serve cool.

Homemade Beef Empanadas

Prep + Cook Time: 25 minutes | Serves: 4

Ingredients

1 lb ground beef
½ onion, diced
1 garlic clove, minced
¼ cup tomato salsa
4 empanada shells

1 egg yolk
2 tsp milk
½ tsp cumin
Salt and black pepper to taste
½ tbsp olive oil

Directions

Grease with olive oil and set to 350 F. Meanwhile, combine the beef, onion, cumin, and garlic, in a bowl. Season with some salt and pepper. Place the beef in the air fryer and cook for 7 minutes, flipping once halfway through.

Stir in the tomato salsa and set aside. In a small bowl, combine the milk and yolk. Place the empanada shells on a dry and clean surface. Divide the beef mixture between the shells. Fold the shells and seal the ends with a fork. Brush with the egg wash. Place on a lined baking sheet and bake at 350 F for 10 minutes. Serve with a cheese dip.

Ground Pork & Apple Burgers

Prep + Cook Time: 25 minutes | Serves: 2

Ingredients

12 oz ground pork
1 apple, peeled and grated
1 cup breadcrumbs
2 eggs, beaten

½ tsp ground cumin
½ tsp ground cinnamon
Salt and black pepper to taste

Directions

In a bowl, add pork, apple, breadcrumbs, cumin, eggs, cinnamon, salt, and black pepper; mix with hands. Shape into 4 even-sized burger patties. Grease the fryer with oil, arrange the patties inside the basket and cook for 14 minutes at 340 F, turning once halfway through.

Chili Roasted Beef

Prep + Cook Time: 4 hrs 20 minutes | Serves: 2

Ingredients

1 lb ground beef
½ tsp salt
2 tbsp soy sauce
½ tsp pepper
Thumb-sized piece of ginger, chopped
3 chilies, deseeded and chopped
4 garlic cloves, chopped

1 tsp brown sugar
Juice of 1 lime
2 tbsp mirin
2 tbsp coriander, chopped
2 tbsp basil, chopped
2 tbsp oil
2 tbsp fish sauce

Directions

Place all ingredients, except the beef, salt and pepper, in a blender; process until smooth. Season the beef with salt and pepper. Place all in a zipper bag; shake well to combine. Marinate in the fridge for 4 hours.

Preheat the air fryer to 350 F. Place the beef in the air fryer and cook for 12 minutes, or more if you like it really well done. Let sit for a couple of minutes before serving. Serve with cooked rice and fresh veggies.

Classic Meatballs with Red Sauce

Prep + Cook Time: 20 minutes | Serves: 4

Ingredients

½ lb ground beef
1 medium onion
1 egg
4 tbsp breadcrumbs

1 tbsp fresh parsley, chopped
½ tbsp thyme leaves, chopped
10 oz of tomato sauce
Salt and black pepper to taste

Directions

Place all ingredients into a bowl and mix very well. Shape the mixture into 10 to 12 balls. Preheat the Air Fryer to 380 F. Place the meatballs in the air fryer basket, and cook them for 10 minutes.

Remove the meatballs to an oven plate. Add in the tomato sauce and bring them back to the Air Fryer. Lower the temperature to 300 F. Cook for 6 more minutes.

Pork Chops in Cream

Prep + Cook Time: 25 minutes | Serves: 4

Ingredients

4 pork chops, center-cut
2 tbsp flour
2 tbsp sour cream

Salt and black pepper
½ cup breadcrumbs

Directions

Coat the chops with flour. Drizzle the cream over and rub gently to coat well. Spread the breadcrumbs onto a bowl, and coat each pork chop with crumbs. Spray the chops with oil and arrange them in the basket of your Air Fryer. Cook for 14 minutes at 380 F, turning once halfway through. Serve with salad, slaw or potatoes.

Tasty Balls

Prep + Cook Time: 30 minutes | Serves: 4

Ingredients

⅓ cup rice
1 lb ground beef
1 tbsp minced onion
2 tbsp green bell peppers, finely chopped
1 tsp celery salt

2 tbsp worcestershire sauce
1 clove garlic
2 cups tomato juice
1 tsp oregano

Directions

Combine the rice, ground beef, onion, celery salt, green peppers and garlic. Shape into balls of 1-inch each.

Arrange the balls in the basket of the Air fryer and cook for 25 minutes at 320 degrees. Meanwhile, heat the tomato juice, the cloves, the oregano and the Worcestershire sauce. Serve the balls warm with the sauce.

Hoisin Beef Veggie Mix

Prep + Cook Time: 55 minutes | Serves: 4

Ingredients

Hoisin Sauce:
2 tbsp soy sauce
1 tbsp peanut butter
½ tsp Sriracha hot sauce

1 tsp sugar
1 tsp rice vinegar
3 cloves garlic, minced

Beef Veggie Mix:
2 lb beef Sirloin, cut in strips
2 yellow peppers, cut in strips
2 green peppers, cut in strips
2 green peppers, cut in strips
2 white onions, cut in strips
1 red onion, cut in strips
2 lb broccoli, cut in florets

2 tbsp soy sauce
2 tsp sesame oil
3 tsp minced garlic
2 tsp ground ginger
½ cup water
1 tbsp olive oil

Directions

Make the hoisin sauce first:
In a pan, add the soy sauce, peanut butter, sugar, hot sauce, rice vinegar, and minced garlic. Bring to simmer over low heat until reduced, about 15 minutes. Stir occasionally using a vessel and let it cool.

For the beef veggie mix: Add to the chilled hoisin sauce, garlic, sesame oil, soy sauce, ginger, and water; mix well.

Add meat, mix with a spoon, and refrigerate for 20 minutes, to marinate. Meanwhile, add the florets, peppers, onions, and olive oil to a bowl; mix to coat well. Add the veggies in the fryer basket and cook for 5 minutes at 400 F. Open the Air Fryer, stir the veggies, and cook further for 5 minutes, if not soft.

Remove the veggies to a serving plate and set aside. Remove the meat from the fridge and drain the liquid into a bowl. Add the beef into the fryer, and cook at 380 F for 8 minutes. Slide out the basket and shake. Cook for 7 more minutes. Remove to the veggie plate; season with salt and pepper and pour the cooking sauce over, to serve.

Friday Night Pork Belly

Prep + Cook Time: 4 hrs 50 minutes | Serves: 6

Ingredients

2 lb pork belly, cut in half, blanched
2 bay leaves
2 tbsp soy sauce
5 garlic cloves, coarsely chopped

1 tbsp peppercorns
1 tbsp peanut oil
1 tsp salt

Directions

Let the blanched pork air fry for 2 hours; pat the excess water, if any. Take a mortar and pestle, and place bay leaves, garlic, salt, peppercorns, and peanut oil in it. Smash until a paste-like consistency has formed. Whisk the paste with the soy sauce. Pierce the skin of the pork belly with a fork or a skewer.

Rub the mixture onto the meat. Wrap the pork with a plastic foil and refrigerate for 2 hours. Preheat the fryer to 350 F. Place the pork inside and cook for 30 minutes. Set to 370 F and cook for 10 more minutes. Serve chilled.

Beef & Cannellini Bean Chili

Prep + Cook Time: 50 minutes | Serves: 6

Ingredients

1 lb ground beef
½ tbsp chili powder
1 tsp salt
1 can (8 oz) cannellini beans
1 tsp chopped cilantro
1 tbsp olive oil
½ tsp parsley

½ cup chopped celery
1 onion, chopped
2 garlic cloves, minced
1 ½ cup vegetable broth
¼ tsp pepper
1 can diced tomatoes
½ cup finely chopped bell peppers

Directions

Preheat the air fryer to 350 F. Place the oil, garlic, onion, bell pepper, and celery, in an ovenproof bowl. Place the bowl in the air fryer and cook for 5 minutes. Add the beef and cook for 6 more minutes. Stir in broth, tomatoes, chili, parsley, and coriander. Let cook for 20 minutes. Stir in beans, salt, and pepper. Cook for 10 more minutes. Sprinkle with cilantro, to serve.

Jalapeno Beef Mozzarella Tacos

Prep + Cook Time: 25 minutes | Serves: 4

Ingredients

8 soft round taco shells
1 beefsteak, sliced
1 cup mozzarella cheese, grated
½ cup fresh cilantro, chopped

1 jalapeno chili, chopped
1 cup corn kernels, canned
Salt and black pepper
Oil for greasing

Directions

Place sliced beef on each taco, top with cheese, cilantro, chili, corn, salt and pepper. Fold gently in half and secure with toothpicks if necessary. Grease the rack with oil and arrange the tacos into the basket. Cook at 380 F for 14 minutes, turning once halfway through. Serve with Mexican sauces and guacamole!

Five Spice Pork Belly

Prep + Cook Time: 3 hrs 10 minutes | Serves: 4

Ingredients

1 ½ lb pork belly, blanched
1 tsp five spice seasoning
½ tsp white pepper

¾ tsp garlic powder
1 tsp salt

Directions

After blanching the pork belly leave it at room temperature for 2 hours to air dry. Pat with paper towels if there is excess water. Preheat the air fryer to 330 F. Take a skewer and pierce the skin as many times as you can, so you can ensure crispiness. Combine the seasonings in a small bowl, and rub it onto the pork.

Place the pork into the air fryer and cook for 30 minutes. Increase the temperature to 350 F and cook for 30 more minutes. Let cool slightly before serving.

Autumn Apple & Onion Pork Chops

Prep + Cook Time: 25 minutes | Serves: 3

Ingredients

Topping:
1 small onion, sliced
2 tbsp olive oil
1 tbsp apple cider vinegar
2 tsp thyme

¼ tsp brown sugar
1 cup sliced apples
2 tsp rosemary

Meat:
¼ tsp smoked paprika
1 tbsp olive oil
3 pork chops

1 tbsp apple cider vinegar
Salt and black pepper to taste

Directions

Preheat the air fryer to 350 F. Place all topping ingredients in a baking dish and then in the air fryer. Cook for 4 minutes. Meanwhile, place the pork chops in a bowl. Add oil, vinegar, paprika, and season with salt and pepper.

Stir to coat them well. Remove the topping from the dish. Add the pork chops in the dish and cook in the air fryer for 10 minutes. Top with the topping, return to the air fryer and cook for 5 more minutes. Serve immediately.

Fast Rib Eye Steak

Prep + Cook Time: 20 minutes | Serves: 4

Ingredients

2 pounds rib eye steak
1 tbsp olive oil

Salt and black pepper to taste

Directions

Preheat your fryer to 350 F. Rub both sides of the steak with oil; season with salt and pepper. Place the steak in your Air Fryer's cooking basket and cook for 8 minutes. Serve and enjoy!

Pork Tenderloins with Apple

Prep + Cook Time: 60 minutes | Serves: 4

Ingredients

4 pork tenderloins
1 apple, wedged
1 cinnamon quill

1 tbsp olive oil
1 tbsp soy sauce
Salt and black pepper

Directions

In a bowl, add pork, apple, cinnamon, olive oil, soy sauce, salt, and black pepper into; stir to coat well. Let sit at room temperature for 25-35 minutes. Put the pork and apples into the air fryer, and a little bit of marinade. Cook at 380 F for 14 minutes, turning once halfway through. Serve hot!

Meatloaf with Worcestershire Sauce

Prep + Cook Time: 35 minutes | Serves: 8

Ingredients

4 lb ground beef
1 tbsp basil
1 tbsp oregano
1 tbsp parsley
1 onion, diced
1 tbsp Worcestershire sauce

3 tbsp ketchup
½ tsp salt
1 tsp ground peppercorns
10 whole peppercorns, for garnishing
1 cup breadcrumbs

Directions

Preheat the air fryer to 350 F. Place the beef in a large bowl. Add all of the ingredients except the whole peppercorns and the breadcrumbs. Mix with your hand until well combined; stir in the breadcrumbs.

Place the meatloaf on a lined baking dish. Place in the air fryer and cook for 25 minutes. Garnish the meatloaf with the whole peppercorns and let cool slightly before serving.

Tomato-Thyme Beef Balls

Prep + Cook Time: 25 minutes | Serves: 6

Ingredients

1 small onion, chopped
¾ pound grounded beef
1 tbsp fresh parsley, chopped
½ tbsp of fresh thyme leaves, chopped

1 whole egg, beaten
3 tbsp Breadcrumbs
Salt and black pepper to taste
Tomato sauce for coating

Directions

Preheat the Air fryer to 390 F, and in a bowl, mix all ingredients, except the tomato sauce; roll the mixture into 10-12 balls.

Place the balls in the cooking basket and cook for 8 minutes. Add tomato sauce to the balls to coat, and cook for 5 more minutes at 300 F. When ready, stir gently and serve with spaghetti.

Herby Beef Loin

Prep + Cook Time: 60 minutes | Serves: 8

Ingredients

2 lb beef loin
½ tsp black pepper, salt
1 tsp thyme
1 tsp rosemary

½ tsp oregano
½ tsp garlic powder
1 tsp onion powder
1 tbsp olive oil

Directions

Preheat the air fryer to 330 F. In a bowl, combine olive oil and seasonings. Rub the mixture onto the beef. Place the beef in the air fryer and cook for 30 minutes. Turn the roast over and cook for 20 to 30 more minutes, until well-roasted. Serve with mushrooms sauce, cooked rice, and steamed veggies.

Garlic Pork Ribs in Honey-BBQ Sauce

Prep + Cook Time: 4 h 35 minutes | Serves: 2

Ingredients

1 lb pork ribs
½ tsp five-spice powder
1 tsp salt
3 garlic cloves, chopped
1 tsp black pepper

1 tsp sesame oil
1 tbsp honey, plus some more for brushing
4 tbsp barbecue sauce
1 tsp soy sauce

Directions

Chop the ribs into smaller pieces and place them in a large bowl. In a smaller bowl, whisk together all other ingredients. Add them to the bowl with the pork, and mix until the pork is fully coated.

Cover the bowl, place it in the fridge, and marinate for 4 hours. Preheat the air fryer to 350 F. Place the ribs in the basket and cook for 15 minutes. Brush the ribs with some honey and cook for another 15 minutes.

Rosemary Lamb Rack with Cashews

Prep + Cook Time: 30 minutes | Serves: 4

Ingredients

3 oz chopped cashews
1 tbsp chopped rosemary
1 ½ lb rack of lamb
1 garlic clove, minced

1 tbsp breadcrumbs
1 egg, beaten
1 tbsp olive oil Salt and black pepper to taste

Directions

Preheat the air fryer to 210 F. Combine olive oil with the garlic, and brush this mixture onto lamb. Meanwhile, combine rosemary, cashews, and crumbs, in a bowl. Brush egg over the lambs, and coat it with the cashew mixture.

Place the lamb into the air fryer's basket, cook for 25 minutes. Increase the temperature to 390 F, and cook for 5 more minutes. Cover with a foil and let sit for a couple of minutes before serving.

Ground Beef Stuffed Cabbage Rolls

Prep + Cook Time: 35 minutes | Serves: 3

Ingredients

½ lb ground beef
8 savoy cabbage leaves
1 small onion, chopped
¼ packet Taco seasoning
1 tbsp cilantro lime rotel
⅔ cup shredded Mexican cheese

2 tsp olive oil
Salt and black pepper to taste
2 cloves garlic, minced
1 tsp chopped cilantro

Directions

Preheat the Air Fryer to 400 F. Grease a skillet with cooking spray and place it over medium heat on a stove top. Add the onions and garlic; sauté until fragrant. Add the beef, pepper, salt, and taco seasoning. Cook until the beef browns while breaking the meat with a vessel as it cooks. Add the cilantro rotel and stir well to combine.

Turn off the heat. Lay 4 of the savoy cabbage leaves on a flat surface and scoop the beef mixture in the center, and sprinkle with the Mexican cheese. Wrap diagonally and double wrap with the remaining 4 cabbage leaves.

Arrange the 4 rolls in the fryer basket and spray with cooking spray. Close the fryer and cook for 8 minutes. Flip the rolls, spray with cooking spray, and continue to cook for 4 minutes. Remove, garnish with cilantro and allow them to cool. Serve with cheese dip.

Beef Tenderloin with Green Sauce

Prep + Cook Time: 30 minutes | Serves: 3

Ingredients

Beef:
2 lb beef tenderloin, cut into strips

½ cup flour

Sauce:
1 tbsp minced ginger
1 tbsp minced garlic
½ cup chopped green onions
2 tbsp olive oil
½ cup soy sauce
½ cup water

¼ cup vinegar
¼ cup sugar
1 tsp cornstarch
½ tsp red chili flakes
Salt and black pepper to taste

Directions

Pour the flour in a bowl, add the beef strips and dredge them in the flour. Spray the fryer basket with cooking spray and arrange the beef strips in it; spray with cooking spray. Cook the beef at 400 F for 4 minutes. Slide out and shake the fryer basket to toss the beef strips. Cook further for 3 minutes; set aside.

To make the sauce, pour the cornstarch in a bowl and mix it with 3 to 4 teaspoons of water until well dissolve; set aside. Place a wok or saucepan over medium heat on a stove top and add the olive oil, garlic, and ginger. Stir continually for 10 seconds. Add the soy sauce, vinegar, and remaining water.

Stir well and bring to boil for 2 minutes. Stir in the sugar, chili flakes, and cornstarch mixture. Add the beef strips, stir and cook for 3 minutes. Stir in the green onions and cook for 1 to 2 minutes. Season with pepper and salt as desired. Turn off the heat. Serve with a side of steamed rice.

Spicy Lamb Balls

Prep + Cook Time: 40 minutes | Serves: 12

Ingredients

1 ½ lb ground lamb
½ cup minced onion
2 tbsp chopped mint leaves
3 garlic cloves, minced
2 tsp paprika
2 tsp coriander seeds

½ tsp cayenne pepper
1 tsp salt
1 tbsp chopped parsley
2 tsp cumin
½ tsp ground ginger

Directions

Soak 24 skewers in water, until ready to use. Preheat the air fryer to 330 F. Combine all ingredients in a large bowl. Mix well with your hands until the herbs and spices are evenly distributed and the mixture is well incorporated.

Shape the lamb mixture into 12 sausage shapes around 2 skewers. Cook for 12 to 15 minutes, or until it reaches the preferred doneness. Serve with tzatziki sauce and enjoy.

Sticky Hoisin Pork Ribs

Prep + Cook Time: 55 minutes | Serves: 6

Ingredients

2 lb pork ribs
2 tbsp char siew sauce
2 tbsp minced ginger
2 tbsp hoisin sauce

2 tbsp sesame oil
1 tbsp honey
4 garlic cloves, minced
1 tbsp soy sauce

Directions

Whisk together all marinade ingredients in a small bowl; coat the ribs well with the mixture. Place in a container with a lid, and refrigerate for 4 hours. Preheat the air fryer to 330 F.

Place the ribs in the basket but do not throw away the liquid from the container; cook for 40 minutes. Stir in the liquid, increase the temperature to 350 F, and cook 10 more minutes.

Awesome Beef Bulgogi with Mushrooms

Prep + Cook Time: 3 hrs 15 minutes | Serves: 1

Ingredients

6 oz beef
½ cup sliced mushrooms

2 tbsp bulgogi marinade
1 tbsp diced onion

Directions

Cut the beef into small pieces and place them in a bowl. Add the bulgogi and mix to coat the beef completely. Cover the bowl and place in the fridge for 3 hours to marinate. Preheat the air fryer to 350 F.

Transfer the beef to a baking dish; stir in the mushroom and onion. Cook for 10 minutes, until nice and tender. Serve with some roasted potatoes and a green salad.

Minty Lamb with Red Potatoes

Prep + Cook Time: 25 minutes | Serves: 2

Ingredients

2 lamb steaks
2 tbsp olive oil
2 garlic cloves, crushed

Salt and black pepper to taste
A handful of fresh mint, chopped
4 red potatoes, cubed

Directions

Rub the steaks with oil, garlic, salt, and black pepper. Put mint in the fryer, and place the steaks on top. Oil the potato chunks and sprinkle with salt and pepper. Arrange the potatoes next to the steaks, and cook on 360 F for 14 minutes, turning once halfway through cooking.

Basil Meatloaf with Parmesan

Prep + Cook Time: 40 minutes | Serves: 5

Ingredients

1 cup tomato basil sauce, divided in 2
1 ½ lb ground beef
1 ¼ cup diced onion
2 tbsp minced garlic
2 tbsp minced ginger
½ cup breadcrumbs
½ cup grated Parmesan cheese

Salt and black pepper to taste to season
2 tsp cayenne pepper
½ tsp dried basil
⅓ cup chopped parsley
2 egg whites

Directions

Preheat the Air Fryer to 360 F. In a bowl, add the beef, half of the tomato sauce, onion, garlic, ginger, breadcrumbs, cheese, salt, pepper, cayenne pepper, dried basil, parsley, and egg whites; mix well.

Grease an 8 or 10-inch pan with cooking spray and scoop the meat mixture into it. Shape the meat into the pan while pressing firmly. Brush the remaining tomato sauce onto meat. Place the pan in the fryer basket and close the Air Fryer; cook for 25 minutes. After 15 minutes, open the fryer, and use a meat thermometer to ensure the meat has reached 160 F internally. If not, cook further for 5 minutes. Remove the pan, drain any excess liquid and fat. Let meatloaf cool for 20 minutes before slicing. Serve with a side of sautéed green beans.

Homemade Beef Liver Soufflé

Prep + Cook Time: 40 minutes | Serves: 4

Ingredients

½ lb of beef liver
3 eggs
3 oz buns

1 cup warm milk
Salt and black pepper to taste

Directions

Cut the liver in slices and put it in the fridge for 15 minutes. Divide the buns into pieces and soak them in milk for 10 minutes. Put the liver in a blender, and add the yolks, the bread mixture, and the spices. Grind the components and stuff in the ramekins. Line the ramekins in the Air Fryer's basket; cook for 20 minutes at 350 F.

Rib Eye Steak with Avocado Sauce

Prep + Cook Time: 35 minutes | Serves: 4

Ingredients

1 ½ lb rib eye steak
2 tsp olive oil
1 tbsp chipotle chili pepper

Salt and black pepper to taste
1 avocado, diced
Juice from ½ lime

Directions

Place the steak on a chopping board. Pour the olive oil over and sprinkle with the chipotle pepper, salt, and black pepper. Use your hands to rub the spices on the meat. Leave it to sit and marinate for 10 minutes.

Preheat the Air Fryer to 400 F. Pull out the fryer basket and place the meat inside. Slide it back into the Air Fryer and cook for 14 minutes. Turn the steak and continue cooking for 6 minutes. Remove the steak, cover with foil, and let it sit for 5 minutes before slicing.

Meanwhile, prepare the avocado salsa by mashing the avocado with potato mash. Add in the lime juice and mix until smooth. Taste, adjust the seasoning, slice and serve with salsa.

Hot Flank Steaks with Roasted Peanuts

Prep + Cook Time: 25 minutes | Serves: 3 to 4

Ingredients

2 lb flank steaks, cut in long strips
2 tbsp fish sauce
2 tbsp soy sauce
2 tbsp sugar
2 tbsp ground garlic

2 tbsp ground ginger
2 tsp hot sauce
1 cup chopped cilantro, divided into two
½ cup roasted peanuts, chopped

Directions

Preheat the Air Fryer to 400 F. In a zipper bag, add the beef, fish sauce, swerve sweetener, garlic, soy sauce, ginger, half of the cilantro, and hot sauce. Zip the bag and massage the ingredients with your hands to mix well.

Open the bag, remove the beef, shake off the excess marinade and place the beef strips in the fryer basket in a single layer; avoid overlapping. Close the Air Fryer and cook for 5 minutes. Turn the beef and cook further for 5 minutes. Dish the cooked meat in a serving platter, garnish with the peanuts and the remaining cilantro.

Authentic Wiener Beef Schnitzel

Prep + Cook Time: 25 minutes | Serves: 4

Ingredients

4 beef schnitzel cutlets
½ cup flour
2 eggs, beaten

Salt and black pepper
1 cup breadcrumbs

Directions

Coat the cutlets in flour and shake off any excess. Dip the coated cutlets into the beaten egg. Sprinkle with salt and black pepper. Then dip into the crumbs and to coat well. Spray them generously with oil and cook for 10 minutes at 360 F, turning once halfway through.

Dreamy Beef Steak with Rice, Broccoli & Green Beans

Prep + Cook Time: 40 minutes | Serves: 2

Ingredients

Beef:

1 lb beef steak,   Salt and black pepper to taste to season

Fried Rice:

2 ½ cups rice   2 tsp vinegar
1 ½ tbsp. soy sauce   1 clove garlic, minced
2 tsp sesame oil   ¼ cup chopped broccoli
2 tsp minced ginger   ¼ cup green beans

Directions

Put the beef on a chopping board and use a knife to cut it in 2-inch strips. Add the beef to a bowl, sprinkle with pepper and salt, and mix it with a spoon. Let it sit for 10 minutes. Preheat the Air Fryer to 400 F. Add the beef to the fryer basket, and cook for 5 minutes. Turn the beef strips with kitchen tongs and cook further for 3 minutes.

Once ready, remove the beef to a safe-oven dish that fits in the fryer's basket. Add the rice, broccoli, green beans, garlic, ginger, sesame oil, vinegar and soy sauce. Mix evenly using a spoon.

Place the dish in the fryer basket, close, and cook at 370 F for 10 minutes. Open the Air Fryer, mix the rice well, and cook for 4 minutes; season with salt and pepper. Dish the rice into serving bowls and serve with hot sauce.

Mustard Pork Chops with Lemon Zest

Prep + Cook Time: 25 minutes | Serves: 3

Ingredients

3 lean pork chops   3 tsp paprika
Salt and black pepper to taste to season   1 ½ tsp oregano
2 eggs, cracked into a bowl   ½ tsp cayenne pepper
1 tbsp water   ¼ tsp dry mustard
1 cup breadcrumbs   1 lemon, zested
½ tsp garlic powder

Directions

Put the pork chops on a chopping board and use a knife to trim off any excess fat. Add the water to the eggs and whisk; set aside. In another bowl, add the breadcrumbs, salt, pepper, garlic powder, paprika, oregano, cayenne pepper, lemon zest, and dry mustard. Use a fork to mix evenly.

Preheat the Air Fryer to 380 F and grease the basket with cooking spray. In the egg mixture, dip each pork chop and then in the breadcrumb mixture. Place the breaded chops in the fryer. Don't spray with cooking spray. The fat in the chops will be enough oil to cook them. Close the Air Fryer and cook for 12 minutes.

Flip to other side and cook for another 5 minutes.

Once ready, place the chops on a chopping board to rest for 3 minutes before slicing and serving. Serve with a side of vegetable fries.

Herbed Beef Roast

Prep + Cook Time: 50 minutes | Serves: 2

Ingredients

2 tsp olive oil
1 lb beef Roast
½ tsp dried rosemary

½ tsp dried thyme
½ tsp dried oregano
Salt and black pepper to taste

Directions

Preheat the Air Fryer to 400 F. Drizzle oil over the beef, and sprinkle with salt, pepper, and herbs. Rub onto the meat with hands. Cook for 45 minutes for medium-rare and 50 minutes for well-done.

Check halfway through, and flip to ensure they cook evenly. Wrap the beef in foil for 10 minutes after cooking to allow the juices to reabsorb into the meat. Slice the beef and serve with a side of steamed asparagus.

Roast Pork Belly with Cumin

Preparation 4 hrs 30 minutes | Serves: 8

Ingredients

1 ½ lb pork belly
1 ½ tsp garlic powder
1 ½ tsp coriander powder
⅓ tsp salt
1 ½ tsp black pepper

1 ½ dried thyme
1 ½ tsp dried oregano
1 ½ tsp cumin powder
3 cups water
1 lemon, halved

Directions

Leave the pork to air fry for 3 hours. In a small bowl, add the garlic powder, coriander powder, ½ tsp of salt, black pepper, thyme, oregano, and cumin powder. After the pork is well dried, poke holes all around it using a fork. Smear the oregano rub thoroughly on all sides with your hands and squeeze the lemon juice all over it.

Leave to sit for 5 minutes. Put the pork in the center of the fryer basket and cook for 30 minutes. Turn the pork with the help of two spatulas, increase the temperature to 350 F and continue cooking for 25 minutes.

Once ready, remove it and place it in on a chopping board to sit for 4 minutes before slicing. Serve the pork slices with a side of sautéed asparagus and hot sauce.

Sunday Night Garlic Beef Schnitzel

Prep + Cook Time: 22 minutes | Serves: 1

Ingredients

2 tbsp olive oil
1 thin beef cutlet
1 egg, beaten
2 oz breadcrumbs

1 tsp paprika
¼ tsp garlic powder
Salt and black pepper to taste

Directions

Preheat the air fryer to 350 F. Combine olive oil, breadcrumbs, paprika, garlic powder, and salt, in a bowl. Dip the beef in with the egg first, and then coat it with the breadcrumb mixture completely. Line a baking dish with parchment paper and place the breaded meat on it. Cook for 12 minutes. Serve and enjoy.

Meatballs with Parsley and Thyme

Prep + Cook Time: 25 minutes | Serves: 6

Ingredients

1 small onion, chopped
¾ pound grounded beef
1 tbsp fresh parsley, chopped
½ tbsp fresh thyme leaves, chopped

1 whole egg, beaten
3 tbsp breadcrumbs
Salt and black pepper to taste
Tomato sauce for coating

Directions

Preheat your Air Fryer to 390 F. In a mixing bowl, mix all the ingredients except tomato sauce. Roll the mixture into 10-12 balls. Place the balls in your air fryer's cooking basket, and cook for 8 minutes. Add tomato sauce to the balls to coat and cook for 5 minutes at 300 F. Gently stir and enjoy!

Garlic Lamb Chops with Thyme

Prep + Cook Time: 30 minutes | Serves: 4

Ingredients

4 lamb chops
1 garlic clove, peeled
1 tbsp plus
2 tsp olive oil

½ tbsp oregano
½ tbsp thyme
½ tsp salt
¼ tsp black pepper

Directions

Preheat the air fryer to 390 F. Coat the garlic clove with 1 tsp. of olive oil and place it in the air fryer for 10 minutes. Meanwhile, mix the herbs and seasonings with the remaining olive oil.

Using a towel or a mitten, squeeze the hot roasted garlic clove into the herb mixture and stir to combine. Coat the lamb chops with the mixture well, and place in the air fryer. Cook for 8 to 12 minutes.

Ginger Rack Rib Steak

Prep + Cook Time: 35 minutes | Serves: 2

Ingredients

1 rack rib steak
Salt to season
1 tsp white pepper
1 tsp garlic powder

½ tsp red pepper flakes
1 tsp ginger powder
1 cup Hot sauce

Directions

Preheat the Air Fryer to 360 F. Place the rib rack on a flat surface and pat dry using a paper towel. Season the ribs with salt, garlic, ginger, white pepper, and red pepper flakes.

Place the ribs in the fryer's basket and cook for 15 minutes. Turn the ribs with kitchen tongs and cook further for 15 minutes. Remove the ribs onto a chopping board and let sit for 3 minutes before slicing. Plate and drizzle hot sauce over and serve.

Bacon-Wrapped Stuffed Pork Tenderloin

Prep + Cook Time: 40 minutes | Serves: 4

Ingredients

16 bacon slices
16 oz pork tenderloin
Salt and black pepper to taste to season
1 cup spinach
3 oz cream cheese

1 small onion, sliced
1 tbsp olive oil
1 clove garlic, minced
½ tsp dried thyme
½ tsp dried rosemary

Directions

Place the tenderloin on a chopping board, cover it with a plastic wrap and pound it using a kitchen hammer to a 2-inches flat and square piece. Trim the uneven sides with a knife to have a perfect square. Set aside on a flat plate. On the same chopping board, place and weave the bacon slices into a square of the size of the pork.

Place the pork on the bacon weave and set aside. Put a skillet over medium heat on a stovetop, add olive oil, onions, and garlic; sauté until transparent. Add the spinach, ½ tsp rosemary, ½ tsp thyme, a bit of salt, and pepper.

Stir with a spoon and allow the spinach to wilt. Stir in the cream cheese, until the mixture is even. Turn off.

Preheat the Air Fryer to 360 F. Spoon and spread the spinach mixture onto the pork loin. Roll up the bacon and pork over the spinach stuffing. Secure the ends with as many toothpicks as necessary. Season with more salt and pepper. Place it in the fryer basket and cook for 15 minutes. Flip to other side and cook for another 5 minutes.

Once ready, remove to a clean chopping board. Let sit for 4 minutes before slicing. Serve with steamed veggies.

American-Style Beef Burgers

Prep + Cook Time: 255 minutes | Serves: 4

Ingredients

Beef:
1 ½ lb ground beef
Salt and black pepper to taste to season
¼ tsp liquid smoke

2 tsp onion powder
1 tsp garlic powder
1 ½ tbsp worcestershire sauce

Burgers:
4 buns
4 trimmed lettuce leaves
4 tbsp mayonnaise

1 large tomato, sliced
4 slices Cheddar cheese

Directions

Preheat the Air Fryer to 370 F. In a bowl, combine the beef, salt, pepper, liquid smoke, onion powder, garlic powder and Worcestershire sauce using your hands. Form 3 to 4 patties out of the mixture. Place the patties in the fryer basket making sure to leave enough space between them.

Ideally, work with two patties at a time. Close the Air Fryer and cook for 10 minutes. Turn the beef with kitchen tongs, reduce the temperature to 350 F, and cook further for 5 minutes. Remove the patties onto a plate. Assemble burgers with the lettuce, mayonnaise, sliced cheese, and sliced tomato.

Basil Pork Patties with Cheddar

Prep + Cook Time: 35 minutes | Serves: 2

Ingredients

½ lb ground pork
1 medium onion, chopped
1 tbsp mixed herbs
2 tsp garlic powder
1 tsp dried basil

1 tbsp tomato puree
1 tsp mustard
Salt and black pepper to taste
2 bread buns, halved

Assembling:

1 large onion, sliced in 2-inch rings
1 large tomato, sliced in 2-inch rings

2 small lettuce leaves, cleaned
4 slices Cheddar cheese

Directions

In a bowl, add the minced pork, chopped onion, mixed herbs, garlic powder, dried basil, tomato puree, mustard, salt, and pepper. Use hands to mix evenly. Form two patties out of the mixture and place them on a flat plate.

Preheat the Air Fryer to 370 F. Place the pork patties in the fryer basket, and cook for 15 minutes. Slide out the basket and turn the patties with a spatula. Reduce the temperature to 350 F and cook for 5 minutes.

Once ready, remove them onto a plate and start assembling the burger. Place two halves of the bun on a clean flat surface. Add the lettuce in both, then a patty each, followed by an onion ring each, a tomato ring each, and then 2 slices of cheddar cheese each. Cover the buns with their other halves. Serve with ketchup and french fries.

Tasty Sausage Bacon Rolls

Prep + Cook Time: 1 hour 44 minutes | Serves: 4

Ingredients

Sausage:

8 bacon strips

8 pork sausages

Relish:

8 large tomatoes
1 clove garlic, peeled
1 small onion, peeled
3 tbsp chopped parsley
A pinch of salt

A pinch of pepper
2 tbsp sugar
1 tsp smoked paprika
1 tbsp white wine vinegar

Directions

Start with the relish; add the tomatoes, garlic, and onion in a food processor. Blitz them for 10 seconds until the mixture is pulpy. Pour the pulp into a saucepan, add the vinegar, salt, pepper, and place it over medium heat.

Bring to simmer for 10 minutes; add the paprika and sugar. Stir with a spoon and simmer for 10 minutes until pulpy and thick. Turn off the heat, transfer the relish to a bowl and chill it for an hour. In 30 minutes after putting the relish in the refrigerator, move on to the sausages. Wrap each sausage with a bacon strip neatly and stick in a bamboo skewer at the end of the sausage to secure the bacon ends.

Open the Air Fryer, place 3 to 4 wrapped sausages in the fryer basket and cook for 12 minutes at 350 F. Ensure that the bacon is golden and crispy before removing them. Repeat the cooking process for the remaining wrapped sausages. Remove the relish from the refrigerator. Serve the sausages and relish with turnip mash.

Delicious Beef Roast with Red Potatoes

Prep + Cook Time: 25 minutes | Serves: 3

Ingredients

2 tbsp olive oil
4 pound top round roast beef
1 tsp salt
¼ tsp fresh ground black pepper

1 tsp dried thyme
½ tsp fresh rosemary, chopped
3 pounds red potatoes, halved
Olive oil, black pepper and salt for garnish

Directions

Preheat your Air Fryer to 360 F. In a small bowl, mix rosemary, salt, pepper and thyme; rub oil onto beef. Season with the spice mixture. Place the prepared meat in your Air Fryer's cooking basket and cook for 20 minutes.

Give the meat a turn and add potatoes, more pepper and oil. Cook for 20 minutes more. Take the steak out and set aside to cool for 10 minutes. Cook the potatoes in your Air Fryer for 10 more minutes at 400 F. Serve hot.

Beef, Mushrooms and Noodles Dish

Prep + Cook Time: 35 minutes | Serves: 5

Ingredients

1½ pounds beef steak
1 package egg noodles, cooked
1 ounce dry onion soup mix
1 can (14.5 oz) cream mushroom soup

2 cups mushrooms, sliced
1 whole onion, chopped
½ cup beef broth
3 garlic cloves, minced?

Directions

Preheat your Air Fryer to 360 F. Drizzle onion soup mix all over the meat. In a mixing bowl, mix the sauce, garlic cloves, beef broth, chopped onion, sliced mushrooms and mushroom soup. Top the meat with the prepared sauce mixture. Place the prepared meat in the air fryer's cooking basket and cook for 25 minutes. Serve with cooked egg noodles.

Lemongrass Pork Chops

Prep + Cook Time: 2 hrs 20 minutes | Serves: 3

Ingredients

3 slices pork chops
2 garlic cloves, minced
1 ½ tbsp sugar
4 stalks lemongrass, trimmed and chopped
2 shallots, chopped

2 tbsp olive oil
1 ¼ tsp soy sauce
1 ¼ tsp fish sauce
1 ½ tsp black pepper

Directions

In a bowl, add the garlic, sugar, lemongrass, shallots, olive oil, soy sauce, fish sauce, and black pepper; mix well. Add the pork chops, coat them with the mixture and allow to marinate for around 2 hours to get nice and savory.

Preheat the Air Fryer to 400 F. Cooking in 2 to 3 batches, remove and shake each pork chop from the marinade and place it in the fryer basket. Cook it for 7 minutes. Turn the pork chops with kitchen tongs and cook further for 5 minutes. Remove the chops and serve with a side of sautéed asparagus.

Effortless Beef Schnitzel

Prep + Cook Time: 25 minutes | Serves: 2

Ingredients

2 tbsp vegetable oil
2 oz breadcrumbs
1 whole egg, whisked

1 thin beef schnitzel, cut into strips
1 whole lemon

Directions

Preheat your fryer to 356 F. In a bowl, add breadcrumbs and oil and stir well to get a loose mixture. Dip schnitzel in egg, then dip in breadcrumbs coat well. Place the prepared schnitzel your Air Fryer's cooking basket and cook for 12 minutes. Serve with a drizzle of lemon juice.

BBQ Pork Ribs

Prep + Cook Time: 5 hrs 30 minutes | Serves: 2 to 3

Ingredients

1 lb pork ribs
1 tsp soy sauce
Salt and black pepper to taste
1 tsp oregano
1 tbsp + 1 tbsp maple syrup

3 tbsp barbecue sauce
2 cloves garlic, minced
1 tbsp cayenne pepper
1 tsp sesame oil

Directions

Put the chops on a chopping board and use a knife to cut them into smaller pieces of desired sizes. Put them in a mixing bowl, add the soy sauce, salt, pepper, oregano, one tablespoon of maple syrup, barbecue sauce, garlic, cayenne pepper, and sesame oil. Mix well and place the pork in the fridge to marinate in the spices for 5 hours.

Preheat the Air Fryer to 350 F. Open the Air Fryer and place the ribs in the fryer basket. Slide the fryer basket in and cook for 15 minutes. Open the Air fryer, turn the ribs using tongs, apply the remaining maple syrup with a brush, close the Air Fryer, and continue cooking for 10 minutes.

Homemade Beef Stroganoff

Prep + Cook Time: 20 minutes | Serves: 3

Ingredients

1 pound thin steak
4 tbsp butter
1 whole onion, chopped
1 cup sour cream

8 oz mushrooms, sliced
4 cups beef broth
16 oz egg noodles, cooked

Directions

Preheat your Air Fryer to 400 F. Using a microwave proof bowl, melt butter in a microwave oven. In a mixing bowl, mix the melted butter, sliced mushrooms, cream, onion, and beef broth.

Pour the mixture over steak and set aside for 10 minutes. Place the marinated beef in your fryer's cooking basket, and cook for 10 minutes. Serve with cooked egg noodles and enjoy!

Hot Pork Skewers

Prep + Cook Time: 1 hour 20 minutes | Serves: 3 to 4

Ingredients

1 lb pork steak, cut in cubes
¼ cup soy sauce
2 tsp smoked paprika
1 tsp powdered chili

1 tsp garlic salt
1 tsp red chili flakes
1 tbsp white wine vinegar
3 tbsp steak sauce

Skewing:

1 green pepper, cut in cubes
1 red pepper, cut in cubes
1 yellow squash, seeded and cut in cubes

1 green squash, seeded and cut in cubes
Salt and black pepper to taste to season

Directions

In a mixing bowl, add the pork cubes, soy sauce, smoked paprika, powdered chili, garlic salt, red chili flakes, white wine vinegar, and steak sauce. Mix them using a ladle. Refrigerate to marinate them for 1 hour.

After one hour, remove the marinated pork from the fridge and preheat the Air Fryer to 370 F.

On each skewer, stick the pork cubes and vegetables in the order that you prefer. Have fun doing this. Once the pork cubes and vegetables are finished, arrange the skewers in the fryer basket and grill them for 8 minutes. You can do them in batches. Once ready, remove them onto the serving platter and serve with salad.

Pork Rack with Macadamia Nuts

Prep + Cook Time: 50minutes | Serves: 2 to 3

Ingredients

1 lb rack of pork
2 tbsp olive oil
1 clove garlic, minced
Salt and black pepper to taste

1 cup chopped macadamia nuts
1 tbsp breadcrumbs
1 egg, beaten in a bowl
1 tbsp rosemary, chopped

Directions

Add the olive oil and garlic to a bowl. Mix vigorously with a spoon to make garlic oil. Place the rack of pork on a chopping board and brush it with the garlic oil using a brush. Sprinkle with salt and pepper.

Preheat the Air Fryer to 250 F. In a bowl, add breadcrumbs, nuts, and rosemary. Mix with a spoon and set aside. Brush the meat with the egg on all sides and sprinkle the nut mixture generously over the pork. Press with hands. Put the coated pork in the fryer basket, close and roast for 30 minutes.

Increase the temperature to 390 F and cook further for 5 minutes. Once ready, remove the meat onto a chopping board. Allow a sitting time of 10 minutes before slicing. Serve with a side of parsnip fries and tomato dip.

Sweet Marinaded Pork Chops

Prep + Cook Time:15 minutes | Serves: 3

Ingredients

3 pork chops, ½-inch thick
Salt and black pepper to taste to season
1 tbsp maple syrup

1 ½ tbsp minced garlic
3 tbsp mustard

Directions

In a bowl, add maple syrup, garlic, mustard, salt, and pepper; mix well. Add the pork and toss it in the mustard sauce to coat well. Slide out the fryer basket and place the chops in the basket; cook at 350 F for 6 minutes.

Open the Air Fryer and flip the pork with a spatula and cook further for 6 minutes. Once ready, remove them onto a serving platter and serve with a side of steamed asparagus.

Savory Pulled Pork with Cheddar and Bacon

Prep + Cook Time: 50 minutes | Serves: 2

Ingredients

½ pork steak
1 tsp steak seasoning
Salt and black pepper to taste
5 thick bacon slices, chopped

1 cup grated Cheddar cheese
½ tbsp worcestershire sauce
2 bread buns, halved

Directions

Preheat the Air Fryer to 400 F. Place the pork steak in a plate and season with pepper, salt, and the steak seasoning. Pat it with your hands. Slide out the fryer basket and place the pork in it. Grill for 15 minutes, turn using tongs, slide the fryer in and continue cooking for 6 minutes.

Once ready, remove the steak onto a chopping board and use two forks to shred the pork into small pieces. Place the chopped bacon in a small heatproof bowl and place the bowl in the fryer's basket.

Close the Air Fryer and cook the bacon at 370 F for 10 minutes. Remove the bacon into a bigger heatproof bowl, add the pulled pork, Worcestershire sauce, and the cheddar cheese. Season with salt and pepper.

Place the bowl in the fryer basket and cook at 350 for 4 minutes. Slide out the fryer basket, stir the mixture with a spoon, slide the fryer basket back in and cook further for 1 minute. Spoon to scoop the meat into the halved buns and serve with a cheese or tomato dip.

Teriyaki Pork Ribs with Tomato Sauce

Prep + Cook Time: 20 minutes | Serves: 3

Ingredients

1 pound pork ribs
1 tsp salt
1 tsp pepper
1 tbsp sugar
1 tsp ginger juice
1 tsp five-spice powder

1 tbsp teriyaki sauce
1 tbsp light soy sauce
1 garlic clove, minced
2 tbsp honey
1 tbsp water
1 tbsp tomato sauce

Directions

In a bowl, mix pepper, sugar, five-spice powder, salt, ginger juice, teriyaki sauce. Add pork ribs to the marinade and let marinate for 2 hours. Preheat your Air Fryer to 350 F.

Add pork ribs to your Air Fryer's cooking basket and cook for 8 minutes. In a separate mixing bowl, mix soy sauce, garlic, honey, water, tomato sauce. Over medium heat, add oil and garlic in a pan and fry for 30 seconds. Add fried pork ribs and pour the prepared sauce. Stir-fry for a few minutes, serve and enjoy!

Tamarind Pork Chops with Caramelized Potatoes

Prep + Cook Time: 45 minutes | Serves: 4

Ingredients

2 tbsp tamarind paste
2 whole caramelized potatoes
1 tbsp garlic, minced
½ cup green mole sauce
3 tbsp corn syrup
1 tbsp olive oil

2 tbsp molasses
4 tbsp southwest seasoning
2 tbsp ketchup
4 pork chops
2 tbsp water

Directions

Preheat your Air Fryer to 350 F. In a bowl, mix all the ingredients except potatoes, pork chops and mole sauce.

Let the pork chops marinate in the mixture for 30 minutes. Place pork chops to your Air Fryer's cooking basket and cook for 25 minutes. Serve with caramelized potatoes and mole sauce.

Oyster Beef Steak with Broccoli

Prep + Cook Time: 35 minutes | Serves: 4

Ingredients

¾ pound circular beef steak, cut into strips
1 pound broccoli, cut into florets
⅓ cup oyster sauce
2 tbsp sesame oil
⅓ cup sherry

1 tsp soy sauce
1 tsp white sugar
1 tsp cornstarch
1 tbsp olive oil
1 garlic clove, minced

Directions

In a bowl, mix cornstarch, sherry, oyster sauce, sesame oil, soy sauce, sugar and beef steaks. Set aside for 45 minutes. Add garlic, oil and ginger to the steaks. Place the steaks in your air fryer's cooking basket and cook for 12 minutes at 390 F.

Beef Rolls with Pesto and Spinach

Prep + Cook Time: 30 minutes | Serves: 4

Ingredients

2 pounds beef steak, sliced
1 tsp pepper
3 tbsp pesto
1 tsp salt

6 slices cheese
¾ cup spinach, chopped
3 oz bell pepper, deseeded and sliced

Directions

Preheat your Air Fryer to 400 F. Top the steak slices with pesto, cheese, spinach, bell pepper. Roll up the slices and secure using a toothpick. Season with salt and pepper accordingly. Place the prepared slices in your Air Fryer's cooking basket and cook for 15 minutes. Serve and enjoy!

Grandma's Ground Beef Balls

Prep + Cook Time: 15 minutes | Serves: 5

Ingredients

1 pound beef, ground
1 tbsp extra-virgin olive oil
1 large red onion, chopped

1 tsp garlic, minced
2 whole eggs, beaten
Salt and black pepper to taste

Directions

Preheat your Air Fryer to 350 F. Using a pan over high heat, heat the oil. Add the chopped onion and garlic, cook for 1 minute until tender; transfer to a bowl. Add ground beef and egg and mix well. Season with salt and pepper. Roll the mixture golf ball shapes. Place the balls in the Air Fryer cooking basket and cook for 4 minutes.

Savory Chili Pork Chops with Rice

Prep + Cook Time: 40 minutes | Serves: 4

Ingredients

2 pork chops
1 lime juice
Salt and black pepper to taste
1 tsp garlic powder
1 ½ cups white rice, cooked
2 tbsp olive oil

1 can (14.5 oz) tomato sauce
1 onion, chopped
3 garlic cloves, minced
½ tsp oregano
1 tsp chipotle chili

Directions

Preheat your Air Fryer to 350 F. Season pork chops with salt, pepper and garlic powder. Next, in a bowl, mix onion, garlic, chipotle, oregano, and tomato sauce. Add the pork to the mixture. Let marinate for an hour.

Remove the meat from the mixture and allow the mixture to sit for 15 minutes. After, place them into the wire basket of your air fryer and cook for 25 minutes; make sure you check them halfway through and turn to ensure they get nicely cooked on both sides. Serve with cooked rice.

Italian-Style Pork Chops

Prep + Cook Time: 30 minutes | Serves: 4

Ingredients

4 slices pork chops, sliced
2-3 tbsp olive oil
Salt and black pepper to taste
1 whole egg, beaten

1 tbsp flour
Breadcrumbs as needed
A bunch of Italian herbs

Directions

Preheat your Air Fryer to 400 F. Mix oil, salt, and pepper to form a marinade. Place the beaten egg in a plate. In a separate plate, add the breadcrumbs. Add pork to the marinade and allow to rest for 15 minutes.

Add one slice in egg and then to breadcrumbs; repeat with all slices. Place the prepared slices in your Air Fryer's cooking basket and cook for 20 minutes. Season with your desired herbs and serve.

Homemade Pork Ratatouille

Prep + Cook Time: 25 minutes | Serves: 4

Ingredients

4 pork sausages

For Ratatouille

1 pepper, chopped

2 zucchinis, chopped

1 eggplant, chopped

1 medium red onion, chopped

1 tbsp olive oil

1-ounce butterbean, drained

15 oz tomatoes, chopped

2 sprigs fresh thyme

1 tbsp balsamic vinegar

2 garlic cloves, minced

1 red chili, chopped

Directions

Preheat your Air Fryer to 392 F. Mix pepper, eggplant, oil, onion, zucchinis, and add to the cooking basket. Roast for 20 minutes. Set aside to cool. Reduce Air Fryer temperature to 356 F. In a saucepan, mix prepared vegetables and the remaining ratatouille ingredients, and bring to a boil over medium heat.

Let the mixture simmer for 10 minutes; season with salt and pepper. Add sausages to your Air Fryer's basket and cook for 10-15 minutes. Serve the sausages with ratatouille.

Sage Sausages Balls

Prep + Cook Time: 20 minutes | Serves: 4

Ingredients

3 ½ oz sausages, sliced

Salt and black pepper to taste

1 cup onion, chopped

3 tbsp breadcrumbs

½ tsp garlic puree

1 tsp sage

Directions

Preheat your Air Fryer to 340 F. In a bowl, mix onions, sausage meat, sage, garlic puree, salt and pepper. Add breadcrumbs to a plate. Form balls using the mixture and roll them in breadcrumbs. Add onion balls in your Air Fryer's cooking basket and cook for 15 minutes. Serve and enjoy!

Party Stuffed Pork Chops

Prep + Cook Time: 40 minutes | Serves: 4

Ingredients

8 pork chops

¼ tsp pepper

4 cups stuffing mix

½ tsp salt

2 tbsp olive oil

4 garlic cloves, minced

2 tbsp sage leaves

Directions

Preheat your Air Fryer to 350 F. Cut a hole in pork chops and fill chops with stuffing mix. In a bowl, mix sage leaves, garlic cloves, oil, salt and pepper. Cover chops with marinade and let marinate for 10 minutes. Place the chops in your Air Fryer's cooking basket and cook for 25 minutes. Serve and enjoy!

Cheddar Pork Meatballs

Prep + Cook Time: 25 minutes | Serves: 4 to 6

Ingredients

1 lb ground pork
1 large onion, chopped
½ tsp maple syrup
2 tsp mustard

½ cup chopped basil leaves
Salt and black pepper to taste
2 tbsp grated Cheddar cheese

Directions

In a mixing bowl, add the ground pork, onion, maple syrup, mustard, basil leaves, salt, pepper, and cheddar cheese; mix well. Use your hands to form bite-size balls. Place in the fryer basket and cook at 400 F for 10 minutes.

Slide out the fryer basket and shake it to toss the meatballs. Cook further for 5 minutes. Remove them onto a wire rack and serve with zoodles and marinara sauce.

Swiss Cheese Ham Muffins

Prep + Cook Time: 25 minutes | Serves: 18

Ingredients

5 whole eggs, beaten
2 ¼ oz ham
1 cup milk
¼ tsp pepper

1 ½ cups Swiss cheese, grated
¼ tsp salt
¼ cup green onion, chopped
½ tsp thyme

Directions

Preheat your Fryer to 350 F. In a bowl, mix beaten eggs, thyme, onion, salt, Swiss cheese, pepper, and milk. Prepare baking forms and place ham slices in each baking form. Top with the egg mixture. Place the prepared muffin forms in your Air Fryer's cooking basket and cook for 15 minutes. Serve and enjoy!

Almond Pork Bites

Prep + Cook Time: 40 minutes | Serves: 10

Ingredients

16 oz sausage meat
1 whole egg, beaten
3 ½ oz onion, chopped
2 tbsp dried sage

2 tbsp almonds, chopped
½ tsp pepper
3 ½ oz apple, sliced
½ tsp salt

Directions

Preheat your Air Fryer to 350 F. In a bowl, mix onion, almonds, sliced apples, egg, pepper and salt. Add the almond mixture and sausage in a Ziploc bag. mix to coat well and set aside for 15 minutes.

Use the mixture to form cutlets. Add cutlets to your fryer's basket and cook for 25 minutes. Serve with heavy cream and enjoy!

Pork Belly with Honey

Prep + Cook Time: 35 minutes | Serves: 8

Ingredients

2 pounds pork belly
½ tsp pepper
1 tbsp olive oil

1 tbsp salt
3 tbsp honey

Directions

Preheat your Air Fryer to 400 F. Season the pork belly with salt and pepper. Grease the basket with oil. Add seasoned meat and cook for 15 minutes. Add honey and cook for 10 minutes more. Serve with green salad.

Cocktail Franks in Blanket

Prep + Cook Time: 20 minutes | Serves: 4

Ingredients

12 oz cocktail franks

8 oz can crescent rolls

Directions

Use a paper towel to pat the cocktail franks to drain completely. Cut the dough in 1 by 1.5-inch rectangles using a knife. Gently roll the franks in the strips, making sure the ends are visible Place in freezer for 5 minutes.

Preheat the fryer to 330 F. Take the franks out of the freezer and place them in the air fryer's basket and cook for 6-8 minutes. Increase the temperature to 390 F. cook for another 3 minutes until a fine golden texture appears.

Smoked Ham with Pears

Prep + Cook Time: 30 minutes | Serves: 2

Ingredients

15 oz pears, halved
8 pound smoked ham
1 ½ cups brown sugar
¾ tbsp allspice

1 tbsp apple cider vinegar
1 tsp black pepper
1 tsp vanilla extract

Directions

Preheat your Air Fryer to 330 F. In a bowl, mix pears, brown sugar, cider vinegar, vanilla extract, pepper, and allspice. Place the mixture in a frying pan and fry for 2-3 minutes. Pour the mixture over ham. Add the ham to the Air Fryer cooking basket and cook for 15 minutes. Serve ham with hot sauce, to enjoy!

Morning Ham and Cheese Sandwich

Prep + Cook Time: 15 minutes | Serves: 4

Ingredients

8 slices whole wheat bread
4 slices lean pork ham

4 slices cheese
8 slices tomato

Directions

Preheat your air fryer to 360 F. Lay four slices of bread on a flat surface. Spread the slices with cheese, tomato, turkey and ham. Cover with the remaining slices to form sandwiches. Add the sandwiches to the Air Fryer cooking basket and cook for 10 minutes.

Amazing Bacon and Potato Platter

Prep + Cook Time: 40 minutes | Serves: 4

Ingredients

4 potatoes, halved
6 garlic cloves, squashed
4 streaky cut rashers bacon

2 sprigs rosemary
1 tbsp olive oil

Directions

Preheat your Air Fryer to 392 F. In a mixing bowl, mix garlic, bacon, potatoes and rosemary; toss in oil. Place the mixture in your Air Fryer's cooking basket and roast for 25-30 minutes. Serve and enjoy!

Corned Beef with Carrots

Prep + Cook Time: 35 minutes | Serves: 3

Ingredients

1 tbsp beef spice
1 whole onion, chopped
4 carrots, chopped

12 oz bottle beer
1½ cups chicken broth
4 pounds corned beef

Directions

Preheat your Air Fryer to 380 F. Cover beef with beer and set aside for 20 minutes. Place carrots, onion and beef in a pot and heat over high heat. Add in broth and bring to a boil. Drain boiled meat and veggies; set aside.

Top with beef spice. Place the meat and veggies in your Air Fryer's cooking basket and cook for 30 minutes.

Cheese Breaded Pork

Prep + Cook Time: 15 minutes | Serves: 6

Ingredients

6 pork chops
6 tbsp seasoned breadcrumbs
2 tbsp Parmesan cheese, grated

1 tbsp melted butter
½ cup mozzarella cheese, shredded
1 tbsp marinara sauce

Directions

Preheat your Air Fryer to 390 F. Grease the cooking basket with cooking spray. In a small bowl, mix breadcrumbs and Parmesan cheese. In another microwave proof bowl, add butter and melt in the microwave.

Brush the pork with butter and dredge into the breadcrumbs. Add pork to the cooking basket and cook for 6 minutes. Turn over and top with marinara sauce and shredded mozzarella; cook for 3 more minutes.

FISH AND SEAFOOD

Barramundi Filles with Lemon-Butter Sauce

Prep + Cook Time: 25 minutes | Serves: 3

Ingredients

3 (½ lb) barramundi fillets
2 lemons, juiced
Salt and black pepper to taste
6 oz butter
¾ cup thickened cream

½ cup white wine
2 bay leaves
15 black peppercorns
2 cloves garlic, minced
2 shallots, chopped

Directions

Preheat the Air Fryer to 390 F. Place the barramundi fillets on a baking paper and put them in the fryer basket. Cook for 15 minutes. Remove to a serving platter without the paper.

Place a small pan over low heat on a stove top. Add the garlic and shallots, and dry fry for 20 seconds. Add the wine, bay leaves, and peppercorns. Stir and allow the liquid to reduce by three quarters, and add the cream. Stir and let the sauce thicken into a dark cream color.

Add the butter, whisk it into the cream until it has fully melted. Add the lemon juice, pepper, and salt. Turn the heat off. Strain the sauce into a serving bowl. Pour the sauce over the fish and serve with a side of rice.

Garlic-Chili Prawns

Prep + Cook Time: 12 minutes | Serves: 8

Ingredients

8 prawns, cleaned
Salt and black pepper
½ tsp ground cayenne
½ tsp chili flakes

½ tsp ground cumin
½ tsp garlic powder

Directions

In a bowl, season the prawns with salt and black pepper. Sprinkle cayenne, flakes, cumin and garlic and stir to coat. Spray the air fryer's basket with oil and arrange the prawns in an even layer. Cook for 8 minutes at 340 F, turning once halfway through. Serve with fresh lettuce leaves or sweet chili/mayo sauce.

Catfish Fillets with Parsley

Prep + Cook Time: 40 minutes | Serves: 2

Ingredients

2 catfish fillets
3 tbsp breadcrumbs
1 tsp cayenne pepper

1 tsp dry fish seasoning, of choice
2 sprigs parsley, chopped
Salt to taste, optional

Directions

Preheat Air Fryer to 400 F. Meanwhile, pour all the dry ingredients, except the parsley, in a zipper bag. Pat dry and add the fish pieces. Close the bag and shake to coat the fish well. Do this with one fish piece at a time.

Lightly spray the fish with olive oil. Arrange them in the fryer basket, one at a time depending on the size of the fish. Close the Air Fryer and cook for 10 minutes. Flip the fish and cook further for 10 minutes. For extra crispiness, cook for 3 more minutes. Garnish with parsley and serve as a lunch accompaniment.

Garlic Salmon with Soy Sauce

Prep + Cook Time: 13 minutes | Serves: 1

Ingredients

1 salmon fillet
1 tbsp soy sauce

¼ tsp garlic powder
Salt and black pepper to taste

Directions

Preheat the Air fryer to 350 F, and combine soy sauce with garlic powder, salt and pepper. Brush the mixture over salmon. Place the salmon onto a sheet of parchment paper and into the air fryer; cook for 10 minutes.

Creamy Crab Croquettes

Prep + Cook Time: 30 minutes | Serves: 4

Ingredients

Filling:
1 ½ lb lump crab meat
3 egg whites, beaten
⅓ cup sour cream
⅓ cup mayonnaise
1 ½ tbsp olive oil
1 red pepper, chopped finely

⅓ cup chopped red onion
2 ½ tbsp chopped celery
½ tsp chopped tarragon
½ tsp chopped chives
1 tsp chopped parsley
1 tsp cayenne pepper

Breading:
1 ½ cup breadcrumbs
2 tsp olive oil
1 cup flour

4 eggs, beaten
Salt to taste

Directions

Place a skillet over medium heat on a stove top, add 1 ½ tbsp olive oil, red pepper, onion, and celery. Sauté for 5 minutes or until sweaty and translucent. Turn off heat. Add the breadcrumbs, the remaining olive oil, and salt to a food processor. Blend to mix evenly; set aside. In 2 separate bowls, add the flour and 4 eggs respectively; set aside.

In a separate bowl, add the crabmeat, mayo, egg whites, sour cream, tarragon, chives, parsley, cayenne pepper, and the celery sauté and mix evenly. Form bite-size balls from the mixture and place into a plate.

Preheat the Air Fryer to 390 F. Dip each crab meatball (croquettes) in the eggs mixture and press them in the breadcrumb mixture. Place the croquettes in the fryer basket, 12 to 15 at a time; avoid overcrowding.

Close the Air Fryer and cook for 10 minutes or until golden brown. Remove them and plate them. Serve the crab croquettes with tomato dipping sauce and a side of vegetable fries.

Baby Octopus with Capers and Fennel Salad

Prep + Cook Time: 50 minutes | Serves: 3

Ingredients

1 lb baby octopus, thoroughly cleaned
1 ½ tbsp olive oil
2 cloves garlic, minced
1 ½ tbsp capers
1 ¼ tbsp balsamic glaze
1 bunch parsley, chopped roughly
1 bunch baby fennel, chopped

1 cup semi-dried tomatoes, chopped
1 red onion, sliced
A handful of arugula
Salt and black pepper to taste
¼ cup chopped grilled Halloumi
1 long red chili, minced
1 ½ cups water

Directions

Pour the water in a pot and bring to boil over medium heat on a stove top. Cut the octopus into bite sizes and add it to the boiling water for 45 seconds; drain the water. Add the garlic, olive oil, and octopus in a bowl. Coat the octopus with the garlic and olive oil. Leave to marinate for 20 minutes.

Preheat the Air Fryer to 390 F. Place the octopus in the fryer basket and grill for 5 minutes. Meanwhile, in a salad mixing bowl, add the capers, halloumi, chili, tomatoes, olives, parsley, red onion, fennel, octopus, arugula, and balsamic glaze. Season with salt and pepper and mix. Serve with a side of toasts.

Rich Seafood Pie

Prep + Cook Time: 60 minutes | Serves: 3

Ingredients

1 cup seafood marinara mix
1 lb russet potatoes, peeled and quartered
1 cup water
1 carrot, grated
½ head baby fennel, grated
1 bunch dill sprigs, chopped
1 sprig parsley, chopped
A handful of baby spinach

1 small tomato, diced
½ celery sticks, grated
2 tbsp butter
1 tbsp milk
½ cup grated Cheddar cheese
1 small red chili, minced
½ lemon, juiced
Salt and black pepper to taste

Directions

Add the potatoes to a pan, pour the water, and bring to a boil over medium heat on a stove top. Use a fork to check that if they are soft and mash-able, after about 12 minutes. Drain the water and use a potato masher to mash. Add the butter, milk, salt, and pepper. Mash until smooth and well mixed; set aside.

In a bowl, add the celery, carrots, cheese, chili, fennel, parsley, lemon juice, seafood mix, dill, tomato, spinach, salt, and pepper; mix well.

Preheat the Air Fryer to 330 F. In a 6 inches casserole dish, add half of the carrots mixture and level. Top with half of the potato mixture and level. Place the dish in the Air Fryer and bake for 20 minutes until golden brown and the seafood is properly cooked. Remove the dish and add the remaining seafood mixture and level out.

Top with the remaining potato mash and level it too. Place the dish back to the fryer and cook at 330 F for 20 minutes. Once ready, ensure that it's well cooked, and remove the dish. Slice the pie and serve with a green salad.

Savory Salmon with Vegetables

Prep + Cook Time: 25 minutes | Serves: 2

Ingredients

2-3 fingerling potatoes, thinly sliced
½ bulb fennel, thinly sliced
4 tbsp melted butter
Salt and black pepper to taste

1-2 tsp fresh dill
2 sockeye salmon fillets (6 oz each)
8 cherry tomatoes, halved
¼ cup fish stock

Directions

Preheat Air Fryer to 400 F, and boil salted water in a small saucepan over medium heat. Add the potatoes and blanch for 2 minutes; drain the potatoes. Cut 2 large-sized rectangles of parchment paper of 13x15 inch size.

In a large bowl, mix potatoes, melted butter, fennel, fresh ground pepper, and salt. Divide the mixture between parchment paper pieces and sprinkle dill on top. Place fillet on top of veggie piles; season with salt and pepper.

Add cherry tomato on top of each veggie pile and drizzle butter; pour fish stock on top. Fold the squares and seal them. Preheat your air fryer to 400 F, and cook the packets for 10 minutes. Garnish with a bit of dill and enjoy!

Mozzarella & Smoked Fish Tart

Prep + Cook Time: 35 minutes | Serves: 5

Ingredients

1 quiche pastry case
5 eggs, lightly beaten
4 tbsp heavy cream
¼ cup finely chopped green onions
¼ cup chopped parsley

1 tsp baking powder
Salt and black pepper
1 lb smoked fish
1 cup shredded mozzarella cheese

Directions

In a bowl, whisk eggs, cream, scallions, parsley, baking powder, salt and black. Add in fish and cheese, stir to combine. Line the air fryer with baking paper. Pour the mixture into the pastry case and place it gently inside the air fryer. Cook for 25 minutes at 360 F. Check past 15 minutes, so it's not overcooked.

Homemade Crispy Fish Fingers

Prep + Cook Time: 20 minutes | Serves: 8

Ingredients

2 fresh white fish fillets, cut into 4 fingers each
1 egg, beaten
½ cup buttermilk

1 cup panko breadcrumbs
Salt and black pepper

Directions

In a bowl, mix egg and buttermilk. On a plate, mix and spread crumbs, salt, and black pepper. Dip each finger into the egg mixture, then roll it up in the crumbs, and spray with olive oil. Arrange them in the air fryer and cook for 10 minutes at 340 F, turning once halfway through. Serve with garlic mayo and lemon wedges.

Friday Night Cod Fish Nuggets

Prep + Cook Time: 20 minutes | Serves: 4

Ingredients

4 Cod fillets
2 tbsp olive oil
2 eggs, beaten

1 cup breadcrumbs
A pinch of salt
1 cup flour

Directions

Preheat the Air Fryer to 390 F. Place the breadcrumbs, olive oil, and salt in a food processor and process until evenly combined. Pour the breadcrumb mixture into a bowl, the eggs into another bowl, and the flour into a third bowl. Toss the cod fillets in the flour, then in the eggs, and then in the breadcrumb mixture.

Place them in the fryer basket, close and cook for 9 minutes. At the 5-minute mark, quickly turn the chicken nuggets over. Once golden brown, remove onto a serving plate and serve with vegetable fries.

Simple Fish and Fries

Prep + Cook Time: 25 minutes | Serves: 4

Ingredients

4 potatoes, cut into thin slices
Salt and black pepper to taste
4 white fish fillets
2 tbsp flour

1 egg, beaten
1 cup breadcrumbs
Salt and black pepper

Directions

Spray the slices with olive oil and season with salt and black pepper. Place them in the air fryer, and cook for 20 minutes at 400 F.

Meanwhile, spread flour on a plate and coat the fish. Dip them in the egg, then into the crumbs and season with salt and black pepper. At the 10 minutes' mark, add the fish to the fryer and cook with the chips. Cook until crispy. Serve with lemon slices, mayo and ketchup.

Chili Crab Cakes

Prep + Cook Time: 20 minutes | Serves: 8

Ingredients

1 lb crabmeat, shredded
2 eggs, beaten
½ cup breadcrumbs
⅓ cup finely chopped green onion
¼ cup parsley, chopped

1 tbsp mayonnaise
1 tsp sweet chili sauce
½ tsp paprika
Salt and black pepper

Directions

In a bowl, add meat, eggs, crumbs, green onion, parsley, mayo, chili sauce, paprika, salt, and black pepper and mix well with hands. Shape into 8 cakes and grease them lightly with oil. Arrange the cakes into a fryer, without overcrowding. Cook for 8 minutes at 400 F, turning once halfway through cooking.

Bacon Wrapped Prawns

Prep + Cook Time: 30 minutes | Serves: 4

Ingredients

8 bacon slices
8 jumbo prawns, peeled and deveined

Lemon Wedges for garnishing

Directions

Wrap each prawn from head to tail with each bacon slice overlapping to keep the bacon in place. Secure the end of the bacon with a toothpick. It's ok not to cover the ends of the cheese with bacon. Refrigerate for 15 minutes.

Preheat the Air Fryer to 400 F. Arrange the bacon wrapped prawns in the fryer's basket, close and cook for 7 minutes or until the bacon is browned and crispy. Transfer prawns to a paper towel to cool for 2 minutes. Remove the toothpicks and serve the bacon wrapped prawns with lemon wedges and a side of steamed green vegetables.

Salmon with Dill-Yogurt Sauce

Prep + Cook Time: 25minutes | Serves: 4

Ingredients

4 (6-oz) salmon pieces
Salt and black pepper to taste
2 tsp olive oil

3 tbsp chopped dill + extra for garnishing
1 cup sour cream
1 cup Greek yoghurt, full fat

Directions

For the dill sauce, in a bowl, mix well the sour cream, yogurt, dill, and salt. Preheat the Air Fryer to 280 F.

Drizzle the olive oil over the salmon, and rub with salt and pepper. Arrange the salmon pieces in the fryer basket and cook them for 15 minutes. Remove salmon to a platter and top with the sauce. Serve with steamed asparagus.

Tuna Sandwich with Mozzarella

Prep + Cook Time: 10 minutes | Serves: 2

Ingredientst

4 slices of white bread
2 small tins of tuna, drained
½ onion, finely chopped

2 tbsp mayonnaise
1 cup mozzarella cheese, shredded

Directions

Lay the bread out onto a board. In a bowl, mix tuna, onion, mayonnaise. Spoon the mixture over two bread slices.

Top with cheese and put the other piece of bread on top. Spray with oil each side and arrange the sandwiches into the air fryer. Cook at 360 F for 6 minutes, turning once halfway through cooking.

Rosemary Fish Fillets

Prep + Cook Time: 20 minutes | Serves: 5

Ingredients

5 frozen fish fillets
5 biscuits, crumbled
3 tbsp flour
1 egg, beaten
A pinch of salt

A pinch of black pepper
¼ tsp rosemary
3 tbsp olive oil divided
A handful of sesame seeds

Directions

Preheat the Air fryer to 390 F. Combine the flour, pepper and salt, in a shallow bowl. In another shallow bowl, combine the sesame seeds, crumbled biscuits, oil, and rosemary. Dip the fish fillets into the flour mixture first, then into the beaten egg, and finally, coat them with the sesame mixture.

Arrange them in the air fryer on a sheet of aluminum foil; cook the fish for 8 minutes. Flip the fillets over and cook for an additional 4 minutes. Serve and enjoy.

Fennel and Herbs Stuffed Trout en Papillote

Prep + Cook Time: 30 minutes | Serves: 2

Ingredients

¾ lb whole trout, scaled and cleaned
¼ bulb fennel, sliced
½ brown onion, sliced
3 tbsp chopped parsley

3 tbsp chopped dill
2 tbsp olive oil
1 lemon, sliced
Salt and black pepper to taste

Directions

In a bowl, add the onion, parsley, dill, fennel, and garlic. Mix and drizzle the olive oil over. Preheat the Air Fryer to 350 F. Open the cavity of the fish and fill with the fennel mixture.

Wrap the fish completely in parchment paper and then in foil. Place the fish in the fryer basket and cook for 10 minutes. Remove the paper and foil, and top with lemon slices. Serve with a side of cooked mushrooms.

Trout in Dill Sauce

Prep + Cook Time: 30 minutes | Serves: 3

Ingredients

3 trout fillets, 5-6 oz each
3 tbsp olive oil

1 pinch salt

Dill Sauce:

½ cup greek yogurt
½ cup sour cream

2 tbsp finely chopped dill
1 pinch salt

Directions

Preheat the Air Fryer to 300 F. Drizzle the trout with oil and season with a pinch of salt. Place the seasoned trout into the Air Fryer's cooking basket. Cook for 20 minutes and top with the dill sauce before serving. For the dill sauce, in a large bowl, mix the yogurt, the sour cream, the chopped dill and salt.

Lemon Garlic Calamari

Prep + Cook Time: 130 minutes | Serves: 3

Ingredients

½ lb calamari rings
½ cup cornmeal or cornstarch
2 large eggs, beaten

2 mashed garlic cloves
1 cup breadcrumbs
lemon juice

Directions

Coat the calamari rings with the cornmeal. The first mixture is prepared by mixing the eggs and the garlic. Dip the calamari in the eggs' mixture. Then dip them in the breadcrumbs. Put the rings in the fridge for 2 hours.

Then, line them in the Air Fryer and add oil generously. Fry for 10 to 13 minutes at 390 F, shaking once halfway through. Serve with garlic mayonnaise and top with lemon juice.

Tasty Cod Fillets Sandwich with Pesto

Prep + Cook Time: 20 minutes | Serves: 4

Ingredients

4 cod fillets
2 tbsp flour
10 capers
4 bread rolls

2 oz breadcrumbs
4 tbsp pesto sauce
4 lettuce leaves
Salt and black pepper to taste

Directions

Preheat the Air fryer to 370 F. Season the fillets with salt and pepper, and coat them with the flour; dip in the breadcrumbs. You should get a really thin layer of breadcrumbs, that's why we don't use eggs for this recipe.

Arrange the fillets onto a baking mat and cook in the fryer for 10 to 15 minutes. Cut the bread rolls in half. Place a lettuce leaf on top of the bottom halves; put the fillets over. Spread a tbsp of pesto sauce on top of each fillet, and top with the remaining halves.

Cheesy Haddock with Lemon

Prep + Cook Time: 15 minutes | Serves: 4

Ingredients

4 haddock fillets
1 cup breadcrumbs
2 tbsp lemon juice
½ tsp black pepper
¼ cup dry potato flakes

1 egg, beaten
¼ cup Parmesan cheese, grated
3 tbsp flour
¼ tsp salt

Directions

Combine the flour, black pepper and salt, in a small bowl. In another bowl, combine the lemon, breadcrumbs, Parmesan cheese, and potato flakes. Dip the fillets in the flour first, then in the beaten egg, and coat them with the lemony crumbs. Arrange on a lined sheet and place in the air fryer. Cook for 8 to 10 minutes at 370 F.

Lime Salmon with Broccoli

Prep + Cook Time: 25 minutes | Serves: 2

Ingredients

2 salmon fillets
1 tsp olive oil
Juice of 1 lime
1 tsp chili flakes

Salt and black pepper
1 head broccoli, cut into florets
1 tsp olive oil
1 tbsp soy sauce

Directions

In a bowl, add oil, lime juice, flakes, salt, and black pepper; rub the mixture onto fillets. Lay the florets into your air fryer and drizzle with oil. Arrange the fillets around or on top and cook at 340 F for 10 minutes. Drizzle the florets with soy sauce to serve!

Party Fish Tacos

Prep + Cook Time: 15 minutes | Serves: 4

Ingredients

4 corn tortillas
1 halibut fillet
2 tbsp olive oil1
½ cup flour, divided
1 can of beer

1 tsp salt
4 tbsp peach salsa
4 tsp chopped cilantro
1 tsp baking powder

Directions

Preheat the Air fryer to 390 F, and combine 1 cup of flour, baking, powder and salt. Pour in some of the beer, enough to form a batter-like consistency. Save the rest of the beer to gulp with the taco.

Slice the fillet into 4 strips and toss them in half cup of flour. Dip them into the beer batter and arrange on a lined baking sheet. Cook in the air fryer for 8 minutes. Meanwhile, spread the peach salsa on the tortillas. Top each tortilla with one fish strip and chopped cilantro.

Salmon Cakes with Celery

Prep + Cook Time: 13 minutes | Serves: 2

Ingredients

4 oz tinned salmon
4 tbsp celery, chopped
4 tbsp spring onion, sliced
4 tbsp wheat germ

4 tbsp olive oil
1 large egg
1 tbsp dill, fresh and chopped
½ tsp garlic powder

Directions

Preheat the Air Fryer to 390 F. In a large bowl, mix the tinned salmon, egg, celery, onion, dill and garlic.

Shape the mixture into 2-inch size balls and roll them in wheat germ. Heat the oil in a skillet and add the salmon balls; carefully flatten them. Then place them in the Air Fryer and fry for 8 minutes. Serve with yogurt or garlic mayo.

Sweet Coconut Shrimp

Prep + Cook Time: 30 minutes | Serves: 2

Ingredients

8 large shrimp
½ cup breadcrumbs
8 oz coconut milk
½ cup shredded coconut
¼ tsp salt
¼ tsp pepper

½ cup orange jam
1 tsp mustard
1 tbsp honey
½ tsp cayenne pepper
¼ tsp hot sauce

Directions

Combine the breadcrumbs, cayenne pepper, shredded coconut, salt, and pepper in a bowl. Dip the shrimp in the coconut milk, first, and then in the coconut crumbs. Arrange on a lined sheet, and cook in the fryer for 20 minutes at 350 F. Meanwhile, whisk the jam, honey, hot sauce, and mustard. Serve shrimp drizzled with the sauce.

Savory Ginger Cod Fillet with Honey

Prep + Cook Time: 15 minutes | Serves: 1

Ingredients

1 cod fillet
1 tsp olive oil
A pinch of sea salt
A pinch of pepper

1 tbsp soy sauce
Dash of sesame oil
¼ tsp ginger powder
¼ tsp honey

Directions

Preheat the Air fryer to 370 degrees. Combine the olive oil, salt and pepper, and brush that mixture over the cod.

Place the cod onto an aluminum sheet and into the air fryer; cook for 6 minutes. Meanwhile, combine the soy sauce, ginger, honey, and sesame oil. Brush the glaze over the cod. Flip the fillet over and cook for 3 more minutes.

Salmon Patties with Mashed Potatoes

Prep + Cook Time: 1 hour 15 minutes | Serves: 4

Ingredients

10 oz cooked salmon
14 oz boiled and mashed potatoes
2 oz flour
A handful of capers

A handful of chopped parsley
1 tsp olive oil
 zest of 1 lemon

Directions

Place the mashed potatoes in a large bowl and flake the salmon over. Stir in capers, parsley, and lemon zest. Shape small cakes out of the mixture. Dust them with flour and place in the fridge to set, for 1 hour. Preheat the air fryer to 350 degrees F. Brush the olive oil over the basket's bottom and add the cakes. Cook for 7 minutes.

Shrimp Risotto with Baby Spinach and Cheese

Prep + Cook Time: 25 minutes | Serves: 4

Ingredients

4 whole eggs, beaten
Pinch salt
½ cup rice, cooked

½ cup baby spinach
½ cup Monterey Jack cheese , grated
½ cup shrimp, chopped and cooked

Directions

Preheat your Air fryer to 320 F, and in a small bowl, add eggs and season with salt and basil; stir until frothy. Spray baking pan with non-stick cooking spray. Add rice, spinach and shrimp to the pan.

Pour egg mixture over and garnish with cheese. Place the pan in the air fryer's basket and cook for 14-18 minutes until the frittata is puffed and golden brown. Serve immediately.

Salmon with Parmesan and Pistachios

Prep + Cook Time: 15 minutes | Serves: 1

Ingredients

1 salmon fillet
1 tsp mustard
3 tbsp pistachios
A pinch of sea salt
A pinch of garlic powder

A pinch of black pepper
1 tsp lemon juice
1 tsp grated Parmesan cheese
1 tsp olive oil

Directions

Preheat the Air fryer to 350 degrees F, and whisk mustard and lemon juice together. Season the salmon with salt, pepper, and garlic powder. Brush the olive oil on all sides. Brush the mustard mixture onto salmon.

Chop the pistachios finely and combine them with the Parmesan cheese; sprinkle on top of the salmon. Place the salmon in the air fryer basket with the skin side down. Cook for 12 minutes, or to your liking.

Herby Crab Balls with Dijon Mustard

Prep + Cook Time: 20 minutes | Serves: 4

Ingredients

½ pound jumbo crab
Lemon juice to taste
2 tbsp parsley, chopped
Old bay seasoning as needed
1 tbsp basil, chopped

3 tbsp real mayo
¼ tsp Dijon mustard
Zest of ½ lemon
¼ cup panko breadcrumbs

Directions

Preheat your Fryer to 400 F, and in a bowl, mix mayo, lemon zest, old bay seasoning, mustard, and oil. Blend crab meat in food processor and season with salt. Transfer to the mixing bowl and combine well.

Form cakes using the mixture and dredge the mixture into breadcrumbs. Place the cakes in your air fryer's basket and cook for 15 minutes. Serve garnished with parsley and lemon juice.

Mom's Crispy Salmon

Prep + Cook Time: 18 minutes | Serves: 2

Ingredients

2 salmon fillets

Salt and ground black pepper, to taste

Directions

Rinse and pat dry the fillets with a paper towel. Coat the fish generously on both sides, with cooking spray. Season with salt and freshly ground pepper. Arrange the fillets skin-side-down in the air fryer and cook for 10 minutes at 350 F turning once halfway through cooking. Serve with lemon wedges and steamed asparagus!

Delicious Crab Cakes

Prep + Cook Time: 55 minutes | Serves: 4

Ingredients

½ cup cooked crab meat
¼ cup chopped red onion
1 tbsp chopped basil
¼ cup chopped celery
¼ cup chopped red pepper
3 tbsp mayonnaise

Zest of half a lemon
¼ cup breadcrumbs
2 tbsp chopped parsley
Old bay seasoning, as desired

Directions

Preheat the Air fryer to 390 F. Place all ingredients in a large bowl, and mix well. Make 4 large crab cakes from the mixture and place them on a lined sheet. Refrigerate for 30 minutes, to set. Spay the air basket with cooking spray and arrange the crab cakes inside it. Cook for 7 minutes on each side, until crispy.

Fenugreek Fried Mussels with White Wine

Prep + Cook Time: 25 minutes | Serves: 4

Ingredients

4 pounds mussels
2 tbsp olive oil
1 cup white wine
2 tsp salt
2 bay leaves
1 tbsp pepper

1 ½ cup flour
1 tbsp fenugreek
2 tbsp vinegar
5 garlic cloves
4 bread slices
½ cup mixed nuts

Directions

Preheat the Air Fryer to 350 F. Add oil, garlic, vinegar, salt, nuts, fenugreek, pepper and bread to a food processor, and process until you obtain a creamy texture. Add bay leaves, wine, and mussels to a pan.

Bring to a boil over medium heat, lower heat to low and simmer the mixture until the mussels have opened up. Take the mussels out and drain; remove from shells. Add flour to the creamy mixture prepared before.

Cover the mussels with the sauce and cook them in your Air Fryer for 10 minutes. Serve with fenugreek to enjoy.

Chili Tuna Cakes

Prep + Cook Time: 50 minutes | Serves: 2

Ingredients

5 oz of canned tuna
1 tsp lime juice
1 tsp paprika
¼ cup flour
½ cup milk

1 small onion, diced
2 eggs
1 tsp chili powder, optional
½ tsp salt

Directions

Place all ingredients in a bowl and mix well to combine. Make two large patties, or a few smaller ones, out of the mixture. Place them on a lined sheet and refrigerate for 30 minutes. Cook the patties for 7 minutes on each side at 350 F.

Spicy Peanut Butter Shrimp

Prep + Cook Time: 15 minutes | Serves: 5

Ingredients

1 ½ pound shrimp
Juice of 1 lemon
1 tsp sugar
3 tbsp peanut oil
2 tbsp cornstarch
2 scallions, chopped

¼ tsp Chinese powder
Chopped chili to taste
1 tsp salt
4 garlic cloves
1 tsp pepper

Directions

Preheat the Air fryer to 370 F, and in a Ziploc bag, mix lemon juice, sugar, pepper, oil, cornstarch, powder, Chinese powder and salt. Add in the shrimp and massage to coat evenly. Let sit for 10 minutes.

Add garlic cloves, scallions and chili to a pan, and fry for a few minutes over medium heat. Place the marinated shrimp, garlic, chili and scallions in your air fryer's basket and cook for 10 minutes, until nice and crispy.

Crispy Calamari Rings

Prep + Cook Time: 20 minutes | Serves: 5

Ingredients

12 oz frozen squid
1 large egg, beaten
1 cup all-purpose flour
1 tsp ground coriander seeds
1 tsp cayenne pepper

½ tsp pepper
½ tsp salt
Lemon wedges, to garnish
olive oil for spray

Directions

In a bowl, mix flour, ground pepper, paprika, cayenne pepper and salt. Dredge calamari in eggs, followed by the floured mixture. Preheat your Air Fryer to 390 F and cook them for 15 minutes, until golden brown. Do it in batches if needed to avoid overcrowding. Garnish with lemon wedges and enjoy!

Gingery Shrimp Medley

Prep + Cook Time: 20 minutes | Serves: 4

Ingredients

1 pound shrimp
2 whole onions, chopped
3 tbsp butter
1 ½ tbsp sugar

2 tbsp soy sauce
2 cloves garlic, chopped
2 tsp lime juice
1 tsp ginger, chopped

Directions

Preheat your Air fryer to 340 F, and in a bowl, mix lime juice, soy sauce, ginger, garlic, sugar and butter.

Add the mixture to a frying pan and warm over medium heat. Add in the chopped onions, and cook for 1 minute until translucent. Pour the mixture over shrimp, toss well and set aside for 30 minutes. Then, place the mixture in the air fryer's basket and cook for 8 minutes.

Scrumptious Alaskan Salmon with Parsley Sauce

Prep + Cook Time: 30 minutes | Serves: 4

Ingredients

For Salmon
4 Alaskan wild salmon fillets, 6 oz each
2 tsp olive oil

A pinch of salt

For Dill Sauce
½ cup heavy cream
½ cup milk

A pinch of salt
2 tbsp chopped parsley

Directions

Preheat your Air fryer to 310 F, and in a mixing bowl, add salmon and drizzle 1 tsp of oil. Season with salt and pepper. Place the salmon in your Air Fryer's cooking basket and cook for 20-25 minutes, until tender and crispy.

In a bowl, mix milk, chopped parsley, salt, and whipped cream. Serve the salmon with the sauce.

Creamy Onion Frittata with Smoked Trout

Prep + Cook Time: 12 minutes | Serves: 6

Ingredients

2 tbsp olive oil
1 onion, sliced
1 egg, beaten
6 tbsp crème fraiche

½ tbsp horseradish sauce
2 trout fillet, hot and smoked
A handful of fresh dill

Directions

Heat oil in a frying pan over medium heat. Add onion and stir-fry until tender; season the onions well. Preheat your Air fryer to 320 F, and in a bowl, mix egg, crème Fraiche, and horseradish. Add cooked onion and trout, and mix well. Place the mixture in your fryer's cooking basket and cook for 20 minutes. Serve and enjoy!

Effortless Fish Nuggets with Garlic & Paprika

Prep + Cook Time: 20 minutes | Serves: 4

Ingredients

28 oz fish fillets
Lemon juice to taste
Salt and black pepper to taste
1 tsp drilled dill
4 tbsp mayonnaise

1 whole egg, beaten
1 tbsp garlic powder
3 ½ oz breadcrumbs
1 tbsp paprika

Directions

Preheat your air fryer to 400 F, and season fish fillets with salt and pepper. In a bowl, mix beaten egg, lemon juice, and mayonnaise. In a separate bowl, mix breadcrumbs, paprika, dill, and garlic powder.

Dredge fillets in egg mixture and then the garlic-paprika mix; repeat until all fillets are prepared. Place the fillets in your Air Fryer's cooking basket and cook for 15 minutes. Serve and enjoy!

Lovely Cod Fillets with Fennel & Grapes

Prep + Cook Time: 15 minutes | Serves: 4

Ingredients

2 black cod fillets
Salt and black pepper to taste
1 cup grapes, halved
1 small fennel bulb, sliced

½ cup pecans
2 tsp white balsamic vinegar
2 tbsp extra virgin olive oil

Directions

Preheat your Air fryer to 400 F, and season the fillets with salt and pepper; drizzle oil on top. Place the fillet in the air fryer basket and cook for 10 minutes; set the fish aside to cool. In a bowl, add grapes, pecans, and fennels. Drizzle oil over the grape mixture, and season with salt and pepper.

Add the mixture to the basket and cook for 3 minutes. Add balsamic vinegar and oil to the mixture, season with salt and pepper. Pour over the fish, and serve.

Parmesan Fish with Pine Nuts

Prep + Cook Time: 15 minutes | Serves: 6

Ingredients

1 Bunch of basil
2 garlic cloves, minced
1 tbsp olive oil
1 tbsp Parmesan cheese , grated

Black pepper and salt to taste
2 tbsp Pine nuts
6 white fish fillet
2 tbsp olive oil

Directions

Season the fillets with salt and pepper. Preheat the Air fryer to 350 F, and cook the fillets inside for 8 minutes.

In a bowl, add basil, oil, pine nuts, garlic and Parmesan cheese; blend with your hand. Serve with the fish and enjoy!

Savory Cod Fish in Soy Sauce

Prep + Cook Time: 20 minutes | Serves: 4

Ingredients

7 ¼ oz codfish fillets
4 tbsp chopped cilantro
Salt to taste
A handful of green onions, chopped
1 cup water

5 slices of ginger
5 tbsp light soy sauce
3 tbsp oil
1 tsp dark soy sauce
5 cubes rock sugar

Directions

Preheat your Air fryer to 360 F, and cover codfish with salt and coriander; drizzle with oil. Place the fish fillet in your air fryer's cooking basket and cook for 15 minutes. Place the remaining ingredients in a frying pan over medium heat; cook for 5 minutes. Serve the fish with the sauce, and enjoy.

Chili-Rubbed Jumbo Shrimp

Prep + Cook Time: 10 minutes | Serves: 2 to 3

Ingredients

1 lb jumbo shrimp
Salt to taste
¼ tsp old bay seasoning

⅓ tsp smoked paprika
¼ tsp chili powder
1 tbsp olive oil

Directions

Preheat the Air fryer to 390 degrees. In a bowl, add the shrimp, paprika, oil, salt, old bay seasoning, and chili powder; mix well. Place the shrimp in the fryer, close and cook for 5 minutes. Serve with mayo and rice.

Delightful Catfish Fillets

Prep + Cook Time: 25 minutes | Serves: 4

Ingredients

4 catfish fillets, rinsed and dried
¼ cup seasoned fish fry

1 tbsp olive oil
1 tbsp parsley, chopped

Directions

Preheat your Air fryer to 400 F, and add seasoned fish fry, and fillets in a large Ziploc bag; massage well to coat. Place the fillets in your Air fryer's cooking basket and cook for 10 minutes. Flip the fish and cook for 2-3 more minutes. Top with parsley and serve.

Shrimp with Smoked Paprika & Cayenne Pepper

Prep + Cook Time: 10 minutes | Serves: 4

Ingredients

5-6 oz tiger shrimp, 12 to 16 pieces
1 tbsp olive oil
½ a tbsp old bay seasoning

¼ a tbsp cayenne pepper
¼ a tbsp smoked paprika
A pinch of sea salt

Directions

Preheat the Air fryer to 380 F, and mix all ingredients in a large bowl. Coat the shrimp with a little bit of oil and spices. Place the shrimp in the Air fryer's basket and fry for 6-7 minutes. Serve with rice or salad.

Speedy Fried Scallops

Prep + Cook Time: 5 minutes | Serves: 6

Ingredients

12 fresh scallops
3 tbsp flour
4 salt and black pepper

1 egg, lightly beaten
1 cup breadcrumbs

Directions

Coat the scallops with flour. Dip into the egg, then into the breadcrumbs. Spray them with olive oil and arrange them in the air fryer. Cook for 6 minutes at 360 F, turning once halfway through cooking.

Simple Lemony Salmon

Prep + Cook Time: 20 minutes | Serves: 2

Ingredients

2 salmon fillets

Salt, to taste
Zest of a lemon

Directions

Spray the fillets with olive oil and rub them with salt and lemon zest. Line baking paper in your air fryer's basket to avoid sticking. Cook the fillets for 10 minutes at 360 F, turning once halfway through. Serve with steamed asparagus and a drizzle of lemon juice.

Fried Cod Nuggets

Prep + Cook Time: 25 minutes | Serves: 4

Ingredients

1 ¼ lb cod fillets, cut into 4 to 6 chunks each
½ cup flour
1 egg

1 tbsp water
1 cup cornflakes
1 tbsp olive oil Salt and black pepper to taste

Directions

Place the oil and cornflakes in a food processor and process until crumbed. Season the fish chunks with salt and pepper. In a bowl, beat the egg along with water. Dredge the chunks in flour first, then dip in the egg, and coat with cornflakes. Arrange on a lined sheet, and cook in the air fryer at 350 F for 15 minutes, until crispy.

Crispy Crab Legs

Prep + Cook Time: 15 minutes | Serves: 3

Ingredients

3 pounds crab legs
2 cups butter

1 cup salted water

Directions

Preheat the Air fryer to 380 F, and dip the crab legs in salted water; let stay for a few minutes. Place the crab legs in the basket and cook for 10 minutes. Melt the butter in a bowl in the microwave. Pour over crab legs to serve.

Quick Shrimp Bowl

Prep + Cook Time: 15 minutes | Serves: 6

Ingredients

1 ¼ pound tiger shrimp
¼ tsp cayenne pepper
½ tsp old bay seasoning

¼ tsp smoked paprika
A pinch of salt
1 tbsp olive oil

Directions

Preheat your Air fryer to 390 F, and in a bowl, mix all listed ingredients. Place the mixture in your air fryer's cooking basket and cook for 5 minutes. Serve with warm rice and a drizzle of lemon juice.

Garlic-Butter Catfish

Prep + Cook Time: 20 minutes | Serves: 2

Ingredients

2 catfish fillets
2 tsp blackening seasoning
Juice of 1 lime

2 tbsp butter, melted
1 garlic clove, mashed
2 tbsp cilantro

Directions

Preheat your Air fryer to 360 degrees F, and in a bowl, blend in garlic, lime juice, cilantro and butter. Divide the sauce into two parts, pour 1 part of the sauce over your fillets; cover the fillets with seasoning.

Place the fillets in your Air fryer's basket and cook for 15 minutes. Serve the cooked fish with remaining sauce.

Delicious Fried Seafood

Prep + Cook Time: 15 minutes | Serves: 4

Ingredients

1 lb fresh scallops, mussels, fish fillets, prawns, shrimp   1 cup breadcrumbs mixed with the zest of 1 lemon
2 eggs, lightly beaten
Salt and black pepper

Directions

Clean the seafood as needed. Dip each piece into the egg; and season with salt and pepper. Coat in the crumbs and spray with oil. Arrange into your air fryer and cook for 6 minutes at 400 F, turning once halfway through.

Easy Salmon Cakes

Prep + Cook Time: 15 minutes | Serves: 2

Ingredients

8 oz salmon, cooked   A handful of parsley, chopped
1 ½ oz potatoes, mashed   Zest of 1 lemon
A handful of capers   1 ¾ oz plain flour

Directions

Carefully flake the salmon. In a bowl, mix flaked salmon, zest, capers, dill, and mashed potatoes. Form small cakes using the mixture and dust the cakes with flour; refrigerate for 60 minutes. Preheat your Air Fryer to 350 and cook the cakes for 7 minutes. Serve chilled.

Cheesy Tilapia Fillets

Prep + Cook Time: 15 minutes | Serves: 4

Ingredients

¾ cup grated Parmesan cheese   ¼ tsp garlic powder
1 tbsp olive oil   ¼ tsp salt
2 tsp paprika   4 tilapia fillets
1 tbsp chopped parsley

Directions

Preheat the Air fryer to 350 F, and mix parsley, Parmesan cheese, garlic, salt, and paprika in a shallow bowl. Brush the olive oil over the fillets, and then coat them with the Parmesan mixture. Place the tilapia onto a lined baking sheet, and then into the Air fryer. Cook for 4 to 5 minutes on all sides.

Rosemary Buttery Prawns

Prep + Cook Time: 1 h 15 minutes | Serves: 2

Ingredients

8 large prawns   ½ tbsp melted butter
3 garlic cloves, minced   Salt and black pepper to taste
1 rosemary sprig, chopped

Directions

Combine garlic, butter, rosemary, salt and pepper, in a bowl. Add the prawns to the bowl and mix to coat them well. Cover the bowl and refrigerate for an hour. Preheat the air fryer to 350 F, and cook for 6 minutes. Increase the temperature to 390 degrees, and cook for one more minute.

Old Bay Tilapia Fillets

Prep + Cook Time: 15 minutes | Serves: 4

Ingredients

1 pound tilapia fillets
1 tbsp old bay seasoning
2 tbsp canola oil

2 tbsp lemon pepper
Salt to taste
2-3 butter buds

Directions

Preheat your Fryer to 400 F, and drizzle oil over tilapia fillet. In a bowl, mix salt, lemon pepper, butter buds, and seasoning; spread on the fish. Place the fillets in the Air fryer and cook for 10 minutes, until tender and crispy.

Sweet Cajun Salmon

Prep + Cook Time: 10 minutes | Serves: 1

Ingredients

1 salmon fillet
¼ tsp brown sugar
Juice of ½ lemon

1 tbsp cajun seasoning
2 lemon wedges
1 tbsp chopped parsley, for garnishing

Directions

Preheat the Air fryer to 350 F, and combine sugar and lemon; coat the salmon with this mixture. Coat with the Cajun seasoning as well. Place a parchment paper into the air fryer and cook the fish for 7 minutes. Serve with lemon wedges and chopped parsley.

Lemon-Garlic Butter Lobster

Prep + Cook Time: 15 minutes | Serves: 3

Ingredients

4 oz lobster tails
1 tsp garlic, minced
1 tbsp butter

Salt and black pepper to taste
½ tbsp lemon Juice

Directions

Add all the ingredients to a food processor, except shrimp, and blend well. Wash lobster and halve using meat knife; clean the skin of the lobster and cover the lobster with the marinade. Preheat your Air fryer to 380 F.

Place the lobster in your Air Fryer's cooking basket and cook for 10 minutes. Serve with fresh herbs and enjoy!

APPETIZERS AND SIDE DISHES

Perfect Crispy Potatoes

Prep + Cook Time: 35 minutes | Serves: 4

Ingredients

1.5 pounds potatoes, halved
2 tbsp olive oil
3 garlic cloves, grated

1 tbsp minced fresh rosemary
1 tsp salt
¼ tsp freshly ground black pepper

Directions

In a bowl, mix potatoes, olive oil, garlic, rosemary, salt, and pepper, until they are well-coated. Arrange the potatoes in the air fryer and cook on 360 F for 25 minutes, shaking twice during the cooking. Cook until crispy on the outside and tender on the inside.

Allspice Chicken Wings

Prep + Cook Time: 45 minutes | Serves: 8

Ingredients

½ tsp celery salt
½ tsp bay leaf powder
½ tsp ground black pepper
½ tsp paprika

¼ tsp dry mustard
¼ tsp cayenne pepper
¼ tsp allspice
2 pounds chicken wings

Directions

Grease the air fryer basket and preheat to 340 F. In a bowl, mix celery salt, bay leaf powder, black pepper, paprika, dry mustard, cayenne pepper, and allspice. Coat the wings thoroughly in this mixture.

Arrange the wings in an even layer in the basket of the air fryer. Cook the chicken until it's no longer pink around the bone, for 30 minutes. Then, increase the temperature to 380 F and cook for 6 minutes more, until crispy on the outside.

Friday Night Pineapple Sticky Ribs

Prep + Cook Time: 30 minutes | Serves: 4

Ingredients

2 lb cut spareribs
7 oz salad dressing
1 (5-oz) can pineapple juice

2 cups water
Garlic salt to taste
Salt and black pepper

Directions

Sprinkle the ribs with salt and pepper, and place them in a saucepan. Pour water and cook the ribs for 12 minutes on high heat. Drain the ribs and arrange them in the fryer; sprinkle with garlic salt. Cook for 15 minutes at 390 F.

Prepare the sauce by combining the salad dressing and the pineapple juice. Serve the ribs drizzled with the sauce.

Egg Roll Wrapped with Cabbage and Prawns

Prep + Cook Time: 50 minutes | Serves: 4

Ingredients

2 tbsp vegetable oil
1-inch piece fresh ginger, grated
1 tbsp minced garlic
1 carrot, cut into strips
¼ cup chicken broth
2 tbsp reduced-sodium soy sauce

1 tbsp sugar
1 cup shredded Napa cabbage
1 tbsp sesame oil
8 cooked prawns, minced
1 egg
8 egg roll wrappers

Directions

In a skillet over high heat, heat vegetable oil, and cook ginger and garlic for 40 seconds, until fragrant. Stir in carrot and cook for another 2 minutes. Pour in chicken broth, soy sauce, and sugar and bring to a boil.

Add cabbage and let simmer until softened, for 4 minutes. Remove skillet from the heat and stir in sesame oil. Let cool for 15 minutes. Strain cabbage mixture, and fold in minced prawns. Whisk an egg in a small bowl. Fill each egg roll wrapper with prawn mixture, arranging the mixture just below the center of the wrapper.

Fold the bottom part over the filling and tuck under. Fold in both sides and tightly roll up. Use the whisked egg to seal the wrapper. Repeat until all egg rolls are ready. Place the rolls into a greased air fryer basket, spray them with oil and cook for 12 minutes at 370 F , turning once halfway through.

Sesame Garlic Chicken Wings

Prep + Cook Time: 55 minutes | Serves: 4

Ingredients

1 pound chicken wings
1 cup soy sauce, divided
½ cup brown sugar
½ cup apple cider vinegar
2 tbsp fresh ginger, minced

2 tbsp fresh garlic, minced
1 tsp finely ground black pepper
2 tbsp cornstarch
2 tbsp cold water
1 tsp sesame seeds

Directions

In a bowl, add chicken wings, and pour in half cup soy sauce. Refrigerate for 20 minutes; drain and pat dry. Arrange the wings in the air fryer and cook for 30 minutes at 380 F, turning once halfway through. Make sure you check them towards the end to avoid overcooking.

In a skillet and over medium heat, stir sugar, half cup soy sauce, vinegar, ginger, garlic, and black pepper. Cook until sauce has reduced slightly, about 4 to 6 minutes.

Dissolve 2 tbsp of cornstarch in cold water, in a bowl, and stir in the slurry into the sauce, until it thickens, for 2 minutes. Pour the sauce over wings and sprinkle with sesame seeds.

Savory Chicken Nuggets with Parmesan Cheese

Prep + Cook Time: 25 minutes | Serves: 4

Ingredients

1 lb chicken breast, boneless, skinless, cubed
½ tsp ground black pepper
¼ tsp kosher salt
¼ tsp seasoned salt

2 tbsp olive oil
5 tbsp plain breadcrumbs
2 tbsp panko breadcrumbs
2 tbsp grated Parmesan cheese

Directions

Preheat the air fryer to 380 F and grease. Season the chicken with pepper, kosher salt, and seasoned salt; set aside. In a bowl, pour olive oil. In a separate bowl, add crumb, and Parmesan cheese.

Place the chicken pieces in the oil to coat, then dip into breadcrumb mixture, and transfer to the air fryer. Work in batches if needed. Lightly spray chicken with cooking spray.

Cook the chicken for 10 minutes, flipping once halfway through. Cook until golden brown on the outside and no more pink on the inside.

Butternut Squash with Thyme

Prep + Cook Time: 25 minutes | Serves: 4

Ingredients

2 cups peeled, butternut squash, cubed
1 tbsp olive oil
¼ tsp salt

¼ tsp black pepper
¼ tsp dried thyme
1 tbsp finely chopped fresh parsley

Directions

In a bowl, add squash, oil, salt, pepper, and thyme, and toss until squash is well-coated. Place squash in the air fryer and cook for 14 minutes at 360 F. When ready, sprinkle with freshly chopped parsley and serve chilled.

Chicken Breasts In Golden Crumb

Prep + Cook Time: 30 minutes | Serves: 4

Ingredients

1 ½ lb chicken breasts, boneless, cut into strips
1 egg, lightly beaten
1 cup seasoned breadcrumbs

Salt and black pepper to taste
½ tsp dried oregano

Directions

Preheat the air fryer to 390 F. Season the chicken with oregano, salt, and black pepper. In a small bowl, whisk in some salt and pepper to the beaten egg. In a separate bowl, add the crumbs. Dip chicken tenders in the egg wash, then in the crumbs.

Roll the strips in the breadcrumbs and press firmly, so the breadcrumbs stick well. Spray the chicken tenders with cooking spray and arrange them in the air fryer. Cook for 14 minutes, until no longer pink in the center, and nice and crispy on the outside.

Yogurt Chicken Tacos

Prep + Cook Time: 25 minutes | Serves: 4

Ingredients

1 cup cooked chicken, shredded
1 cup shredded mozzarella cheese
¼ cup salsa
¼ cup Greek yogurt

Salt and ground black pepper
8 flour tortillas

Directions

In a bowl, mix chicken, cheese, salsa, and yogurt, and season with salt and pepper. Spray one side of the tortilla with cooking spray. Lay 2 tbsp of the chicken mixture at the center of the non-oiled side of each tortilla.

Roll tightly around the mixture. Arrange taquitos into your air fryer basket, without overcrowding. Cook in batches if needed. Place the seam side down, or it will unravel during cooking crisps. Cook for 12 to 14 minutes, or until crispy, at 380 F.

Flawless Kale Chips

Prep + Cook Time: 25 minutes | Serves: 4

Ingredients

4 cups chopped kale leaves, stems removed
2 tbsp olive oil
1 tsp garlic powder

½ tsp salt
¼ tsp onion powder
¼ tsp black pepper

Directions

In a bowl, mix kale and oil together, until well-coated. Add in garlic, salt, onion, and pepper and toss until well-coated. Arrange half the kale leaves to air fryer, in a single layer.

Cook for 8 minutes at 350 F, shaking once halfway through. Remove chips to a sheet to cool; do not touch.

Cheese Fish Balls

Prep + Cook Time: 45 minutes | Serves: 6

Ingredients

1 cup smoked fish, flaked
2 cups cooked rice
2 eggs, lightly beaten
1 cup grated Grana Padano cheese

¼ cup finely chopped thyme
Salt and black pepper to taste
1 cup panko crumbs

Directions

In a bowl, add fish, rice, eggs, Parmesan cheese, thyme, salt and pepper into a bowl; stir to combine. Shape the mixture into 12 even-sized balls. Roll the balls in the crumbs then spray with oil.

Arrange the balls into the fryer and cook for 16 minutes at 400 F, until crispy.

Vermicelli Noodles & Vegetables Rolls

Prep + Cook Time: 30 minutes | Serves: 8

Ingredients

8 spring roll wrappers
1 cup cooked and cooled vermicelli noodles
2 garlic cloves, finely chopped
1 tbsp minced fresh ginger
2 tbsp soy sauce

1 tsp sesame oil
1 red bell pepper, seeds removed, chopped
1 cup finely chopped mushrooms
1 cup finely chopped carrot
½ cup finely chopped scallions

Directions

In a saucepan, add garlic, ginger, soy sauce, pepper, mushroom, carrot and scallions, and stir-fry over high heat for a few minutes, until soft. Add in vermicelli noodles; remove from the heat.

Place the spring roll wrappers onto a working board. Spoon dollops of veggie and noodle mixture at the center of each spring roll wrapper. Roll the spring rolls and tuck the corners and edges in to create neat and secure rolls.

Spray with oil and transfer them to the air fryer. Cook for 12 minutes at 340 F, turning once halfway through. Cook until golden and crispy. Serve with soy or sweet chili sauce.

Beef Balls with Mixed Herbs

Prep + Cook Time: 30 minutes | Serves: 4

Ingredients

1 lb ground beef
1 onion, finely chopped
3 garlic cloves, finely chopped
2 eggs
1 cup breadcrumbs

½ cup fresh mixed herbs
1tbsp mustard
Salt and black pepper to taste
Olive oil

Directions

In a bowl, add beef, onion, garlic, eggs, crumbs, herbs, mustard, salt, and pepper and mix with hands to combine.

Shape into balls and arrange them in the air fryer's basket. Drizzle with oil and cook for 16 minutes at 380 F, turning once halfway through.

Roasted Pumpkin Seeds

Prep + Cook Time: 50 minutes | Serves: 4

Ingredients

1 cup pumpkin seeds, pulp removed, rinsed
1 tbsp butter, melted
1 tbsp brown sugar

1 tsp orange zest
½ tsp cardamom
½ tsp salt

Directions

Cook the seeds for 4 minutes at 320 F, in your air fryer, to avoid moisture. In a bowl, whisk melted butter, sugar, zest, cardamom and salt. Add the seeds to the bowl and toss to coat well. Transfer the seeds to the air fryer and cook for 35 minutes at 300 F, shaking the basket every 10-12 minutes. Cook until lightly browned.

Buttery Parmesan Broccoli Florets

Prep + Cook Time: 25 minutes | Serves: 2

Ingredients

2 tbsp butter, melted
1 egg white
1 garlic clove, grated
¼ tsp salt

A pinch of black pepper
½ lb broccoli florets
⅓ cup grated Parmesan cheese

Directions

In a bowl, whisk together the butter, egg, garlic, salt, and black pepper. Toss in broccoli to coat well. Top with Parmesan cheese and; toss to coat. Arrange broccoli in a single layer in the air fryer, without overcrowding.

Cook in batches for 10 minutes at 360 F. Remove to a serving plate and sprinkle with Parmesan cheese.

Cauliflower Buffalo Wings

Prep + Cook Time: 25 minutes | Serves: 4

Ingredients

3 tbsp butter, melted
3 tbsp Buffalo hot sauce
1 egg white
1 cup panko breadcrumbs

½ tsp salt
¼ tsp freshly ground black pepper
½ head of cauliflower, cut into florets

Directions

In a bowl, stir in butter, hot sauce, and egg white. Mix breadcrumbs with salt and pepper, in a separate bowl. Toss the florets in the hot sauce mixture until well-coated.

Toss the coated cauliflower in crumbs until coated, then transfer the coated florets to the air fryer. Spray with cooking spray. Cook for 18 minutes at 340 F. Cook in batches if needed.

Chili Garlic Sweet Potato Wedges

Prep + Cook Time: 30 minutes | Serves: 2

Ingredients

1 sweet potato, cut into wedges
1 tbsp olive oil
¼ tsp salt
½ tsp chili powder

½ tsp garlic powder
½ tsp smoked paprika
½ tsp dried thyme
A pinch cayenne pepper

Directions

In a bowl, mix olive oil, salt, chili powder, garlic powder, smoked paprika, thyme, and cayenne. Toss in the potato wedges, until well-coated. Arrange the wedges evenly in the air fryer, and cook for 25 minutes at 380 F, flipping once halfway through.

Spicy Beef Meatballs with Mustard

Prep + Cook Time: 25 minutes | Serves: 3

Ingredients

½ lb ground beef
1 small finger ginger, crushed
1 tbsp hot sauce
3 tbsp vinegar
1 ½ tsp lemon juice

½ cup tomato ketchup, reduced sugar
2 tbsp sugar
¼ tsp dry mustard
Salt and black pepper to taste, if needed

Directions

In a bowl, add beef, ginger, hot sauce, vinegar, lemon juice, tomato ketchup, sugar, mustard, pepper, and salt, and mix well using a spoon. Shape 2-inch sized balls, with hands. Add the balls to the fryer without overcrowding.

Cook at 370 F for 15 minutes, shaking once halfway through. Cook in batches if needed. Serve with tomato or cheese dip.

Cheesy Rice Croquettes

Prep + Cook Time: 45 minutes | Serves: 4

Ingredients

2 cups cooked rice
1 brown onion, chopped
2 garlic cloves, chopped
2 eggs, lightly beaten
½ cup grated Parmesan cheese

Salt and black pepper to taste
½ cup breadcrumbs
1 tsp dried mixed herbs

Directions

Combine rice, onion, garlic, eggs, Parmesan cheese, salt and pepper. Shape into 10 croquettes. Spread the crumbs onto a plate and coat each croquette in the crumbs. Spray each croquette with oil.

Arrange the croquettes in the air fryer and cook for 16 minutes at 380 F, turning once halfway through cooking. They should be golden and crispy. Serve with plum sauce.

American-Style BBQ Chicken Pizza

Prep + Cook Time: 15 minutes | Serves: 1

Ingredients

1 piece naan bread

¼ cup barbeque sauce
¼ cup shredded mozzarella cheese

¼ cup shredded Monterrey Jack cheese
2 tbsp red onion, thinly sliced
½ chicken herby sausage
Chopped cilantro or parsley, for garnish

Directions

Spray naan's bread bottom with cooking spray and arrange it in the air fryer. Brush well with barbeque sauce, sprinkle mozzarella cheese, Monterrey Jack cheese, and red onion on top. Top with the sausage over and spray the crust with cooking spray. Cook for 8 minutes in a preheated air fryer at 400 F.

Effortless Pepperoni Pizza

Prep + Cook Time: 25 minutes | Serves: 2

Ingredients

8 ounces fresh pizza dough

⅓ cup tomato sauce

⅓ cup mozzarella cheese, shredded
8 pepperonis, sliced
Flour, to dust

Directions

On a floured surface, place dough and dust with flour. Stretch with hands into an air-fryer fitting shape. Spray the air fryer basket with cooking spray and arrange the pizza inside.

Brush generously with sauce, leaving some space at the border. scatter with mozzarella and top with pepperonis. Cook for 15 minutes, or until crispy, at 340 F.

Crispy Potatoes

Prep + Cook Time: 45 minutes | Serves: 4

Ingredients

4 yukon gold potatoes, clean and dried
2 tbsp olive oil

Salt and ground black pepper to taste

Directions

Rub each potato with half tbsp of olive oil. Season generously with salt and pepper, and arrange them in the air fryer. Cook for 40 minutes at 400 F.

Let cool slightly, then make a slit on top. Use a fork to fluff the insides of the potatoes. Fill the potato with cheese or garlic mayo.

Cheddar Sausages Balls with Oregano

Prep + Cook Time: 50 minutes | Serves: 8

Ingredients

1 ½ lb ground sausages
2 ¼ cups Cheddar cheese, shredded
1 ½ cup flour
¾ tsp baking soda
4 eggs

¾ cup sour cream
1 tsp dried oregano
1 tsp smoked paprika
2 tsp garlic powder
½ cup liquid coconut oil

Directions

In a pan over medium heat, add the sausages and brown for 3-4 minutes. Drain the excess fat and set aside. In a bowl, sift in baking soda, and flour. Set aside. In another bowl, add eggs, sour cream, oregano, paprika, coconut oil, and garlic powder. Whisk to combine well. Combine the egg and flour mixtures using a spatula.

Add the cheese and sausages. Fold in and let it sit for 5 minutes to thicken. Rub your hands with coconut oil and mold out bite-size balls out of the batter. Place them on a tray, and refrigerate for 15 minutes. Then, add them in the air fryer, without overcrowding. Cook for 10 minutes per round, at 400 F, in batches if needed.

Jalapeno Popper Chicken with Bacon

Prep + Cook Time: 40 minutes | Serves: 4

Ingredients

8 Jalapeno peppers, halved lengthwise and seeded
4 chicken breasts, butterflied and halved
6 oz cream cheese
6 oz Cheddar cheese

16 slices bacon
1 cup breadcrumbs
Salt and black pepper to taste
2 eggs

Directions

Season the chicken with pepper and salt on both sides. In a bowl, add cream cheese, cheddar, a pinch of pepper and salt. Mix well. Take each jalapeno and spoon in the cheese mixture to the brim. On a working board, flatten each piece of chicken and lay 2 bacon slices each on them. Place a stuffed jalapeno on each laid out chicken and bacon set, and wrap the jalapenos in them.

Preheat the air fryer to 350 F. Add the eggs to a bowl and pour the breadcrumbs in another bowl. Also, set a flat plate aside. Take each wrapped jalapeno and dip it into the eggs and then in the breadcrumbs. Place them on the flat plate. Lightly grease the fryer basket with cooking spray. Arrange 4-5 breaded jalapenos in the basket, and cook for 7 minutes.

Prepare a paper towel lined plate; set aside. Once the timer beeps, open the fryer, turn the jalapenos, and cook further for 4 minutes. Once ready, remove them onto the paper towel lined plate. Repeat the cooking process for the remaining jalapenos. Serve with a sweet dip for an enhanced taste.

Whole Chicken with BBQ Sauce

Prep + Cook Time: 35 minutes | Serves: 3

Ingredients

1 whole small chicken, cut into pieces
1 tsp salt
1 tsp smoked paprika

1 tsp garlic powder
1 cup BBQ sauce

Directions

Mix salt, paprika, and garlic powder and coat chicken pieces. Place them skin-side down in the air fryer. Cook for around 18 minutes at 400 F, until slightly golden. Remove to a plate and brush with barbecue sauce.

Wipe fryer out from the chicken fat. Return the chicken to the air fryer, skin-side up, and cook for 5 minutes at 340 F. Serve with more barbecue sauce.

Grandma's Chicken Thighs

Prep + Cook Time: 30 minutes | Serves: 4

Ingredients

1 pound chicken thighs
½ tsp salt

¼ tsp black pepper
¼ tsp garlic powder

Directions

Season the thighs with salt, pepper, and garlic powder. Arrange thighs, skin side down, in the air fryer and cook until golden brown, for 20 minutes at 350 F.

Dill Pickles with Parmesan

Prep + Cook Time: 35 minutes | Serves: 4

Ingredients

3 cups Dill Pickles, sliced, drained
2 eggs
2 tsp water

1 cup Grated Parmesan cheese
1 ½ cups breadcrumbs, smooth
Black pepper to taste

Directions

Add the breadcrumbs and black pepper to a bowl and mix well; set aside. In another bowl, crack the eggs and beat with the water. Set aside. Add the cheese to a separate bowl; set aside.

Preheat the Air Fryer to 400 F.

Pull out the fryer basket and spray it lightly with cooking spray. Dredge the pickle slices it in the egg mixture, then in breadcrumbs and then in cheese. Place them in the fryer without overlapping.

Slide the fryer basket back in and cook for 4 minutes. Turn them and cook for further for 5 minutes, until crispy. Serve with a cheese dip.

Delicious Chicken Wings with Alfredo Sauce

Prep + Cook Time: 60 minutes | Serves: 4

Ingredients

1 ½ pounds chicken wings, pat- dried
Salt to taste

½ cup Alfredo sauce

Directions

Preheat the air fryer to 370 F. Season the wings with salt. Arrange them in the air fryer, without touching.

Cook in batches if needed, for 20 minutes, until no longer pink in the center. Increase the temperature to 390 F and cook for 5 minutes more. Remove to a big bowl and coat well with the sauce, to serve.

Saturday Night Chicken Wings

Prep + Cook Time: 45 minutes | Serves: 3

Ingredients

15 chicken wings
Salt and black pepper to taste
⅓ cup chili sauce

⅓ cup butter
½ tbsp vinegar

Directions

Preheat the Air Fryer to 360 F. Season the wings with pepper and salt. Add them to the air fryer and cook for 35 minutes. Toss every 5 minutes. Once ready, remove them into a bowl. Over low heat, melt the butter in a saucepan. Add the vinegar and hot sauce. Stir and cook for a minute.

Turn the heat off. Pour the sauce over the chicken. Toss to coat well.

Transfer the chicken to a serving platter.Serve with a side of celery strips and blue cheese dressing.

Garlic Lemon Roasted Chicken

Prep + Cook Time: 60 minutes | Serves: 4

Ingredients

1 chicken (around 3.5 lb), rinsed, pat-dried
1 tbsp olive oil
1 tsp salt

¼ tsp black pepper
1 lemon, cut into quarters
5 garlic cloves

Directions

Rub chicken with olive oil and season with salt and pepper. Stuff with lemon and garlic cloves into the cavity.

Arrange chicken, breast-side down, into the air fryer. Tuck the legs and wings tips under. Cook for 45 minutes at 350 F. Let rest for 5-6 minutes, then carve and enjoy.

Easy Crunchy Garlic Croutons

Prep + Cook Time: 20 minutes | Serves: 4

Ingredients

2 cups bread, cubed
2 tbsp butter, melted

Garlic salt and black pepper to taste

Directions

In a bowl, toss the bread with butter, garlic salt, and pepper until well-coated. Place the cubes in the air fryer and cook for 12 minutes at 380 F, or until golden brown and crispy.

Simple Chicken Breasts

Prep + Cook Time: 30 minutes | Serves: 4

Ingredients

4 boneless, skinless chicken breasts
1 tsp salt and black pepper

1 tsp garlic powder

Directions

Spray the breasts and the air fryer tray with cooking spray. Rub chicken with salt, garlic powder, and black pepper. Arrange the breasts in the basket. Cook in batches if needed. Cook for 20 minutes at 360 F, until nice and crispy.

Stuffed Mushrooms with Rice and Cheese

Prep + Cook Time: 30 minutes | Serves: 10

Ingredients

10 Swiss brown mushrooms
Olive oil to brush the mushrooms
1 cup cooked brown rice

1 cup grated Grana Padano cheese
1 tsp dried mixed herbs
Salt and black pepper

Directions

Brush every mushroom with oil and lay onto a board. In a bowl, mix rice, cheese, herbs, salt and pepper. Stuff the mushrooms with the mixture. Arrange the mushrooms in the air fryer and cook for 14 minutes at 360 F. Make sure the mushrooms cooked until golden and the cheese has melted. Serve with fresh herbs.

Chickpeas with Rosemary and Sage

Prep + Cook Time: 20 minutes | Serves: 4

Ingredients

2 (14.5-ounce) cans chickpeas, rinsed, dried
2 tbsp olive oil
1 tsp dried rosemary

½ tsp dried thyme
¼ tsp dried sage
¼ tsp salt

Directions

In a bowl, mix together chickpeas, oil, rosemary, thyme, sage, and salt. Transfer them to the air fryer and spread in an even layer. Cook for 14 minutes at 380 F, shaking once, halfway through cooking.

Traditional French Fries

Prep + Cook Time: 25 minutes | Serves: 2

Ingredients

2 russet potatoes, washed, dried, cut strips

2 tbsp olive oil
Salt and freshly ground black pepper to taste

Directions

Spray the air fryer basket or rack with cooking spray. In a bowl, toss the strips with olive oil until well-coated, and season with salt and pepper.

Arrange in the air fryer and cook for 18 minutes at 400 F, turning once halfway through.

Check for crispiness and serve immediately, with garlic aioli, ketchup or crumbled cheese.

Goat Cheese & Pancetta Bombs

Prep + Cook Time: 25 minutes | Serves: 10

Ingredients

16 oz soft goat cheese
2 tbsp fresh rosemary, finely chopped
1 cup almonds, chopped into small pieces

Salt and black pepper
15 dried plums, chopped
15 pancetta slices

Directions

Line the air fryer basket with baking paper. In a bowl, add cheese, rosemary, almonds, salt, pepper and plums; stir well. Roll into balls and wrap with a pancetta slice. Arrange the bombs in the fryer and cook for 10 minutes at 400 F.

Check at the 5-minute mark, to avoid overcooking. When ready, let cool before removing them from the air fryer. Serve with toothpicks!

Mini Creamy Salmon Quiches

Prep + Cook Time: 20 minutes | Serves: 15

Ingredients

15 mini tart cases
4 eggs, lightly beaten
½ cup heavy cream
Salt and black pepper

3 oz smoked salmon
6 oz cream cheese, divided into 15 pieces
6 fresh dill

Directions

Mix together eggs and cream in a pourable measuring container. Arrange the tarts into the air fryer. Pour in mixture into the tarts, about halfway up the side and top with a piece of salmon and a piece of cheese. Cook for 10 minutes at 340 F, regularly check to avoid overcooking. Sprinkle dill and serve chilled.

Mixed Nuts with Cinnamon

Prep + Cook Time: 25 minutes | Serves: 5

Ingredients

½ cup pecans
½ cup walnuts
½ cup almonds
A pinch cayenne pepper

2 tbsp sugar
2 tbsp egg whites
2 tsp cinnamon

Directions

Add the pepper, sugar, and cinnamon to a bowl and mix them well; set aside. In another bowl, mix in the pecans, walnuts, almonds, and egg whites. Add the spice mixture to the nuts and give it a good mix. Lightly grease the fryer basket with cooking spray.

Pour in the nuts, and cook them for 10 minutes. Stir the nuts using a wooden vessel, and cook for further for 10 minutes. Pour the nuts in the bowl. Let cool before crunching on them.

Cheese Sticks with Thai Sauce

Prep + Cook Time: 2 hrs 20 minutes | Serves: 4

Ingredients

12 mozzarella string cheese
2 cups breadcrumbs
3 eggs

1 cup sweet thai sauce
4 tbsp skimmed milk

Directions

Pour the crumbs in a medium bowl. Crack the eggs into another bowl and beat with the milk. One after the other, dip each cheese sticks in the egg mixture, in the crumbs, then egg mixture again and then in the crumbs again.

Place the coated cheese sticks on a cookie sheet and freeze for 1 to 2 hours. Preheat the Air Fryer to 380 F. Arrange the sticks in the fryer without overcrowding. Cook for 5 minutes, flipping them halfway through cooking to brown evenly. Cook in batches. Serve with a sweet thai sauce.

Maple Shrimp with Coconut

Prep + Cook Time: 30 minutes | Serves: 5

Ingredients

1 lb jumbo shrimp, peeled and deveined
¾ cup shredded coconut
1 tbsp maple syrup

½ cup breadcrumbs
⅓ cup cornstarch
½ cup milk

Directions

Pour the cornstarch in a zipper bag, add shrimp, zip the bag up and shake vigorously to coat with the cornstarch. Mix the syrup and milk in a bowl and set aside. In a separate bowl, mix the breadcrumbs and shredded coconut. Open the zipper bag and remove each shrimp while shaking off excess starch.

Dip each shrimp in the milk mixture and then in the crumbs mixture while pressing loosely to trap enough crumbs and coconut. Place the coated shrimp in the fryer without overcrowding. Cook 12 minutes at 350 F, flipping once halfway through. Cook until golden brown. Serve with a coconut based dip.

Cheese Crisps

Ready in about: 25 minutes | Serves: 3

Ingredients

4 tbsp grated cheese + extra for rolling
1 cup flour + extra for kneading
¼ tsp chili powder
½ tsp baking powder

3 tsp butter
A pinch of salt
Water

Directions

In a bowl, mix in the cheese, flour, baking powder, chili powder, butter, and salt. The mixture should be crusty. Add some drops of water and mix well to get a dough. Remove the dough on a flat surface.

Rub some extra flour in your palms and on the surface, and knead the dough for a while. Using a rolling pin, roll the dough out into a thin sheet. With a pastry cutter, cut the dough into your desired lings' shape. Add the cheese lings in the basket, and cook for 6 minutes at 350 F, flipping once halfway through.

Chorizo with Mushroom Pita Bread Pizzas

Prep + Cook Time: 25 minutes | Serves: 5

Ingredients

5 pita bread
5 tbsp marinara sauce
10 rounds chorizo
10 button mushrooms, sliced

10 fresh basil leaves
2 cups grated cheddar cheese
1 tsp chili flakes

Directions

Spray the pitas with oil and scatter the sauce over. Top with chorizo, mushrooms, basil, cheddar and chili flakes. Cook for 14 minutes at 360 F, checking it at least once halfway through not to overcook them.

Avocado-Bacon Rolls

Prep + Cook Time: 40 minutes | Serves: 6

Ingredients

12 thick strips bacon
3 large avocados, sliced
⅓ tsp salt

⅓ tsp chili powder
⅓ tsp cumin powder

Directions

Stretch the bacon strips to elongate and use a knife to cut in half to make 24 pieces. Wrap each bacon piece around a slice of avocado from one end to the other end. Tuck the end of bacon into the wrap. Arrange on a flat surface and season with salt, chili and cumin on both sides.

Arrange 4 to 8 wrapped pieces in the fryer and cook at 350 F for 8 minutes, or until the bacon is browned and crunchy, flipping halfway through to cook evenly. Remove onto a wire rack and repeat the process for the remaining avocado pieces.

Spicy Calamari with Cilantro and Green Olives

Prep + Cook Time: 25 minutes | Serves: 3

Ingredients

½ lb calamari rings
½ piece coriander, chopped
2 strips chili pepper, chopped

1 tbsp olive oil
1 cup pimiento-stuffed green olives, sliced
Salt and black pepper to taste

Directions

In a bowl, add rings, chili pepper, salt, black pepper, oil, and coriander. Mix and let marinate for 10 minutes. Pour the calamari into an oven-safe bowl, that fits into the fryer basket.

Slide the fryer basket out, place the bowl in it, and slide the basket back in. Cook for 15 minutes stirring every 5 minutes using a spoon, at 400 F. After 15 minutes, and add in the olives.

Stir, close and continue to cook for 3 minutes. Once ready, transfer to a serving platter. Serve warm with a side of bread slices and mayonnaise.

Fried Button Mushrooms with Cheese

Prep + Cook Time: 55 minutes | Serves: 4

Ingredients

1 lb small Button mushrooms, cleaned
2 cups breadcrumbs
2 eggs, beaten

Salt and black pepper to taste
2 cups Parmigiano Reggiano cheese, grated

Directions

Preheat the Air Fryer to 360 F. Pour the breadcrumbs in a bowl, add salt and pepper and mix well. Pour the cheese in a separate bowl and set aside. Dip each mushroom in the eggs, then in the crumbs, and then in the cheese.

Slide out the fryer basket and add 6 to 10 mushrooms. Cook them for 20 minutes, in batches, if needed. Serve with cheese dip.

Parmesan Zucchini Crisps

Prep + Cook Time: 20 minutes | Serves: 3

Ingredients

3 medium zucchinis
1 cup breadcrumbs
2 eggs, beaten
1 cup grated Parmesan cheese

Salt and black pepper to taste
1 tsp smoked paprika

Directions

With a mandolin cutter, slice the zucchinis thinly. Use paper towels to press out excess liquid. In a bowl, add crumbs, salt, pepper, cheese, and paprika. Mix well and set aside. Set a wire rack or tray aside. Dip each zucchini slice in egg and then in the cheese mix while pressing to coat them well.

Place them on the wire rack. Spray the coated slices with oil. Put the slices in the fryer basket in a single layer without overlapping. Cook at 350 F for 8 minutes for each batch. Serve sprinkled with salt and with a spicy dip.

Delicious Cheesy Onion Rings

Prep + Cook Time: 20 minutes | Serves: 3

Ingredients

1 onion, peeled and sliced into 1-inch rings
¾ cup Parmesan cheese
2 medium eggs, beaten
1 tsp garlic powder

A pinch of salt
1 cup flour
1 tsp paprika powder

Directions

Add the eggs to a bowl; set aside In another bowl, add cheese, garlic powder, salt, flour, and paprika. Mix with a spoon. Dip each onion ring in egg, then in the cheese mixture, in the egg again and finally in the cheese mixture.

Add the rings to the basket and cook them for 8 minutes at 350 F. Remove onto a serving platter and serve with a cheese or tomatoes dip.

Garlic Bruschetta with Cheddar Cheese

Prep + Cook Time: 25 minutes | Serves: 10

Ingredients

10 slices French baguette
Olive oil
3 garlic cloves, minced

1 cup grated cheddar cheese
1 tsp dried oregano
Salt and black pepper to taste

Directions

Brush the bread with oil and sprinkle with garlic. Scatter the cheese on top, then oregano, salt and pepper. Arrange the slices in the fryer and cook for 14 minutes at 360 F, turning once halfway through cooking.

Garlic Chicken Nuggets

Prep + Cook Time: 1 hour 20 minutes | Serves: 4

Ingredients

2 chicken breasts, bones removed
2 tbsp paprika
2 cups milk
2 eggs
4 tsp onion powder

1 ½ tsp garlic powder
Salt and black pepper to taste
1 cups flour
2 cups breadcrumbs

Directions

Cut the chicken into 1-inch chunks. In a bowl, mix in paprika, onion, garlic, salt, pepper, flour, and breadcrumbs. In another bowl, crack the eggs, add the milk and beat them together. Prepare a tray. Dip each chicken chunk in the egg mixture, place them on the tray, and refrigerate for 1 hour.

Preheat the Air Fryer to 370 F. Roll each chunk in the crumb mixture. Place the crusted chicken in the fryer's basket. Spray with cooking spray. Cook for 8 minutes at 360 F, flipping once halfway through. Serve with a tomato dip or ketchup. Yum!

Red Potatoes Cheese Balls

Prep + Cook Time: 50 minutes | Serves: 6

Ingredients

2 cups crumbled Cottage cheese
2 cups grated Parmesan cheese
2 red potatoes, peeled and chopped
1 medium onion, finely chopped
1 ½ tsp red chili flakes
1 green chili, finely chopped

Salt to taste
4 tbsp chopped coriander leaves
1 cup flour
1 cup breadcrumbs
Water

Directions

Place the potatoes in a pot, add water and bring them to boil over medium heat for 25 to 30 minutes until soft. Turn off the heat, drain the potatoes through a sieve, and place in a bowl. With a potato masher, mash the potatoes and leave to cool.

Add the cottage cheese, Parmesan cheese, onion, red chili flakes, green chili, salt, coriander, and flour to the potato mash. Use a wooden spoon to mix the ingredients well, then, use your hands to mold out bite-size balls. Pour the crumbs in a bowl and roll each cheese ball lightly in it.

Place them on a tray. Put 8 to 10 cheese balls in the fryer basket, and cook for 15 minutes at 350 F. Repeat the cooking process for the remaining cheese balls. Serve with tomato-basil dip.

Simply Crispy Brussels Sprouts

Prep + Cook Time: 15 minutes | Serves: 2

Ingredients

½ pound Brussels sprouts, trimmed and halved
1 tbsp olive oil

½ tsp salt
¼ tsp black pepper

Directions

In a bowl, mix Brussels sprouts, oil, salt, and pepper. Place Brussels sprouts in air fryer basket. Cook for 10 minutes at 380 F. Serve with sautéed onion rings.

Tasty Spicy Potatoes

Prep + Cook Time: 25 minutes | Serves: 4

Ingredients

3 potatoes, sliced, rinsed
2 tsp olive oil
2 tsp cayenne pepper

1 tsp paprika
Salt and black pepper to taste

Directions

Place the fries into a bowl and sprinkle with oil, cayenne, paprika, salt, and black pepper. Toss and place them in the fryer. Cook for 14 minutes at 360 F, until golden and crispy. Give it a toss after 7-8 minutes.

Herby Chips with Garlic

Prep + Cook Time: 60 minutes | Serves: 2

Ingredients

2 potatoes, sliced
2 tbsp olive oil
3 garlic cloves, crushed

1 tsp each of fresh rosemary, thyme, oregano, chopped
Salt and black pepper to taste

Directions

In a bowl, add oil, garlic, herbs, salt and pepper, and toss with hands until well-coated. Arrange the slices in the air fryer's basket and cook for 14 minutes at 360 F, shaking it every 4-5 minutes. Enjoy with onion dip.

Homemade Radish Chips

Prep + Cook Time: 30 minutes | Serves: 4

Ingredients

10 radishes, leaves removed and cleaned
Salt to season

Water

Directions

Using a mandolin, slice the radishes thinly. Place them in a pot and cover them with water. Heat the pot on a stovetop, and bring to boil, until the radishes are translucent, for 4 minutes. After 4 minutes, drain the radishes through a sieve; set aside. Grease the fryer basket with cooking spray.

Add in the radish slices and cook for 8 minutes, flipping once halfway through. Cook until golden brown, at 400 F. Meanwhile, prepare a paper towel-lined plate. Once the radishes are ready, transfer them to the paper towel-lined plate. Season with salt, and serve with ketchup or garlic mayo.

Scallion Bacon Fries

Prep + Cook Time: 25 minutes | Serves: 4

Ingredients

2 large russet potatoes, sauce and cut strips
5 slices bacon, chopped
2 tbsp vegetable oil
2½ cups Cheddar cheese, shredded

3 oz melted cream cheese
Salt and black pepper to taste
¼ cup scallions, chopped

Directions

Boil salted water in a large sized pot. Add potatoes to the salted water and allow to boil for 4 minutes until blanched. Strain the potatoes in a colander and rinse thoroughly with cold water to remove starch from the surface. Dry them with a kitchen towel. Preheat your Air Fryer to 400 F.

Add chopped bacon to your Air Fryer's cooking basket and cook for 4 minutes until crispy, making sure to give the basket a shake after 2 minutes; set aside. Add dried potatoes to the cooking basket and drizzle oil on top to coat. Cook for 25 minutes, shaking the basket every 5 minutes. Season with salt and pepper after 12 minutes.

Once cooked, transfer the fries to an 8-inch pan. In a bowl, mix 2 cups of cheddar cheese with cream cheese. Pour over the potatoes and add in crumbled bacon. Place the pan into the air fryer's cooking basket and cook for 5 more minutes at 340 F. Sprinkle chopped scallions on top and serve with your desired dressing.

Amazing Brie Cheese Croutons

Prep + Cook Time: 20 minutes | Serves: 1

Ingredients

2 tbsp olive oil
1 tbsp french herbs

7 oz brie cheese, chopped
2 slices bread, halved

Directions

Preheat your Air Fryer to 340 degrees F. Using a bowl, mix oil with herbs. Dip the bread slices in the oil mixture to coat. Place the coated slices on a flat surface. Lay the brie cheese on the slices. Place the slices into your air fryer's basket and cook for 7 minutes. Once the bread is ready, cut into cubes.

Italian Fried Fresh Pasta

Prep + Cook Time: 25 minutes | Serves: 6

Ingredients

2 packages fresh agnolotti
1 cup flour
Salt and black pepper

4 eggs, beaten
2 cups breadcrumbs

Directions

Mix flour with salt and black pepper. Dip the pasta into the flour, then into the egg, and finally in the breadcrumbs. Spray with oil and arrange in the air fryer in an even layer.

Set to 400 F and cook for 14 minutes, turning once halfway through cooking. Cook until nice and golden. Serve with goat cheese.

Nut & Raisin Topped Crispy Cauliflower

Prep + Cook Time: 23 minutes | Serves: 4

INGREDIENTS

1 head of cauliflower
⅓ cup olive oil
⅓ cup golden raisins

⅓ cup toasted pine nuts
1 cup hot water
A pinch of salt

DIRECTIONS

Preheat the Air fryer to 380 F and add the oil and the pine nuts; cook for 2 minutes, then set aside.

In a bowl, pour 1 cup of hot water and add the raisins; set aside. Core the head of the cauliflower using a knife and cut it into medium-sized pieces. In a pan, boil 5 cups of water and add the cut florets and leave them there until the water boils again.

Remove the cauliflower florets from the pan and transfer them to a large bowl; add the olive oil and salt. Place about half of the florets in the preheated Air fryer and cook them for 10-12 minutes. Repeat the process with the rest of the cauliflower florets. Drain the raisins in a strainer. and toss them over the florets and the pine nuts.

Gourmet Beef Sticks

Prep + Cook Time: 2 hrs 10 minutes | Serves: 3

Ingredients

1 lb ground beef
3 tbsp sugar
A pinch garlic powder

A pinch chili powder
Salt to taste
1 tsp liquid smoke

Directions

Place the meat, sugar, garlic powder, chili powder, salt and liquid smoke in a bowl. Mix with a spoon. Mold out 4 sticks with your hands, place them on a plate, and refrigerate for 2 hours. Cook at 350 F. for 10 minutes, flipping once halfway through.

Friday Night Onion Rings with Buttermilk

Prep + Cook Time: 30 minutes | Serves: 4

INGREDIENTS

2 sweet onions
2 cups buttermilk
2 cups pancake mix

2 cups water
1 package cornbread mix
1 tsp salt

DIRECTIONS

Preheat the Air fryer to 370 F and slice the onions into rings. Combine the pancake mix with the water. Line a baking sheet with parchment paper. Dip the rings in the cornbread mixture first, and then in the pancake batter.

Place half of the onion rings onto the sheet and then into the Air fryer; cook for 8 to 12 minutes, and repeat one more time. Serve with salsa rosa or garlic mayo.

Tasty Carrot Chips

Prep + Cook Time: 20 minutes | Serves: 2

Ingredients

3 large carrots, washed and peeled

Salt to taste

Directions

Using a mandolin slicer, slice the carrots very thinly heightwise. Put the carrot strips in a bowl and season with salt to taste. Grease the fryer basket lightly with cooking spray, and add the carrot strips. Cook at 350 F for 10 minutes, stirring once halfway through.

Crispy Calamari Rings

Prep + Cook Time: 10 minutes | Serves: 4

INGREDIENTS

1 lb calamari (squid), cut in rings
¼ cup flour

2 large beaten eggs
1 cup breadcrumbs

DIRECTIONS

Coat the calamari rings with the flour and dip them in the eggs' mixture. Then, dip in the breadcrumbs. Refrigerate for 2 hours. Line them in the Air Fryer and apply oil generously; cook for 9 minutes at 380° F. Serve with garlic mayo and lemon wedges.

Homemade Cheese Sticks

Prep + Cook Time: 5 minutes | Serves: 12

Ingredients

6 (6 oz) bread cheese
2 tbsp butter

2 cups panko crumbs

Directions

Put the butter in a bowl and melt in the microwave, for 2 minutes; set aside. With a knife, cut the cheese into equal sized sticks. Brush each stick with butter and dip into panko crumbs. Arrange the cheese sticks in a single layer on the fryer basket. Cook at 390 F for 10 minutes. Flip them halfway through, to brown evenly; serve warm.

Homemade Cod Fingers

Prep + Cook Time: 25 minutes | Serves: 3

Ingredients

2 cups flour
Salt and black pepper to taste
1 tsp seafood seasoning
2 whole eggs, beaten
1 cup cornmeal

1 pound cod fillets, cut into fingers
2 tbsp milk
2 eggs, beaten
1 cup breadcrumbs

Directions

Preheat your Air Fryer to 400 F. In a bowl, mix beaten eggs with milk. In a separate bowl, mix flour, cornmeal, and seafood seasoning. In another mixing bowl, mix spices with the eggs. In a third bowl, pour the breadcrumbs.

Dip cod fingers in the seasoned flour mixture, followed by a dip in the egg mixture and finally coat with breadcrumb. Place the prepared fingers in your air fryer's cooking basket and cook for 10 minutes.

Spaghetti with Carbonara Sauce

Prep + Cook Time: 30 minutes | Serves: 4

INGREDIENTS

½ lb. white button mushrooms, sliced
½ cup of water
1 tsp butter
2 garlic cloves, chopped

12 oz spaghetti, cooked
14 oz carbonara mushroom sauce (store bought)
Salt and black pepper to taste

DIRECTIONS

Preheat the Air fryer to 300 F, add the butter and garlic; cook for 3 minutes. Add the mushrooms and cook for 5 more minutes.

Stir in mushroom carbonara sauce and water; season with salt and pepper and cook for 18 minutes. Stir in the spaghetti and cook for 1 minute more.

Sweet Juicy Pickle Chips with Buttermilk

Prep + Cook Time: 20 minutes | Serves: 3

Ingredients

36 sweet pickle chips
1 cup buttermilk
3 tbsp smoked paprika

2 cups flour
¼ cup cornmeal
Salt and black pepper to taste

Directions

Preheat your Air Fryer to 400 F. Using a bowl mix flour, paprika, pepper, salt, cornmeal and powder. Place pickles in buttermilk and set aside for 5 minutes. Dip the pickles in the spice mixture and place them in the air fryer's cooking basket. Cook for 10 minutes.

Grandma's Apple Cinnamon Chips

Prep + Cook Time: 25 minutes | Serves: 2

Ingredients

1 tsp sugar
1 tsp salt
1 whole apple, sliced

½ tsp cinnamon
Confectioners' sugar for serving

Directions

Preheat your Air Fryer to 400 F. In a bowl, mix cinnamon, salt and sugar; add the apple slices. Place the prepared apple spices in your fryer's cooking basket and bake for 8 minutes. Dust with confectioners' sugar and serve.

Crunchy Cheesy Twists

Prep + Cook Time: 45 minutes | Serves: 8

INGREDIENTS

2 cups cauliflower florets, steamed
1 egg
3 ½ oz oats
1 red onion, diced

1 tsp mustard
5 oz cheddar cheese
Salt and black pepper to taste

DIRECTIONS

Preheat the Air fryer to 350 F, and place the oats in a food processor and pulse until they are the consistency of breadcrumbs.

Place the steamed florets in a cheesecloth and squeeze out the excess liquid. Place the florets in a large bowl. Add the rest of the ingredients to the bowl. Mix well with hands to combine the ingredients completely.

Take a little bit of the mixture and twist it into a straw. Place on a lined baking sheet and repeat with the rest of the mixture. Cook for 10 minutes, turn over and cook for an additional 10 minutes.

Homemade Tortilla Chips

Prep + Cook Time: 55 minutes | Serves: 6

Ingredients

1 cup flour
Salt and black pepper to taste

1 tbsp golden flaxseed meal
2 cups shredded Cheddar cheese

Directions

Melt cheddar cheese in the microwave for 1 minute. Once melted, add the flour, salt, flaxseed meal, and pepper. Mix well with a fork. On a board, place the dough, and knead it with hands while warm until the ingredients are well combined. Divide the dough into 2 and with a rolling pin, roll them out flat into 2 rectangles.

Use a pastry cutter, to cut out triangle-shaped pieces and line them in 1 layer on a baking dish. Grease the fryer basket lightly with cooking spray. Arrange some triangle chips in 1 layer in the fryer basket without touching or overlapping; spray them with cooking spray. Close the Air Fryer and cook for 8 minutes. Serve with a cheese dip.

Cheese Eggplant Boats with Ham and Parsley

Prep + Cook Time: 17 minutes | Serves: 2

INGREDIENTS

1 eggplant
4 ham slices, chopped
1 cup shredded mozzarella cheese , divided

1 tsp dried parsley
Salt and black pepper to taste

DIRECTIONS

Preheat the Air fryer to 330 F, peel the eggplant and cut it lengthwise in half; scoop some of the flesh out. Season with salt and pepper. Divide half the mozzarella cheese between the eggplants and place the ham on top of the mozzarella. Top with the remaining mozzarella cheese, sprinkle with parsley and cook for 12 minutes.

Savory Rutabaga Chips

Prep + Cook Time: 20 minutes | Serves: 12

Ingredients

1 rutabaga, sliced
1 tsp olive oil

1 tsp soy sauce
Salt to taste

Directions

Preheat your Air Fryer to 400 F. In a bowl, mix oil, soy sauce and salt to form a marinade. Add rutabaga pieces and allow to stand for 5 minutes. Cook in your air fryer for 5 minutes, tossing once halfway through cooking.

Italian-Style Salmon Croquettes with Vegetables

Prep + Cook Time: 40 minutes | Serves: 4

Ingredients

1 (15 oz) tinned salmon, deboned and flaked
1 cup grated onion
1 ½ cups grated carrots
3 large eggs
1 ½ tbsp chopped chives
4 tbsp mayonnaise

4 tbsp breadcrumbs
2 ½ tsp Italian seasoning
Salt and black pepper to taste
2 ½ tsp lemon juice

Directions

In a bowl, add salmon, onion, carrots, eggs, chives, mayo, crumbs, Italian seasoning, pepper, salt, and lemon juice and mix well. With hands, form 2-inch thick oblong balls from the mixture, resembling croquette shape. Put them on a flat tray and refrigerate for 45 minutes. Grease the air fryer's basket with cooking spray.

Remove the croquettes from the fridge and arrange in a single layer, in the fryer, without overcrowding. Spray with cooking spray. Cook for 10 minutes, flipping once, until crispy at, 400 F. Serve with a dill-based dip.

Parsley Chicken Croquettes

Prep + Cook Time: 20 minutes | Serves: 4

Ingredients

4 chicken breasts
1 whole egg
Salt and black pepper to taste
1 cup oats, crumbled

½ tsp garlic powder
1 tbsp parsley
1 tbsp thyme

Directions

Preheat your Air Fryer to 360 F. Pulse chicken breast in a processor food until well blended. Add seasoning to the chicken alongside garlic, parsley, thyme and mix well. In a bowl, add beaten egg and beat until the yolk is mixed.

In a separate bowl, add crumbled oats. Form croquettes using the chicken mixture and dip in beaten egg, and finally in oats until coated. Place the nuggets in your fryer's cooking basket. Cook for 10 minutes, making sure to keep shaking the basket after every 5 minutes.

Baked Radish and Mozzarella Salad

Prep + Cook Time: 35 minutes | Serves: 4

INGREDIENTS

1 lb. radishes, green parts too
1 large red onion, sliced
½ lb. mozzarella, sliced
2 tbsp olive oil, plus more for drizzling

2 tbsp balsamic glaze
1 tsp dried basil
1 tsp dried parsley
1 tsp salt

DIRECTIONS

Preheat the Air fryer to 350 F, wash the radishes and dry them by patting with paper towels. Cut them in half and place in a large bowl; add the onion slices in. Stir in salt, basil, parsley and olive oil. Place in the fryer and cook for 30 minutes; toss them twice.

Stir in the mozzarella immediately so that it begins to melt. Stir in balsamic glaze and drizzle with olive oil, to serve.

Mushrooms with Cheddar Cheese and Italian Herbs

Prep + Cook Time: 20 minutes | Serves: 2

Ingredients

2-3 tbsp olive oil
Salt and black pepper to taste
10 button mushrooms
2 cups mozzarella cheese, chopped

2 cups cheddar cheese, chopped
3 tbsp mixture of Italian herbs
1 tbsp dried dill

Directions

Wash the mushrooms thoroughly under cold water and clean. Preheat your Air Fryer to 340 F. In a bowl, mix oil, salt, pepper, herbs, and dill to form a marinade. Add button mushrooms to the marinade and toss to coat well.

In a separate bowl, mix both kinds of cheese. Stuff each mushroom with the cheese mixture. Place the mushrooms in your air fryer's cooking basket and cook for 10 minutes.

Party Mozzarella Cheese Sticks

Prep + Cook Time: 40 minutes | Serves: 2

INGREDIENTS

8 oz mozzarella cheese
1 tsp garlic powder
1 egg

1 cup breadcrumbs
½ tsp salt
Olive oil

DIRECTIONS

Cut the mozzarella into 6 strips. Whisk the egg along with the salt and garlic powder, in a bowl. Dip the mozzarella into the egg mixture first, and then into the breadcrumbs. Arrange them on a platter and place in the freezer for about 20 to 30 minutes.

Preheat the fryer to 370 F and grease with olive oil. Arrange the mozzarella sticks inside and cook for 5 minutes. Make sure to turn them over at least 2 times, to ensure even cooking until golden on all sides. Serve with marinara sauce or garlic mayo.

Feta, Prosciutto and Quinoa Salad

Prep + Cook Time: 10 minutes | Serves: 2

INGREDIENTS

1 cup cooked quinoa
½ cup crumbled feta cheese
¼ cup chopped olives
2 prosciutto slices, chopped

1 tsp olive oil
½ red bell pepper, chopped
Salt and black pepper to taste

DIRECTIONS

Preheat the Air fryer to 350 degrees F, place the olive oil and pepper and cook for 2 minutes. Add the prosciutto and cook for 3 more minutes. Meanwhile, combine the quinoa, feta, and olives, in an ovenproof bowl. Stir in cooked prosciutto and peppers, and season with salt and pepper. Place the bowl in the basket of the Air fryer and cook for 1 minute.

Minty Cheese with Watermelon and Kalamata Olives

Prep + Cook Time: 15 minutes | Serves: 4

INGREDIENTS

8 thick watermelon slices
12 kalamata olives
8 oz halloumi cheese
2 tbsp chopped parsley

2 tbsp chopped mint
Juice and zest of 1 lemon
Salt and black pepper to taste
Olive oil

DIRECTIONS

Preheat the Air fryer to 350 F, season the watermelon with salt and pepper, and gently brush them with olive oil. Place in the Air fryer and cook for about 4 minutes. Brush the cheese with olive oil and add it to the Air fryer; cook for 4 minutes. Place them on a platter and serve with olives and sprinkled with herbs, and lemon zest and juice.

Easy Chicken Tenderloins

Prep + Cook Time: 15 minutes | Serves: 4

INGREDIENTS:

2 tbsp oil
2 oz breadcrumbs

1 large whisked egg
6 chicken tenderloins

DIRECTIONS

Preheat the Air fryer to 360 F, and combine the oil with the crumbs. Keep mixing and stirring until the mixture gets crumbly. Dip the chicken in the egg wash. Dip the chicken in the crumbs mix, making sure it is evenly and fully covered.

Cook for 12 minutes. Serve the dish and enjoy its crispy taste with Dijon mustard.

Turkey Balls with Minty Sauce

Prep + Cook Time: 22 minutes | Serves: 4

INGREDIENTS

Meatballs:

1 ½ tbsp chopped parsley

1 lb. ground lamb

4 oz ground turkey

1 tbsp chopped mint

1 egg white

2 garlic cloves, chopped

2 tsp harissa

1 tsp pepper

1 tsp salt

¼ cup olive oil

1 tsp cumin

1 tsp coriander

Yogurt:

¼ cup chopped mint

¼ cup sour cream

½ cup yogurt

2 tbsp buttermilk

1 garlic clove, minced

¼ tsp salt

DIRECTIONS

Preheat the Air fryer to 390 F and combine all meatball ingredients, in a large bowl. Wet your hands and make meatballs out of the mixture; cook them for 8 minutes. Work in batches if needed. Meanwhile, combine all yogurt ingredients in another bowl. Serve the meatballs topped with yogurt.

Homemade Eggplant Chips

Prep + Cook Time: 20 minutes | Serves: 3

INGREDIENTS

2 eggplants

¼ cup flour

¼ cup olive oil

½ cup water

DIRECTIONS

Preheat the Air fryer to 390 F and cut the eggplants in slices of half inch each. In a big bowl, mix the flour, olive oil, water, and the eggplants; slowly coat the eggplants. Cook for 12 minutes or until they start to brown. Repeat this process until all eggplant slices are cooked. Serve with yogurt or tomato sauce.

Delicious Parsnip Fries

Prep + Cook Time: 15 minutes | Serves: 3

INGREDIENTS

6 large parsnips

⅓ cup olive oil

⅓ cup cornstarch

⅓ cup water

1 pinch of salt

DIRECTIONS

Preheat the Air fryer to 390 F, peel and cut the parsnips to ½ inch by 3 inches. Mix the cornstarch, olive oil, water and parsnips, in a large bowl. Combine the ingredients and coat the parsnips. Fry the parsnips for around 12 minutes. Serve and enjoy!

Cilantro Baby Carrots

Prep + Cook Time: 25 minutes | Serves: 4

INGREDIENTS

1 ¼ lb. baby carrots
2 tbsp olive oil
1 tsp cumin seeds
½ tsp cumin powder

½ tsp garlic powder
1 handful cilantro, chopped
1 tsp salt
½ tsp black pepper

DIRECTIONS

Preheat the Air fryer to 370 F, and place the baby carrots in a large bowl. Add cumin seeds, cumin, olive oil, salt, garlic powder, and pepper, and stir to coat them well. Place the baby carrots in the basket and cook for 20 minutes. Place on a platter and sprinkle with chopped cilantro.

Tasty Eggplant Chips with Yogurt Sauce

Prep + Cook Time: 20 minutes | Serves: 2

INGREDIENTS

2 eggplants
⅓ cup olive oil
⅓ cup cornstarch

½ cup water
a pinch of salt
1 cup of yogurt

DIRECTIONS

Preheat the Air Fryer to 370 F, and cut the eggplants in slices of ½-inch each. In a bowl, mix the cornstarch, water, olive oil, and the eggplants; carefully coat the eggplants. Cook in the Air fryer for around 15 minutes or until the eggplant starts to brown. Repeat the process until all eggplant slices are fried. Serve with yogurt or tomato sauce!

Italian-Style Sausage Bowl

Prep + Cook Time: 20 minutes | Serves: 4

Ingredients

1 lb Italian Sausage chopped
4 Eggs
1 cup Artichoke hearts, chopped
1 Sweet Onion, diced

2 cups Monterrey Jack, shredded
Salt and black pepper to taste
Fresh Cilantro to garnish

Directions

Place a skillet over medium heat on a stove top, and brown the sausage for a few minutes. Drain any excess fat derived from cooking and set aside. Grease a casserole dish that fits in the basket, with cooking spray, and arrange the sausage at the bottom.

Top with onion and serrano pepper; spread the cheese on top. In a bowl beat the eggs, and season with salt and black pepper. Pour the mixture in the casserole. Place the casserole dish in the fryer basket, and cook at 340 F for 15 minutes. Carefully remove the casserole and serve with fresh cilantro.

Delicious Mozzarella and Parmesan Sticks

Prep + Cook Time: 15 minutes | Serves: 6

Ingredients

Marinara sauce
12 sticks mozzarella cheese
¼ cup flour

2 cups breadcrumbs
2 whole eggs
¼ cup Parmesan cheese, grated

Directions

Preheat your air fryer to 350 F. Pour breadcrumbs in a bowl. Beat the eggs in a separate bowl. In a third bowl, mix Parmesan cheese and flour. Dip each cheese stick the flour mixture, then in eggs and finally in breadcrumbs. Place the sticks on a cookie sheet and freeze for 1 to 2 hours.

Put the sticks in your air fryer's basket and cook for 7 minutes, turning them once. Place on a serving plate, and serve with marinara sauce.

Celery Salmon Balls

Prep + Cook Time: 15 minutes | Serves: 2

INGREDIENTS

6 oz tinned salmon
1 large egg
4 tbsp chopped celery
4 tbsp spring onion, sliced

1 tbsp dill, fresh and chopped
½ tbsp garlic powder
5 tbsp breadcrumbs
3 tbsp olive oil

DIRECTIONS

Preheat the Air fryer to 370 F and in a large bowl, mix salmon, egg, celery, onion, dill, and garlic powder. Shape the mixture into golf-ball-sized balls and roll them in the crumbs; heat the oil in a skillet.

Add the balls and slowly flatten them. Then, transfer them to the Air fryer and fry for about 10 minutes. Serve with cream cheese.

Thyme and Carrot Cookies

Prep + Cook Time: 30 minutes | Serves: 8

Ingredients

6 carrots, sliced
Salt and black pepper to taste
1 tbsp parsley

1¼ oz oats
1 whole egg, beaten
1 tbsp thyme

Directions

Preheat your Air Fryer to 360 F. In a saucepan, add carrots and cover with hot water. Heat over medium heat for 10 minutes, until tender. Remove the oiled carrots in a plate. Season with salt, pepper and parsley and mash using a fork. Add the beaten egg, oats, and thyme as you continue mashing to mix well.

Form the batter into cookie shapes. Place in your air fryer's cooking basket and cook for 15 minutes until edges are browned.

Party Macaroni Quiche with Greek Yogurt

Prep + Cook Time: 30 minutes | Serves: 4

Ingredients

8 tbsp leftover macaroni with cheese
Extra cheese for serving
Pastry as much needed for forming 4 shells
Salt and black pepper to taste

1 tsp garlic puree
2 tbsp Greek yogurt
2 whole eggs
11¾ oz milk

Directions

Preheat the fryer to 360 F. Roll the pastry to form 4 shells. Place them in the Air Fryer's basket. In a bowl, mix leftover macaroni with cheese, yogurt, eggs and milk and garlic puree. Pour this mixture over the pastry shells. Top with the cheese evenly. Place the basket into the Air Fryer, and cook for 20 minutes.

Garlic & Cremini Mushroom Pilaf

Prep + Cook Time: 40 minutes | Serves: 6

Ingredients

3 tbsp olive oil
4 cups heated vegetable stock
2 cups long-grain rice
1 onion, chopped

2 garlic cloves, minced
2 cups cremini mushrooms, chopped
Salt and ground black pepper to taste
1 tbsp fresh chopped parsley, or to taste

Directions

Preheat your Air Fryer to 400 F. Place a frying pan over medium heat. Add oil, onion, garlic, and rice; cook for 5 minutes. Pour the vegetable stock and mushrooms and whisk well. Season with salt and pepper to taste.

Transfer to your air fryer's basket and cook for 20 minutes. Serve sprinkled with fresh chopped parsley.

Cabbage Wedges with Parmesan

Prep + Cook Time: 30 minutes | Serves: 4

INGREDIENTS

½ head of cabbage, cut into 4 wedges
4 tbsp butter, melted
2 cup Parmesan cheese, grated

Salt and black pepper to taste
1 tsp smoked paprika

DIRECTIONS

Preheat the Air fryer to 330 degrees F and line a baking sheet with parchment paper. Brush the butter over the cabbage wedges.

Season with salt and pepper. Coat the cabbage with the Parmesan cheese and arrange on the baking sheet; sprinkle with paprika. Cook for 15 minutes, then flip the wedges over and cook for an additional 10 minutes. Serve with yogurt dip.

Feta Lime Corn

Prep + Cook Time: 20 minutes | Serves: 2

INGREDIENTS

2 ears of corn
Juice of 2 small limes
2 tsp paprika

4 oz feta cheese
Olive oil

DIRECTIONS

Preheat the Air fryer to 370 F, peel the corn and remove the silk. Place the feta cheese in the freezer. Drizzle some olive oil into the Air fryer. Place the corn and cook for 15 minutes. Squeeze the juice of 1 lime on top of each ear of corn. Take the cheese out of the freezer and grate onto corn.

Bacon & Potato Salad with Mayonnaise

Prep + Cook Time: 10 minutes | Serves: 1

Ingredients:

4 lb boiled and cubed potatoes
15 bacon slices, chopped
2 cups shredded cheddar cheese
15 oz sour cream

2 tbsp mayonnaise
1 tsp salt
1 tsp pepper
1 tsp dried herbs, any

DIRECTIONS

Preheat the Air fryer to 350 F, and combine the potatoes, bacon, salt, pepper, and herbs, in a large bowl. Transfer to a baking dish that fits in your Air fryer. Cook for about 7 minutes. Remove and stir in sour cream and mayonnaise, to serve.

Creamy Eggplant Cakes

Prep + Cook Time: 20 minutes | Serves: 4

INGREDIENTS

1 ½ cups flour
1 tsp cinnamon
3 eggs
2 tsp baking powder
2 tbsp sugar
1 cup milk

2 tbsp butter, melted
1 tbsp yogurt
½ cup shredded eggplant
Pinch of salt
2 tbsp cream cheese

DIRECTIONS

Preheat the Air fryer to 350 F, and on a bowl, whisk the eggs along with the sugar, salt, cinnamon, cream cheese, flour, and baking powder. In another bowl, combine all of the liquid ingredients. Gently combine the dry and liquid mixtures; stir in eggplant.

Line the muffin tins and pour the batter inside; cook for 12 minutes. Check with a toothpick: you may need to cook them for an additional 2 to 3 minutes.

Spicy Pumpkin-Ham Fritters

Prep + Cook Time: 10 minutes | Serves: 4

INGREDIENTS

1 oz ham, chopped
1 cup dry pancake mix
1 egg
2 tbsp canned puree pumpkin
1 oz cheddar, shredded

½ tsp chili powder
3 tbsp of flour
1 oz beer
2 tbsp scallions, chopped

DIRECTIONS

Preheat the Air fryer to 370 F and in a bowl, mix the pancake mix and chili powder. Add the egg, puree pumpkin, beer, shredded cheddar, ham and scallions. Roll the mixture in 3 tbsp. of flour.

Arrange the balls into the basket and cook for 8 minutes. Drain on paper towel before serving.

Savory Parsley Crab Cakes

Prep + Cook Time: 20 minutes | Serves: 6

Ingredients

1 lb. crab meat, shredded
2 eggs, beaten
½ cup breadcrumbs
⅓ cup finely chopped green onion
¼ cup parsley, chopped

1 tbsp mayonnaise
1 tsp sweet chili sauce
½ tsp paprika
Salt and black pepper
Olive oil to spray

Directions

In a bowl, add meat, eggs, crumbs, green onion, parsley, mayo, chili sauce, paprika, salt and black pepper; mix well with hands.

Shape into 6 cakes and grease them lightly with oil. Arrange them in the fryer, without overcrowding. Cook for 8 minutes at 400 F, turning once halfway through.

Party Pumpkin Wedges

Prep + Cook Time: 30 minutes | Serves: 3

Ingredients

½ pumpkin, washed and cut into wedges
1 tbsp paprika
1 whole lime, squeezed
1 cup paleo dressing

1 tbsp balsamic vinegar
Salt and black pepper to taste
1 tsp turmeric

Directions

Preheat your Air Fryer to 360 F. Add the pumpkin wedges in your air fryer's cooking basket, and cook for 20 minutes. In a mixing bowl, mix lime juice, vinegar, turmeric, salt, pepper and paprika to form a marinade. Pour the marinade over pumpkin, and cook for 5 more minutes.

Lemony Dip and Potato Chips

Prep + Cook Time: 25 minutes | Serves: 3

INGREDIENTS

3 large potatoes
1 cup sour cream
2 scallions, white part minced

3 tbsp olive oil.
½ tsp lemon juice
salt and black pepper

DIRECTIONS

Preheat the Air fryer to 350 F and slice the potatoes into thin slices; do not peel them. Soak them in water for 10 minutes, then dry them and spray with oil.

Fry the potato slices in two separate batches for 15 minutes; season with salt and pepper.

To prepare the dip, mix the sour cream, olive oil, the scallions, the lemon juice, salt and pepper.

Bok Choy Crisps

Prep + Cook Time: 10 minutes | Serves: 2

INGREDIENTS

2 tbsp olive oil
4 cups packed bok choy
1 tsp vegan seasoning

1 tbsp yeast flakes
Sea salt, to taste

DIRECTIONS

In a bowl, mix oil, bok choy, yeast and vegan seasoning. Dump the coated kale in the Air fryer's basket.

Set the temperature to 360 F and cook for to 5 minutes. Shake after 3 minutes.

Serve sprinkled with sea salt.

Ham Rolls with Vegetables and Walnuts

Prep + Cook Time: 15 minutes | Serves: 4

INGREDIENTS

8 rice leaves
4 carrots
4 slices ham
2 oz walnuts, finely chopped
1 zucchini

1 clove garlic
1 tbsp olive oil
1 tbsp ginger powder
¼ cup basil leaves, finely chopped
Salt and black pepper to taste

DIRECTIONS

In a cooking pan, pour olive oil and add the zucchini, carrots, garlic, ginger and salt; cook on low heat for 10 minutes.

Add the basil and walnuts, and keep stirring. Soak the rice leaves in warm water. Then fold one side above the filling and roll in.

Cook the rolls in the preheated Air fryer for 5 minutes at 300 F.

Garlic Potato Chips

Prep + Cook Time: 50 minutes | Serves: 3

Ingredients

3 whole potatoes, cut into thin slices
¼ cup olive oil
1 tbsp garlic

½ cup cream
2 tbsp rosemary

Directions

Preheat your Air Fryer to 390 F. In a bowl, add oil, garlic and salt to form a marinade. In a separate bowl, add potato slices and top with cold water. Allow sitting for 30 minutes. Drain the slices and transfer them to marinade.

Allow sitting for 30 minutes. Lay the potato slices onto your Air Fryer's cooking basket and cook for 20 minutes. After 10 minutes, give the chips a turn, sprinkle with rosemary and serve.

Simple Parmesan Sandwich

Prep + Cook Time: 20 minutes | Serves: 1

Ingredients

2 tbsp Parmesan cheese, shredded
2 scallions
2 tbsp butter

2 slices bread
¾ cup cheddar cheese

Directions

Preheat your Air Fryer to 360 F. Lay the bread slices on a flat surface. On one slice, spread the exposed side with butter, followed by cheddar and scallions. On the other slice, spread butter and then sprinkle cheese.

Bring the buttered sides together to form sand. Place the sandwich in your Air Fryer's cooking basket and cook for 10 minutes. Serve with berry sauce.

Homemade Cheddar Biscuits

Prep + Cook Time: 35 minutes | Serves: 8

Ingredients

½ cup + 1 tbsp butter
2 tbsp sugar
3 cups flour

1 ⅓ cups buttermilk
½ cup Cheddar cheese, grated

Directions

Preheat your Air Fryer to 380 F. Lay a parchment paper on a baking plate. In a bowl, mix sugar, flour, ½ cup butter, cheese and buttermilk to form a batter. Make 8 balls from the batter and roll in flour.

Place the balls in your air fryer's cooking basket and flatten into biscuit shapes. Sprinkle cheese and the remaining butter on top. Cook for 30 minutes, tossing every 10 minutes. Serve warm.

Molasses Cashew Delight

Prep + Cook Time: 20 minutes | Serves: 12

Ingredients

3 cups cashews
3 tbsp liquid smoke

2 tsp salt
2 tbsp molasses

Directions

Preheat your Air Fryer to 360 F. In a bowl, add salt, liquid, molasses, and cashews; toss to coat well. Place the coated cashews in your Air Fryer's cooking basket and cook for 10 minutes, shaking the basket every 5 minutes.

Ham and Cheese Grilled Sandwich

Prep + Cook Time: 15 minutes | Serves: 2

Ingredients

4 slices bread
¼ cup butter

2 slices ham
2 slices cheese

Directions

Preheat your Air Fryer to 360 degrees F. Place 2 bread slices on a flat surface. Spread butter on the exposed surfaces. Lay cheese and ham on two of the slices. Cover with the other 2 slices to form sandwiches. Place the sandwiches in the cooking basket and cook for 5 minutes.

Simply Parsnip Fries

Prep + Cook Time: 15 minutes | Serves: 3

INGREDIENTS

4 large parsnips
¼ cup flour
¼ cup olive oil

¼ cup water
A pinch of salt

DIRECTIONS

Preheat the Air Fryer to 390 F and cut the parsnip to a half inch by 3 inches. In a bowl, mix the flour, olive oil, water, and parsnip. Mix well and coat. Line the fries in the Air fryer and cook for 15 minutes.

Serve with yogurt and garlic paste.

Crispy Eggplant Fries

Prep + Cook Time: 20 minutes Serves: 2

Ingredients

1 eggplant, sliced
1 tsp olive oil

1 tsp soy sauce
Salt to taste

Directions

Preheat your Air Fryer to 400 F. Make a marinade of 1 tsp oil, soy sauce and salt. Mix well. Add in the eggplant slices and let stand for 5 minutes. Place the prepared eggplant slices in your Air Fryer's cooking basket and cook for 5 minutes. Serve with a drizzle of maple syrup.

Amul Cabbage Canapes

Prep + Cook Time: 15 minutes | Serves: 2

Ingredients

1 whole cabbage, washed and cut in rounds
1 cube Amul cheese
½ carrot, cubed

¼ onion, cubed
¼ capsicum, cubed
Fresh basil to garnish

Directions

Preheat your Air Fryer to 360 F. Using a bowl, mix onion, carrot, capsicum and cheese. Toss to coat everything evenly. Add cabbage rounds to the Air Fryer's cooking basket.

Top with the veggie mixture and cook for 5 minutes. Serve with a garnish of fresh basil.

Feta Butterbeans with Crispy Bacon

Prep + Cook Time: 10 minutes | Serves: 2

Ingredients

1 (14 oz) can butter beans
1 tbsp chives
3 ½ oz feta

Black pepper to taste
1 tsp olive oil
3 ½ oz bacon, sliced

Directions

Preheat your Air Fryer to 340 F. Blend beans, oil and pepper using a blender. Arrange bacon slices on your Air Fryer's cooking basket. Sprinkle chives on top and cook for 10 minutes. Add feta cheese to the butter bean blend and stir. Serve bacon with the dip.

French Beans with Toasted Almonds

Prep + Cook Time: 25 minutes | Serves: 5

Ingredients

1 ½ pounds French beans, washed and drained
1 tbsp salt
1 tbsp pepper

½ pound shallots, chopped
3 tbsp olive oil
½ cup almonds, toasted

Directions

Preheat your Air Fryer to 400 F. Put a pan over medium heat, mix beans in hot water and oil until tender, about 5-6 minutes. Mix the boiled beans with oil, shallots, salt, and pepper. Add the mixture to your Air Fryer's cooking basket and cook for 20 minutes. Serve with almonds and enjoy!

Shrimp with Spices

Prep + Cook Time: 15 minutes | Serves: 3

Ingredients

½ pound shrimp, sauce and deveined
½ tsp Cajun seasoning
Salt as needed

1 tbsp olive oil
¼ tsp black pepper
¼ tsp paprika

Directions

Preheat your Air Fryer to 390 F. Using a bowl, make the marinade by mixing paprika, salt, pepper, oil and seasoning. Cut shrimp and cover with marinade. Place the prepared shrimp in your Air Fryer's cooking basket and cook for 10 minutes, flipping halfway through.

Brussels Sprouts with Garlic

Prep + Cook Time: 25 minutes | Serves: 4

Ingredients

1 block brussels sprouts
½ tsp garlic, chopped
2 tbsp olive oil

½ tsp black pepper
Salt to taste

Directions

Wash the Brussels thoroughly under cold water and trim off the outer leaves, keeping only the head of the sprouts. In a bowl, mix oil and garlic. Season with salt and pepper. Add prepared sprouts to this mixture and let rest for 5 minutes. Place the coated sprouts in your air fryer's cooking basket and cook for 15 minutes.

Yogurt Masala Cashew

Prep + Cook Time: 25 minutes | Serves: 2

Ingredients

8 oz Greek yogurt
2 tbsp mango powder
8¾ oz cashew nuts
Salt and black pepper to taste

1 tsp coriander powder
½ tsp masala powder
½ tsp black pepper powder

Directions

Preheat your Fryer to 240 F. In a bowl, mix all powders. Season with salt and pepper. Add cashews and toss to coat well. Place the cashews in your air fryer's basket and cook for 15 minutes. Serve with a garnish of basil.

Savory Curly Potatoes

Prep + Cook Time: 20 minutes | Serves: 2

Ingredients

2 whole potatoes
1 tbsp extra-virgin olive oil

Salt and black pepper to taste
1 tsp paprika

Directions

Preheat your Fryer to 350 F. Wash the potatoes thoroughly under cold water and pass them through a spiralizer to get curly shaped potatoes. Place the potatoes in a bowl and coat with oil. Transfer them to your air fryer's cooking basket and cook for 15 minutes. Sprinkle a bit of salt and paprika, to serve.

French-Style Fries

Prep + Cook Time: 35 minutes | Serves: 6

Ingredients

6 medium russet potatoes, sauce
2 tbsp olive oil

Salt to taste

Directions

Cut potatoes into ¼ by 3-inch pieces and place in a bowl with cold water; let soak for 30 minutes. Strain and allow to dry. Preheat your Air Fryer to 360 F. Drizzle oil on the dried potatoes and toss to coat. Place the potatoes in your air fryer's cooking basket and cook for 30 minutes. Season with salt and pepper, to serve.

Bacon Wrapped Asparagus

Serves: 4 | Prep + Cook Time: 25 minutes | Serves: 4

Ingredients

20 spears asparagus
4 bacon slices
1 tbsp olive oil

1 tbsp sesame oil
1 tbsp brown sugar
1 garlic clove, crushed

Directions

Preheat your Air Fryer to 380 F. In a bowl, mix the oils, sugar and crushed garlic. Separate the asparagus into 4 bunches (5 spears in 1 bunch) and wrap each bunch with a bacon slice. Coat the bunches with the sugar and oil mix. Place the bunches in your air fryer's cooking basket and cook for 8 minutes. Serve immediately.

Cheese and Chives Scones

Serves: 10 | Prep + Cook Time: 25 minutes | Serves: 10

Ingredients

6 ¼ oz flour
Salt and black pepper to taste
¾ oz butter
1 tsp chives

1 whole egg
1 tbsp milk
2 ¾ cheddar cheese, shredded

Directions

Preheat your Air Fryer to 340 F. In a bowl, mix butter, flour, cheddar cheese, chives, milk and egg to get a sticky dough. Dust a flat surface with flour. Roll the dough into small balls. Place the balls in your Air Fryer's cooking basket and cook for 20 minutes. Serve and enjoy!

Pineapple and Mozzarella Pizza

Prep + Cook Time: 15 minutes | Serves: 2

INGREDIENTS

2 tortillas
8 ham slices
8 mozzarella slices

8 thin pineapple slices
2 tbsp tomato sauce
1 tsp dried parsley

DIRECTIONS

Preheat the Air fryer to 330 F and spread the tomato sauce onto the tortillas. Arrange 4 ham slices on each tortilla. Top the ham with the pineapple, top the pizza with mozzarella and sprinkle with parsley. Cook for 10 minutes and enjoy.

Marinara Chicken Breasts

Prep + Cook Time: 25 minutes | Serves: 2

Ingredients

2 chicken breasts, skinless, beaten, ½ inch thick
1 egg, beaten
½ cup breadcrumbs
A pinch of salt and black pepper

2 tbsp marinara sauce
2 tbsp Grana Padano cheese, grated
2 slices mozzarella cheese

Directions

Dip the breasts into the egg, then into the crumbs and arrange in the Air fryer. Cook for 5 minutes on 400 F. When ready, turn over and drizzle with marinara sauce, Grana Padano and mozzarella cheese. Cook for 5 more minutes at 400 F. Serve with rice.

Homemade Prosciutto Cheese Croquettes

Prep + Cook Time: 50 minutes | Serves: 6

INGREDIENTS

1 lb. cheddar cheese
12 slices of prosciutto
1 cup flour

2 eggs, beaten
4 tbsp olive oil
1 cup breadcrumbs

DIRECTIONS

Cut the cheese into 6 equal pieces. Wrap each piece of cheese with 2 prosciutto slices. Place them in the freezer just enough to set. I left mine for about 5 minutes; note that they mustn't be frozen.

Meanwhile, preheat the Air fryer to 390 F, and dip the croquettes into the flour first, then in the egg, and coat with the breadcrumbs. Place the olive oil in the basket and cook the croquettes for 8 minutes, or until golden.

BREAKFAST

Lemon Vanilla Cupcakes with Yogurt Frost

Ready in about: 25 minutes | Serves: 5

Ingredients

Lemon Frosting:

1 cup natural yogurt
Sugar to taste
1 orange, juiced

1 tbsp orange zest
7 oz cream cheese

Cake:

2 lemons, quartered
½ cup flour + extra for basing
¼ tsp salt
2 tbsp sugar
1 tsp baking powder

1 tsp vanilla extract
2 eggs
½ cup softened butter
2 tbsp milk

Directions

In a bowl, add the yogurt and cream cheese. Mix until smooth. Add the orange juice and zest; mix well. Gradually add the sweetener to your taste while stirring until smooth. Make sure the frost is not runny. Set aside.

For cup cakes: Place the lemon quarters in a food processor and process it until pureed. Add the baking powder, softened butter, milk, eggs, vanilla extract, sugar, and salt. Process again until smooth.

Preheat the Air Fryer to 400 F. Flour the bottom of 10 cupcake cases and spoon the batter into the cases ¾ way up. Place them in the Air Fryer and bake for 7 minutes. Once ready, remove and let cool. Design the cupcakes with the frosting.

Almond, Cinnamon Berry Oat Bars

Ready in about: 40 minutes | Serves: 10

Ingredients

3 cups rolled oats
½ cup ground almonds
½ cup flour
1 tsp baking powder
1 tsp ground cinnamon

3 eggs, lightly beaten
½ cup canola oil
⅓ cup milk
2 tsp vanilla extract
2 cups mixed berries

Directions

Spray a baking pan that fits in your air fryer with cooking spray.

In a bowl, add oats, almonds, flour, baking powder and cinnamon into and stir well. In another bowl, whisk eggs, oil, milk, and vanilla.

Stir the wet ingredients gently into the oat mixture. Fold in the berries. Pour the mixture in the pan and place in the fryer. Cook for 30 minutes at 330 F. When ready, check if the bars are nice and soft.

Cheesy Potato & Spinach Frittata

Ready in about: 35 minutes | Serves: 4

Ingredients

3 cups potato cubes, boiled
2 cups spinach, chopped
5 eggs, lightly beaten
¼ cup heavy cream

1 cup grated mozzarella cheese
½ cup parsley, chopped
Fresh thyme, chopped
Salt and black pepper to taste

Directions

Spray the air fryer's basket with oil. Arrange the potatoes inside.

In a bowl, whisk eggs, cream, spinach, mozzarella, parsley, thyme, salt and pepper, and pour over the potatoes. Cook for 16 minutes at 400 F, until nice and golden.

Thiny Caprese Sandwich with Sourdough Bread

Ready in about: 25 minutes | Serves: 2

Ingredients

4 slices sourdough bread
2 tbsp mayonnaise
2 slices ham
2 lettuce leaves

1 tomato, sliced
2 slices mozzarella cheese
Salt and black pepper to taste

Directions

On a clean board, lay the sourdough slices and spread with mayonnaise. Top 2 of the slices with ham, lettuce, tomato and mozzarella. Season with salt and pepper.

Top with the remaining two slices to form two sandwiches. Spray with oil and transfer to the air fryer. Cook for 14 minutes at 340 F, flipping once halfway through cooking. Serve hot!

Cinnamon Mango Bread

Ready in about: 60 minutes | Serves: 8

Ingredients

½ cup melted butter
1 egg, lightly beaten
½ cup brown sugar
1 tsp vanilla extract
3 ripe mango, mashed

1 ½ cups plain flour
1 tsp baking powder
½ tsp grated nutmeg
½ tsp ground cinnamon

Directions

Spray a loaf tin, that fits in the air fryer, with cooking spray and line with baking paper. In a bowl, whisk melted butter, egg, sugar, vanilla and mango. Sift in flour, baking powder, nutmeg and cinnamon and stir without overmixing.

Pour the batter into the tin and place it the air fryer. Cook for 35 minutes at 300 F. Make sure to check at the 20-25-minute mark. When ready, let cool before slicing it.

Creamy Mushroom and Spinach Omelet

Ready in about: 10 minutes | Serves: 2

Ingredients

4 eggs, lightly beaten
2 tbsp heavy cream
2 cups spinach, chopped
1 cup chopped mushrooms

3 oz feta cheese, crumbled
A handful of fresh parsley, chopped
Salt and black pepper

Directions

Spray your air fryer basket with cooking spray. In a bowl, whisk eggs and until combined. Stir in spinach, mushrooms, feta, parsley, salt and pepper.

Pour into the basket and cook for 6 minutes at 350 F. Serve immediately with a touch of tangy tomato relish.

Cheddar Cheese Hash Browns

Ready in about: 25 minutes | Serves: 4

Ingredients

4 russet potatoes, peeled, grated
1 brown onion, chopped
3 garlic cloves, chopped
½ cup grated cheddar cheese

1 egg, lightly beaten
Salt and black pepper
3 tbsp finely thyme sprigs

Directions

In a bowl, mix with hands potatoes, onion, garlic, cheese, egg, salt, black pepper and thyme. Spray the fryer with cooking spray.

Press the hash brown mixture into the basket and cook for 9 minutes at 400 F., shaking once halfway through cooking. When ready, ensure the hash browns are golden and crispy.

Cherry in Vanilla Almond Scones

Ready in about: 30 minutes | Serves: 4

Ingredients

2 cups flour
⅓ cup sugar
2 tsp baking powder
½ cup sliced almonds
¾ cup chopped cherries, dried

¼ cup cold butter, cut into cubes
½ cup milk
1 egg
1 tsp vanilla extract

Directions

Line air fryer basket with baking paper. Mix together flour, sugar, baking powder, almonds and dried cherries. Rub the butter into the dry ingredients with hands to form a sandy, crumbly texture. Whisk together egg, milk and vanilla extract.

Pour into the dry ingredients and stir to combine. Sprinkle a working board with flour, lay the dough onto the board and give it a few kneads. Shape into a rectangle and cut into squares. Arrange the squares in the air fryer's basket and cook for 14 minutes at 390 F. Serve immediately.

Sweet Caramel French Toast

Ready in about: 15 minutes | Serves: 3

Ingredients

6 slices white bread
2 eggs
¼ cup heavy cream

⅓ cup sugar mixed with 1 tsp ground cinnamon
6 tbsp caramel
1 tsp vanilla extract

Directions

In a bowl, whisk eggs and cream. Dip each piece of bread into the egg and cream. Dip the bread into the sugar and cinnamon mixture until well-coated. On a clean board, lay the coated slices and spread three of the slices with about 2 tbsp of caramel each, around the center.

Place the remaining three slices on top to form three sandwiches. Spray the air fryer basket with oil. Arrange the sandwiches into the fryer and cook for 10 minutes at 340 F, turning once halfway through cooking.

Bacon Egg Muffins with Chives

Ready in about: 30 minutes | Serves: 10

Ingredients

10 eggs, lightly beaten
10 bacon rashers, cut into small pieces
½ cup chopped chives

1 brown onion, chopped
1 cup grated cheddar cheese
Salt and black pepper

Directions

Spray a 10-hole muffin pan with cooking spray. In a bowl, add eggs, bacon, chives, onion, cheese, salt and pepper, and stir to combine. Pour into muffin pans and place inside the fryer. Cook for 12 minutes at 330 F, until nice and set.

Honeyed Banana & Hazelnut Cupcakes

Ready in about: 40 minutes | Serves: 6

Ingredients

½ cup melted butter
½ cup honey
2 eggs, lightly beaten
4 ripe bananas, mashed
1 tsp vanilla extract
2 cups flour

1 tsp baking powder
½ tsp baking soda
1 tsp ground cinnamon
½ cup chopped hazelnuts
½ cup dark chocolate chips

Directions

Spray 10-hole muffin with oil spray. In a bowl, whisk butter, honey, eggs, banana and vanilla, until well-combine. Sift in flour, baking powder, baking soda and cinnamon without overmixing.

Stir in the hazelnuts and chocolate into the mixture. Pour the mixture into the muffin holes and place in the air fryer. Cook for 30 minutes at 350 F, checking them at the around 20-minute mark.

Crunchy Cinnamon Toast Sticks

Ready in about: 15 minutes | Serves: 3

Ingredients

5 slices bread
3 eggs
Salt and black pepper to taste
1 ½ tbsp butter

⅛ tsp cinnamon powder
A pinch nutmeg powder
A pinch clove powder

Directions

Preheat the Air Fryer to 350 F. In a bowl, add clove powder, eggs, nutmeg powder, and cinnamon powder. Beat well using a whisk. Season with salt and pepper. Use a bread knife to apply butter on both sides of the bread slices and cut them into 3 or 4 strips.

Dip each strip in the egg mixture and arrange them in one layer in the fryer's basket. Cook for 2 minutes. Once ready, pull out the fryer basket and spray the toasts with cooking spray. Flip the toasts and spray the other side with cooking spray. Slide the basket back to the fryer and cook for 4 minutes. Check regularly to prevent them from burning. Once the toasts are golden brown, remove them onto a serving platter. Dust with cinnamon and serve with syrup.

Buttery Scramble Eggs

Ready in about: 11 minutes | Serves: 2

Ingredients

2 slices bread
2 eggs

Salt and black pepper to taste
2 tbsp butter

Directions

Place a 3 X 3 cm heatproof bowl in the fryer's basket and brush with butter. Make a hole in the middle of the bread slices with a bread knife and place in the heatproof bowl in 2 batches.

Break an egg into the center of each hole. Season with salt and pepper. Close the Air Fryer and cook for 4 minutes at 330 F. Turn the bread with a spatula and cook for another 4 minutes.

Paprika & Pickles Fritters

Ready in about: 15 minutes | Serves: 2

INGREDIENTS

8 medium pickles
1 egg, beaten
½ cup breadcrumbs
1 tsp paprika

4 tbsp flour
1 tbsp olive oil
Salt, to taste

DIRECTIONS

Preheat the Air fryer to 350 F and cut the pickles lengthwise; pat them dry. Combine the flour, paprika and salt, in a small bowl. In another bowl, combine the breadcrumbs and olive oil. Dredge in the flour first, dip them in the beaten egg, and then coat them with the crumbs. Arrange on a lined baking sheet and place in the Air fryer. Cook for 10 minutes.

Cheesy Sausage Egg Dish

Ready in about: 20 minutes | Serves: 6

Ingredients

1 lb minced breakfast sausage
6 eggs
1 red pepper, diced
1 green pepper, diced
1 yellow pepper, diced

1 sweet onion, diced
2 cups Cheddar cheese, shredded
Salt and black pepper to taste
fresh parsley to garnish

Directions

Place a skillet over medium heat on a stove top, add the sausage and cook until brown, stirring occasionally. Once done, drain any excess fat derived from cooking and set aside.

Grease a casserole dish that fits into the fryer basket with cooking spray, and arrange the sausage on the bottom. Top with onion, red pepper, green pepper, and yellow pepper. Spread the cheese on top.

In a bowl, beat the eggs and season with salt and black pepper. Pour the mixture over the casserole. Place the casserole dish in the air basket, and bake at 355 F for 13-15 minutes. Serve warm garnished with fresh parsley.

Veggie Carrot & Brocoli Cheddar Quiche

Ready in about: 50 minutes | Serves: 2

Ingredients

4 eggs
1 cup whole milk
2 medium broccoli, cut into florets
2 medium tomatoes, diced
4 medium carrots, diced

¼ cup Feta cheese, crumbled
1 cup grated Cheddar cheese
Salt and black pepper to taste
1 tsp chopped parsley
1 tsp dried thyme

Directions

Put the broccoli and carrots in a food steamer and cook until soft, about 10 minutes. In a jug, crack in the eggs, add the parsley, salt, pepper, and thyme. Using a whisk, beat the eggs while adding the milk gradually until a pale mixture is attained.

Once the broccoli and carrots are ready, strain them through a sieve and set aside. In a 3 X 3 cm quiche dish, add the carrots and broccoli. Put the tomatoes on top, then the feta and cheddar cheese following. Leave a little bit of cheddar cheese. Pour the egg mixture over the layering and top with the remaining cheddar cheese.

Place the dish in the Air Fryer and cook at 350 F for 20 minutes.

Tasty Onion & Chili Hash Browns

Ready in about: 50 minutes | Serves: 3

Ingredients

1 pound potatoes, peeled and shredded
Salt and black pepper to taste
1 tsp garlic powder
1 tsp chili flakes

1 tsp onion powder
1 egg, beaten
1 tbsp olive oil

Directions

Place a skillet over medium heat on a stove top, add the olive oil and potatoes. Sauté until evenly golden, about 10 minutes. Transfer to a bowl and let cool completely. After they have cooled, add in the egg, pepper, salt, chili flakes, onion powder, and garlic powder; mix well.

In a flat plate, spread the mixture and pat firmly with your fingers. Refrigerate for 20 minutes and preheat the Air Fryer to 350 F. Remove from the fridge and divide into equal sizes.

Grease the fryer basket with cooking spray and add in the patties. Cook at 350 F for 15 minutes; flip and cook for 6 more minutes. Serve with sunshine eggs.

Banana and Peanut Butter Cake

Ready in about: 50 minutes | Serves: 2

Ingredients

1 cup plus
1 tbsp flour
¼ tsp baking soda
1 tsp baking powder
⅓ cup sugar
2 mashed bananas
¼ cup vegetable oil

1 egg, beaten
1 tsp vanilla extract
¾ cup chopped walnuts
¼ tsp salt
2 tbsp peanut butter
2 tbsp sour cream
 for greasing

Directions

Preheat the air fryer to 330 degrees F. Spray a small baking dish, that fits inside, with cooking spray or grease with butter. Combine the flour, salt, baking powder, and baking soda, in a bowl.

In another bowl, combine bananas, oil, egg, peanut butter, vanilla, sugar, and sour cream. Combine both mixtures gently. Stir in the chopped walnuts. Pour the batter into the dish. Cook for 40 minutes and serve cool.

Sweet Apricot Scones with Almonds

Ready in about: 30 minutes | Serves: 4

Ingredients

2 cups flour
⅓ cup sugar
2 tsp baking powder
½ cup sliced almonds
¾ cup chopped dried apricots

¼ cup cold butter, cut into cubes
½ cup milk
1 egg
1 tsp vanilla extract

Directions

Line Air fryer basket with baking paper. Mix together flour, sugar, baking powder, almonds and apricots. Rub the butter into the dry ingredients with hands to form a sandy, crumbly texture. Whisk together egg, milk and vanilla extract.

Pour into the dry ingredients and stir to combine. Sprinkle a working board with flour, lay the dough onto the board and give it a few kneads. Shape into a rectangle and cut into 8 squares. Arrange the squares in the basket and cook for 14 minutes at 390 F.

Vanilla Brownies with White Chocolate & Walnuts

Ready in about: 35 minutes | Serves: 6

Ingredients

6 oz. dark chocolate
6 oz. butter
¾ cup white sugar
3 eggs
2 tsp vanilla extract

¾ cup flour
¼ cup cocoa powder
1 cup chopped walnuts
1 cup white chocolate chips

Directions

Line a pan inside your Air fryer with baking paper. In a saucepan, melt chocolate and butter over low heat. Do not stop stirring until you obtain a smooth mixture. Let cool slightly, whisk in eggs and vanilla. Sift flour and cocoa and stir to mix well.

Sprinkle the walnuts over and add the white chocolate into the batter. Pour the batter into a pan that fits in the fryer, and cook for 20 minutes at 340 F. Serve with raspberry syrup and ice cream.

Gratined Nutmeg Potatoes

Ready in about: 45 minutes | Serves: 6

INGREDIENTS

5 large potatoes
½ cup sour cream
½ cup grated cheese
½ cup milk

½ tsp nutmeg
½ tsp black pepper
½ tsp salt

DIRECTIONS

Preheat the Air fryer to 390 F, peel and slice the potatoes. In a bowl, combine the sour cream, milk, pepper, salt and nutmeg. Place the potato slices in the bowl with the milk mixture and stir to coat them well.

Transfer the whole mixture to a baking dish. Cook for 25 minutes, then sprinkle grated cheese on top and cook for 10 more minutes.

Cheesy Eggs with Fried Potatoes

Ready in about: 24 minutes | Serves: 3

INGREDIENTS

3 potatoes, sliced
2 eggs, beaten
2 oz cheddar cheese

1 tbsp all-purpose flour
100 ml coconut cream

DIRECTIONS

Remove the skin of the thin sliced potatoes and place them in the Air Fryer; cook for 12 minutes at 350° F.

To prepare the sauce, mix the two beaten eggs, coconut cream and flour until the cream mixture thickens. Remove the potatoes from the fryer, line them in the ramekin and top with the cream mixture and the cheese. Cover and cook for 12 more minutes.

Crunchy Asparagus with Cheese

Ready in about: 30 minutes | Serves: 6

INGREDIENTS

1 lb. asparagus spears
¼ cup flour
1 cup breadcrumbs

½ cup Parmesan cheese , grated
2 eggs, beaten
Salt and black pepper to taste

DIRECTIONS

Preheat the Air fryer to 370 F and combine the breadcrumbs and Parmesan, in a small bowl. Season with salt and pepper. Line a baking sheet with parchment paper. Dip half of the spears into the flour first, then into the eggs, and finally coat with crumbs.

Arrange them on the sheet and bake for about 8 to 10 minutes. Repeat with the other half of the spears. Serve with melted butter, hollandaise sauce or freshly squeezed lemon.

Breaded Cauliflowers in Alfredo Sauce

Ready in about: 20 minutes | Serves: 4

INGREDIENTS

4 cups cauliflower florets
1 tbsp butter, melted
¼ cup alfredo sauce

1 cup breadcrumbs
1 tsp sea salt

DIRECTIONS

Whisk the alfredo sauce along with the butter. In a shallow bowl, combine the breadcrumbs with the sea salt. Dip each cauliflower floret into the alfredo mixture first, and then coat in the crumbs. Drop the prepared florets into the Air fryer.

Set the temperature to 350 F and set the timer for 15 minutes. Shake the florets twice.

Savory Cheddar & Cauliflower Tater Tots

Ready in about: 35 minutes | Serves: 10

INGREDIENTS

2 lb. cauliflower florets, steamed
5 oz cheddar cheese
1 onion, diced
1 cup breadcrumbs
1 egg, beaten

1 tsp chopped parsley
1 tsp chopped oregano
1 tsp chopped chives
1 tsp garlic powder
Salt and black pepper to taste

DIRECTIONS

Mash the cauliflower and place it in a large bowl. Add the onion, parsley, oregano, chives, garlic powder, some salt and pepper, and cheddar cheese. Mix with your hands until fully combined and form 12 balls out of the mixture.

Line a baking sheet with paper. Dip half of the tater tots into the egg and then coat with breadcrumbs. Arrange them on the baking sheet and cook in the fryer at 350 minutes for 15 minutes. Repeat with the other half.

Crunchy Empanadas Filled with Chorizo & Bell Pepper

Ready in about: 15 minutes | Serves: 3

INGREDIENTS

9 oz pizza dough
6 oz chorizo, cubed
2 tbsp of parsley

1 shallot, finely chopped
½ red bell pepper, cubed

DIRECTIONS

In a skillet, mix the chorizo, the bell pepper and the shallot and fry on low heat for around 5 minutes. Switch off the heat and add the parsley. Set the mixture aside and preheat the Air Fryer to 350 F. Using a pin, roll the dough to half inch of thickness.

With a water glass or steel rings, cut the dough in 22-23 rounds of 2 inches each. Scoop 1 spoon of the chorizo mixture on each of the rounds. Press all edges between the thumb and the index finger to create a scallop shape. Cook the empanadas in the fryer for 8 minutes or until brown.

Easy Walnut Banana Muffins

Ready in about: 15 minutes | Serves: 4

Ingredients

1 cup flour
¼ cup mashed banana
¼ cup powdered sugar
1 tsp milk

1 tsp chopped walnuts
½ tsp baking powder
¼ cup oats
¼ cup butter, room temperature

Directions

Preheat the Air Fryer to 320 degrees F. Place the sugar, walnuts, banana, and butter in a bowl and mix to combine. In another bowl, combine the flour, baking powder and oats.

Combine the two mixtures and stir in the milk. Grease a muffin tin and pour the batter in. Cook for 10 minutes.

Ham & Cheese Pinwheels

Ready in about: 25 minutes | Serves: 6

INGREDIENTS

1 sheet puff pastry
8 ham slices

1 ½ cups Gruyere cheese , grated
4 tsp Dijon mustard

DIRECTIONS

Preheat the Air fryer to 370 F and place the pastry on a lightly floured flat surface. Brush the mustard over and then arrange the ham slices; top with the cheese. Start at the shorter edge and roll up the pastry.

Wrap it in a plastic foil and place in the freezer for half an hour, until it becomes firm and easy to cut. Meanwhile, slice the pastry into 6 rounds. Line a baking sheet with parchment paper and lay on the pinwheels on; cook for 9 minutes. Serve with pizza sauce.

Saucy Vegetable Chicken

Ready in about: 25 minutes | Serves: 4

Ingredients

4 boneless and skinless chicken breasts cut into cubes
2 carrots, sliced
1 red bell pepper, cut into strips
1 yellow bell pepper, cut into strips

1 cup snow peas
15 oz broccoli florets
1 scallion, sliced

Sauce:

3 tbsp soy sauce
2 tbsp oyster sauce
1 tbsp brown sugar
1 tsp sesame oil
1 tsp cornstarch

1 tsp sriracha
2 garlic cloves, minced
1 tbsp grated ginger
1 tbsp rice wine vinegar

Directions

Preheat the air fryer to 370 degrees F. Place the chicken, bell peppers, and carrot, in a bowl. In another bowl, combine the sauce ingredients. Coat the chicken mixture with the sauce.

Place on a lined baking sheet and cook for 5 minutes. Add snow peas and broccoli and cook for an additional 8 to 10 minutes. Serve garnished with scallion.

Smoky Cheese & Mustard Rarebit

Ready in about: 15 minutes | Serves: 2

Ingredients

3 slices bread
1 tsp smoked paprika
2 eggs

1 tsp dijon mustard
4 ½ oz cheddar cheese, grated
Salt and black pepper to taste

Directions

Toast the bread in the Air Fryer to your liking. In a bowl, whisk the eggs, stir in the mustard, cheddar and paprika. Season with salt and pepper. Spread the mixture on the toasts. Cook the slices for 10 minutes at 360 degrees F.

Simple Butter Eggs

Ready in about: 11 minutes | Serves: 2

Ingredients

2 slices Bread
2 Eggs

Salt and black pepper to taste
2 tbsp Butter

Directions

Place a 3 X 3 inches heatproof bowl in the fryer basket and brush with butter. Make a hole in the middle of the bread slices with a bread knife and place in the heatproof bowl in 2 batches. Break an egg into the center of each hole. Season with salt and pepper.

Cook for 4 minutes at 330 F, and turn the bread with a spatula; cook for another 4 minutes.

Cinnamon & Banana Bread

Ready in about: 60 minutes | Serves: 8

Ingredients

½ cup melted butter
1 egg, lightly beaten
½ cup brown sugar
1 tsp vanilla extract
3 ripe bananas, mashed

1 ½ cups plain flour
1 tsp baking powder
½ tsp grated nutmeg
½ tsp ground cinnamon

Directions

Spray a loaf tin, that fits in the Air fryer, with cooking spray and line with baking paper. In a bowl, whisk melted butter, egg, sugar, vanilla and bananas. Sift in flour, baking powder, nutmeg and cinnamon and stir without overmixing. Pour the batter into the tin and place it the Air fryer; cook for 35 minutes at 300 F, checking once at the 20-minute mark. When ready, let cool before slicing.

Creamy Ham & Cheese Mini Quiches

Ready in about: 30 minutes | Serves: 8

Ingredients

1 shortcrust pastry
3 oz chopped ham
½ cup grated cheese
4 eggs, beaten

3 tbsp Greek yogurt
¼ tsp garlic powder
¼ tsp salt
¼ tsp black pepper

Directions

Preheat the air fryer to 330 degrees F. Take 8 ramekins and sprinkle them with flour to avoid sticking. Cut the shortcrust pastry into 8 equal pieces to make 8 mini quiches. Line the ramekins with the pastry. Combine all of the other ingredients in a bowl. Divide the filling between the ramekins and cook for 20 minutes in the air fryer.

Caprese Muffins with Mayonnaise

Ready in about: 20 minutes | Serves: 2

Ingredients

2 slices bread
2 prosciutto slices, chopped
2 eggs
4 tomato slices
¼ tsp balsamic vinegar

2 tbsp grated mozzarella
¼ tsp maple syrup
2 tbsp mayonnaise
Salt and black pepper to taste
 for greasing

Directions

Preheat the air fryer to 320 F. Grease two large ramekins. Place one bread slice on the bottom of each ramekin. Arrange 2 tomato slices on top of each bread slice. Divide the mozzarella between the ramekins.

Crack the eggs over the mozzarella. Drizzle with maple syrup and balsamic vinegar. Season with some salt and pepper. Cook for 10 minutes, or until desired. Top with mayonnaise.

Corn & Chorizo Frittata

Ready in about: 12 minutes | Serves: 2

Ingredients

3 eggs
1 large potato, boiled and cubed
½ cup frozen corn
½ cup feta cheese, crumbled

1 tbsp chopped parsley
½ chorizo, sliced
3 tbsp olive oil
Salt and black pepper to taste

Directions

Pour the olive oil into the air fryer and preheat it to 330 degrees F. Cook the chorizo until slightly browned. Beat the eggs with some salt and pepper in a bowl. Stir in all of the remaining ingredients. Pour the mixture into the air fryer, give it a stir, and cook for 6 minutes.

Yogurt & Cream Cheese Zucchini Cake

Ready in about: 20 minutes | Serves: 4

Ingredients

1 ½ cups flour
1 tsp cinnamon
3 eggs
2 tsp baking powder
2 tbsp sugar
1 cup milk

2 tbsp butter, melted
1 tbsp yogurt
½ cup shredded zucchini
A pinch of salt
2 tbsp cream cheese

Directions

Preheat the air fryer to 350 degrees F. In a bowl, whisk the eggs along with the sugar, salt, cinnamon, cream cheese, flour, and baking powder. In another bowl, combine all of the liquid ingredients.

Gently combine the dry and liquid mixtures. Stir in zucchini. Line the muffin tins with baking paper, and pour the batter inside them. Arrange in the air fryer and cook for 15 minutes. Check with a toothpick.

Raspeberries Maple Pancakes

Ready in about: 15 minutes | Serves: 4

Ingredients

2 cups all-purpose flour
1 cup milk
3 eggs, beaten
1 tsp baking powder
1 cup brown sugar

1 ½ tsp vanilla extract
½ cup frozen raspberries, thawed
2 tbsp maple syrup
A pinch of salt
 for greasing

Directions

Preheat the air fryer to 390 degrees F. In a bowl, mix the flour, baking powder, salt, milk, eggs, vanilla extract, sugar, and maple syrup, until smooth. Stir in the raspberries. Do it gently to avoid coloring the batter.

Grease a baking dish or spray it with cooking spray. Drop the batter onto the dish. Just make sure to leave some space between the pancakes. If there is some batter left, repeat the process. Cook for 10 minutes.

Tasty Cheddar Omelet

Ready in about: 15 minutes | Serves: 1

Ingredients

2 eggs
2 tbsp grated cheddar cheese
1 tsp soy sauce

½ onion, sliced
¼ tsp pepper
1 tbsp olive oil

Directions

Whisk the eggs along with the pepper and soy sauce. Preheat the air fryer to 350 degrees F. Heat the olive oil and add the egg mixture and the onion. Cook for 8 to 10 minutes. Top with the grated cheddar cheese.

Buttery Cheese Sandwich

Ready in about: 10 minutes | Serves: 1

Ingredients

2 tbsp butter
2 slices bread

3 slices American cheese

Directions

Preheat the air fryer to 370 degrees F. Spread one tsp of butter on the outside of each of the bread slices. Place the cheese on the inside of one bread slice. Top with the other slice. Cook in the air fryer for 4 minutes. Flip the sandwich over and cook for an additional 4 minutes. Serve cut diagonally.

Olives & Tomato Tart with Feta Cheese

Ready in about: 40 minutes | Serves: 2

Ingredients

4 eggs
½ cup chopped tomatoes
1 cup crumbled feta cheese
1 tbsp chopped basil
1 tbsp chopped oregano

¼ cup chopped kalamata olives
¼ cup chopped onion
2 tbsp olive oil
½ cup milk
Salt and black pepper to taste

Directions

Preheat the air fryer to 340 degrees F. Brush a pie pan with olive oil. Beat the eggs along with the milk and some salt and pepper. Stir in all of the remaining ingredients. Pour the egg mixture into the pan. Cook for 30 minutes.

Creamy Vanilla Berries Pastry

Ready in about: 20 minutes | Serves: 3

Ingredients

3 pastry dough sheets
2 tbsp mashed strawberries
2 tbsp mashed raspberries

¼ tsp vanilla extract
2 cups cream cheese
1 tbsp honey

Directions

Preheat the air fryer to 375 degrees F. Divide the cream cheese between the dough sheets and spread it evenly. In a small bowl, combine the berries, honey and vanilla. Divide the mixture between the pastry sheets. Pinch the ends of the sheets, to form puff. Place the puffs on a lined baking dish. Place the dish in the air fryer and cook for 15 minutes.

Prosciutto & Salami Omelet

Ready in about: 20 minutes | Serves: 2

Ingredients

1 beef sausage, chopped
4 slices prosciutto, chopped
3 oz salami, chopped
1 cup grated mozzarella cheese

4 eggs
1 tbsp chopped onion
1 tbsp ketchup

Directions

Preheat the air fryer to 350 degrees F. Whisk the eggs with the ketchup, in a bowl. Stir in the onion. Brown the sausage in the air fryer for 2 minutes. Meanwhile, combine the egg mixture, mozzarella cheese, salami and prosciutto. Pour the egg mixture over the sausage and give it a stir. Cook for 10 minutes.

Hazelnut Bread Pudding with Honey & Raisins

Ready in about: 45 minutes | Serves: 3

Ingredients

8 slices of bread
½ cup buttermilk
¼ cup honey
1 cup milk
2 eggs
½ tsp vanilla extract

2 tbsp butter, softened
¼ cup sugar
4 tbsp raisins
2 tbsp chopped hazelnuts
Cinnamon for garnish

Directions

Preheat the air fryer to 310 degrees F. Beat the eggs along with the buttermilk, honey, milk, vanilla, sugar and butter. Stir in raisins and hazelnuts. Cut the bread into cubes and place them, in a bowl. Pour the milk mixture over the bread. Let soak for 10 minutes. Cook the bread pudding for 30 minutes and garnish with cinnamon.

Speedy Bacon & Egg Sandwich

Ready in about: 10 minutes | Serves: 1

Ingredients

1 whole egg, cracked
1 slice English bacon

1 slice bread
½ cup butter

Directions

Preheat your Air Fryer to 400 degrees F. Spread butter on one side of the bread slice. Add the cracked egg on top and season with salt and pepper. Place bacon on top. Arrange the bread slice in your Air Fryer's cooking basket and cook for 3-5 minutes. Serve and enjoy!

Parmesan Sausage Frittata with Tomatoes

Ready in about: 15 minutes | Serves: 1

Ingredients

½ sausage, chopped
Salt and black pepper to taste
A bunch of parsley, chopped
3 whole eggs
1 tbsp olive oil

1 slice bread
4 cherry tomatoes, halved
1 slice bread
2 tbsp parmesan, shredded for garnish

Directions

Preheat your Air Fryer to 360 degrees F. Place tomatoes and sausages in your air fryer's cooking basket and cook for 5 minutes. In a bowl, mix baked tomatoes, sausages, eggs, salt, parsley, parmesan, oil and pepper.

Add the bread to the air fryer cooking basket and cook for 5 minutes. Add the frittata mixture over baked bread and top with parmesan. Serve and enjoy!

Cheesy Berry-Flavored French Toast

Ready in about: 15 minutes | Serves: 4

Ingredients

2 eggs, beaten
4 slices bread
3 tbsp sugar
1 ½ cups corn flakes

⅓ cup milk
¼ tsp nutmeg
4 tbsp berry-flavored cheese
¼ tsp salt

Directions

Preheat your Air Fryer to 400 degrees F. In a bowl, mix sugar, eggs, nutmeg, salt and milk. In a separate bowl, mix blueberries and cheese. Take 2 bread slices and pour the blueberry mixture over the slices.

Top with the milk mixture. Cover with the remaining two slices to make sandwiches. Dredge the sandwiches over cornflakes to coat well. Lay the sandwiches in your air fryer's cooking basket and cook for 8 minutes. Serve with berries and syrup.

Peppery Tofu & Green Onion Omelet with Soy Sauce

Ready in about: 20 minutes | Serves: 1

Ingredients

1 small Japanese tofu, cubed
3 whole eggs
Pepper to taste
1 tsp coriander
1 tsp cumin

2 tbsp soy sauce
2 tbsp green onion, chopped
Olive oil
1 whole onion, chopped

Directions

In a bowl, mix eggs, soy sauce, cumin, pepper, oil, and salt. Add cubed tofu to baking forms and pour the egg mixture on top. Place the prepared forms in the air fryer cooking basket and cook for 10 minutes at 400 F. Serve with a sprinkle of coriander and green onion.

Cinnamon Pineapples Grilled with Honey

Ready in about: 15 minutes | Serves: 2

Ingredients

1 tsp cinnamon
5 pineapple slices
½ cup brown sugar

1 tbsp basil, chopped for garnish
1 tbsp honey, for garnish

Directions

Preheat your air fryer to 340 degrees F. In a small bowl, mix brown sugar and cinnamon. Drizzle the sugar mixture over your pineapple slices and set aside for 20 minutes.

Place the pineapple rings in the air fryer cooking basket and cook for 10 minutes. Flip the pineapples and cook for 10 minutes more. Serve with basil and a drizzle of honey.

Creamy Beacon & Thyme Omelet Cups

Ready in about: 25 minutes | Serves: 4

Ingredients

4 crusty rolls
5 eggs, beaten
A pinch of salt
½ tsp thyme, dried

3 strips precooked bacon, chopped
2 tbsp heavy cream
4 Gouda cheese mini wedges, thin slices

Directions

Preheat your air fryer 330 degrees F. Cut the tops off the rolls and remove the inside with your fingers. Line the rolls with a slice of cheese and press down, so the cheese conforms to the inside of the roll. In a bowl, mix eggs with heavy cream, bacon, thyme, salt and pepper.

Stuff the rolls with the egg mixture. Lay the rolls in your air fryer's cooking basket and bake for 8 to 12 minutes or until the eggs become puffy and the roll shows a golden brown texture.

Easy Murshroom & Turkey Sandwich

Ready in about: 15 minutes | Serves: 1

Ingredients

⅓ cup shredded leftover turkey
⅓ cup sliced mushrooms
1 tbsp butter, divided
2 tomato slices

½ tsp red pepper flakes
¼ tsp salt
¼ tsp black pepper
1 hamburger bun

Directions

Melt half of the butter and add the mushrooms. Cook for 4 minutes. Meanwhile, cut the bun in half and spread the remaining butter on the outside of the bun. Place the turkey on one half of the bun.

Arrange the mushroom slices on top of the turkey. Place the tomato slices on top of the mushrooms. Sprinkle with salt pepper and red pepper flakes. Top with the other bun half. Cook for 5 minutes at 350 F.

Cheesy Bacon & Turkey Calzone

Ready in about: 20 minutes | Serves: 4

Ingredients

Pizza dough
4 oz cheddar cheese, grated
1 oz mozzarella cheese
1 oz bacon, diced
2 cups cooked and shredded turkey
1 egg, beaten

1 tsp thyme
4 tbsp tomato paste
1 tsp basil
1 tsp oregano
Salt and black pepper to taste

Directions

Preheat the air fryer to 350 degrees F. Divide the pizza dough into 4 equal pieces so you have the dough for 4 small pizza crusts. Combine the tomato paste, basil, oregano, and thyme, in a small bowl.

Brush the mixture onto the crusts just make sure not to go all the way and avoid brushing near the edges on one half of each crust, place ½ turkey, and season the meat with some salt and pepper.

Top the meat with some bacon. Combine the cheddar and mozzarella and divide it between the pizzas, making sure that you layer only one half of the dough. Brush the edges of the crust with the beaten egg. Fold the crust and seal with a fork. Cook for 10 minutes.

Salty Parsnip Hash Browns

Ready in about: 20 minutes | Serves: 2

Ingredients

1 large parsnip, grated
3 eggs, beaten
½ tsp garlic powder
¼ tsp nutmeg

1 tbsp olive oil
1 cup flour
Salt and black pepper to taste

Directions

Heat olive oil in the air fryer at 390 degrees F. In a bowl, combine flour, eggs, parsnip, nutmeg, and garlic powder. Season with salt and pepper. Form patties out of the mixture. Arrange in the air fryer and cook for 15 minutes.

Creamy Bacon & Egg Wraps with Spicy Salsa

Ready in about: 15 minutes | Serves: 3

Ingredients

3 tortillas
2 previously scrambled eggs
3 slices bacon, cut into strips

3 tbsp salsa
3 tbsp cream cheese, divided
1 cup grated pepper Jack cheese

Directions

Preheat the air fryer to 390 degrees F. Spread one tbsp. of cream cheese onto each tortilla. Divide the eggs and bacon between the tortillas evenly. Top with salsa. Sprinkle some grated cheese over. Roll up the tortillas. Cook for 10 minutes.

Sweet Strawberries Pancake

Ready in about: 30 minutes | Serves: 4

Ingredients

3 eggs, beaten
2 tbsp unsalted butter
½ cup flour

2 tbsp sugar, powdered
½ cup milk
1½ cups fresh strawberries, sliced

Directions

Preheat your Air Fryer to 330 degrees F. Add butter to a pan and melt over low heat. In a bowl, mix flour, milk, eggs and vanilla until fully incorporated. Add the mixture to the pan with melted butter.

Place the pan in your air fryer's cooking basket and cook for 12-16 minutes until the pancake is fluffy and golden brown. Drizzle powdered sugar and toss sliced strawberries on top.

Spinach & Kale Balsamic Chicken

Ready in about: 20 minutes | Serves: 1

Ingredients

½ cup baby spinach leaves
½ cup shredded romaine
3 large kale leaves, chopped
4 oz chicken breasts, cut into cubes

3 tbsp olive oil, divided
1 tsp balsamic vinegar
1 garlic clove, minced
Salt and black pepper to taste

Directions

Place the chicken, 1 tbsp. olive oil and garlic, in a bowl. Season with salt and pepper and toss to combine.

Put on a lined baking dish and cook for 14 minutes at 390F. Meanwhile, place the greens in a large bowl. Add the remaining olive oil and balsamic vinegar. Season with salt and pepper and toss to combine. Top with the chicken.

Creamy Parmesan & Ham Shirred Eggs

Ready in about: 20 minutes | Serves: 2

Ingredients

2 tsp butter, for greasing
4 eggs, divided
2 tbsp heavy cream
4 slices of ham
3 tbsp Parmesan cheese

¼ tsp paprika
¾ tsp salt
¼ tsp pepper
2 tsp chopped chives

Directions

Preheat the air fryer to 320 degrees F. Grease a pie pan with the butter. Arrange the ham slices on the bottom of the pan to cover it completely. Whisk one egg along with the heavy cream, salt and pepper, in a small bowl.

Pour the mixture over the ham slices. Crack the other eggs over the ham. Sprinkle with Parmesan cheese. Cook for 14 minutes. Season with paprika, garnish with chives and serve with bread.

Quick Paprika Eggs

Ready in about: 15 minutes | Serves: 6

Ingredients

6 large eggs

1 tsp paprika

Directions

Preheat your air fryer 300 degrees F. Lay the eggs in your air fryer's basket and bake for at least 8 minutes for a slightly runny yolk or 12 to 15 minutes for a firmer yolk. Using tongs, place the eggs in a bowl with icy water. Allow to cool in cold water for 5 minutes before cracking the shell under water. Serve sprinkled with paprika.

Classic Cheddar Cheese Omelet

Ready in about: 15 minutes | Serves: 1

Ingredients

2 eggs, beaten
Black pepper to taste
1 cup cheddar cheese, shredded

1 whole onion, chopped
2 tbsp soy sauce

Directions

Preheat your Air Fryer to 340 degrees F. Drizzle soy sauce over the chopped onions. Place the onions in your air fryer's cooking basket and cook for 8 minutes. In a bowl, mix the beaten eggs with salt and pepper.

Pour the egg mixture over onions (in the cooking basket) and cook for 3 minutes. Add cheddar cheese over eggs and bake for 2 more minutes. Serve and enjoy!

Buttered Apple & Brie Cheese Sandwich

Ready in about: 8 - 10 minutes | Serves: 1

Ingredients

2 bread slices
½ apple, thinly sliced

2 tsp butter
2 oz brie cheese, thinly sliced

Directions

Spread butter on the outside of the bread slices. Arrange apple slices on the inside of one bread slice. Place brie slices on top of the apple. Top with the other slice of bread. Cook for 5 minutes at 350 F. Serve cut diagonally.

Fresh Kale & Cottage Omelet

Ready in about: 15 minutes | Serves: 1

Ingredients

3 eggs
3 tbsp cottage cheese
3 tbsp chopped kale
½ tbsp chopped basil

½ tbsp chopped parsley
Salt and black pepper to taste
1 tsp olive oil

Directions

Heat oil at 330 F. Beat the eggs with salt and pepper, in a bowl. Stir in the rest of the ingredients. Pour the mixture into the air fryer and cook for 10 minutes, until slightly golden and set.

Vanilla & Cinnamon Toast Toppet

Ready in about: 10 minutes | Serves: 6

Ingredients

12 slices bread
½ cup sugar
1 ½ tsp cinnamon

1 stick of butter, softened
1 tsp vanilla extract

Directions

Preheat the air fryer to 400 degrees F. Combine all ingredients, except the bread, in a bowl. Spread the buttery cinnamon mixture onto the bread slices. Place the bread slices in the air fryer. Cook for 5 minutes.

Parsley Onion & Feta Tart

Ready in about: 30 minutes | Serves: 3

Ingredients

3½ pounds Feta cheese
Black pepper to taste
1 whole onion, chopped
2 tbsp parsley, chopped

1 egg yolk
Olive oil for drizzling
5 sheets frozen filo pastry

Directions

Cut each of the 5 filo sheets into three equal sized strips. Cover the strips with oil. In a bowl, mix onion, pepper, feta, salt, egg yolk, and parsley.

Make triangles using the cut strips and add a little bit of the feta mixture on top of each triangle. Place the triangles in fryer's basket and cook for 3 minutes at 400 F. Serve with a drizzle of oil and green onions.

Tomato, Basil & Mozzarella Breakfast

Ready in about: 7 minutes | Serves: 1

Ingredients

2 slices of bread
4 tomato slices
4 mozzarella slices

1 tbsp olive oil
1 tbsp chopped basil
Salt and black pepper to taste

Directions

Preheat the air fryer to 370 degrees F. Place the bread slices in the air fryer and toast for 3 minutes. Arrange two tomato slices on each bread slice. Season with salt and pepper.

Top each slice with 2 mozzarella slices. Return to the air fryer and cook for 1 minute more. Drizzle the caprese toasts with olive oil and top with chopped basil.

Cinnamon-Orange Toast

Ready in about: 15 minutes | Serves: 6

Ingredients

12 slices bread
½ cup sugar
1 stick butter

1½ tbsp vanilla extract
1½ tbsp cinnamon
2 oranges, zested

Directions

In a microwave proof bowl, mix butter, sugar and vanilla extract. Warm and stir the mixture for 30 seconds until everything melts. Add in orange zest. Pour the mixture over bread slices. Lay the bread slices in your air fryer's cooking basket and cook for 5 minutes at 400 F. Serve with fresh banana and berry sauce.

Herby Parmesan Bagel

Ready in about: 6 minutes | Serves: 1

Ingredients

2 tbsp butter, softened
1 tsp dried basil
1 tsp dried parsley
1 tsp garlic powder

1 tbsp Parmesan cheese
Salt and black pepper to taste
1 bagel

Directions

Preheat the air fryer to 370 degrees. Cut the bagel in half. Place in the air fryer and cook for 3 minutes. Combine the butter, Parmesan, garlic, basil, and parsley in a small bowl. Season with salt and pepper, to taste. Spread the mixture onto the toasted bagel. Return the bagel to the air fryer and cook for an additional 3 minutes.

Porridge with Honey & peanut Butter

Ready in about: 5 minutes | Serves: 4

Ingredients

2 cups steel cut oats
1 cup flax seeds
1 tbsp peanut butter

1 tbsp butter
4 cups milk
4 tbsp honey

Directions

Preheat the air fryer to 390 degrees F. Combine all of the ingredients in an ovenproof bowl. Place in the air fryer and cook for 5 minutes. Stir and serve.

Classic Bacon & Egg English Muffin

Ready in about: 10 minutes | Serves: 1

Ingredients

1 egg
1 English muffin

2 slices of bacon
Salt and black pepper to taste

Directions

Preheat the air fryer to 395 F. Crack the egg into a ramekin. Place the muffin, egg and bacon in the air fryer. Cook for 6 minutes. Let cool slightly so you can assemble the sandwich. Cut the muffin in half. Place the egg on one half and season with salt and pepper. Arrange the bacon on top. Top with the other muffin half.

Peppery Sausage & Parsley Patties

Ready in about: 20 minutes | Serves: 4

Ingredients

1 lb ground Italian sausage
¼ cup breadcrumbs
1 tsp dried parsley
1 tsp red pepper flakes

½ tsp salt
¼ tsp black pepper
¼ tsp garlic powder
1 egg, beaten

Directions

Preheat the air fryer to 350 degrees F. Combine all of the ingredients in a large bowl. Line a baking sheet with parchment paper. Make patties out of the sausage mixture and arrange them on the baking sheet. Cook for 15 minutes, flipping once halfway through cooking.

Air Fried Mac and Cheese

Ready in about: 15 minutes | Serves: 2

Ingredients

1 cup cooked macaroni
1 cup grated cheddar cheese
½ cup warm milk

1 tbsp Parmesan cheese
Salt and black pepper to taste

Directions

Preheat the air fryer to 350 degrees F. Add the macaroni to an ovenproof baking dish. Stir in the cheddar and milk. Season with salt and pepper, to taste. Place the dish in the air fryer and cook for 10 minutes. Sprinkle with Parmesan cheese, to serve.

Prosciutto & Mozzarella Crostini

Ready in about: 7 minutes | Serves: 1

Ingredients

½ cup finely chopped tomatoes
3 oz chopped mozzarella
3 prosciutto slices, chopped

1 tbsp olive oil
1 tsp dried basil
6 small slices of French bread

Directions

Preheat the air fryer to 350 degrees F. Place the bread slices and toast for 3 minutes. Top the bread with tomatoes, prosciutto and mozzarella. Sprinkle the basil over the mozzarella. Drizzle with olive oil. Return to the air fryer and cook for 1 more minute, enough to become melty and warm.

SWEETS AND DESSERTS

Vanilla Lemon Cheesecake

Ready in about: 80 minutes + chilling time | Serves: 8

Ingredients

8 oz graham crackers, crushed
4 oz butter, melted
16 oz plain cream cheese
3 eggs

3 tbsp sugar
1 tbsp vanilla extract
Zest of 2 lemons

Directions

Line a cake tin, that fits in your Air fryer, with baking paper. Mix together the crackers and butter, and press at the bottom of the tin. In a bowl, add cream cheese, eggs, sugar, vanilla and lemon zest and beat with a hand mixer until well combined and smooth. Pour the mixture into the tin, on top of the cracker's base. Cook for 40-45 minutes at 350 F, checking it to ensure it's set but still a bit wobbly. Let cool, then refrigerate overnight.

Cinnamon Baked Apples with Raisins & Walnuts

Ready in about: 35 minutes | Serves: 2

Ingredients

2 granny smith apples, cored, bottom intact
2 tbsp butter, cold
3 tbsp sugar

3 tbsp crushed walnuts
2 tbsp raisins
1 tsp cinnamon

Directions

In a bowl, add butter, sugar, walnuts, raisins and cinnamon; mix with fingers until you obtain a crumble. Arrange the apples in the Air fryer. Stuff the apples with the filling mixture. Cook for 30 minutes at 400 F.

Vanilla Chocolate Brownies with Walnuts

Ready in about: 35 minutes | Serves: 10

Ingredients

6 oz dark chocolate
6 oz butter
¾ cup white sugar
3 eggs
2 tsp vanilla extract

¾ cup flour
¼ cup cocoa powder
1 cup chopped walnuts
1 cup white chocolate chips

Directions

Line a pan inside your Air fryer with baking paper. In a saucepan, melt chocolate and butter over low heat. Do not stop stirring until you obtain a smooth mixture. Let cool slightly, whisk in eggs and vanilla. Sift flour and cocoa and stir to mix well. Sprinkle the walnuts over and add the white chocolate into the batter. Pour the batter into the pan and cook for 20 minutes at 340 F. Serve with raspberry syrup and ice cream.

Raspberry Chocolate Cake

Ready in about: 40 minutes | Serves: 8

Ingredients

1 ½ cups flour
⅓ cup cocoa powder
2 tsp baking powder
¾ cup white sugar
¼ cup brown sugar
⅔ cup butter

2 tsp vanilla extract
1 cup milk
1 tsp baking soda
2 eggs
1 cup freeze-dried raspberries
1 cup chocolate chips

Directions

Line a cake tin with baking powder. In a bowl, sift flour, cocoa and baking powder. Place the sugars, butter, vanilla, milk and baking soda into a microwave-safe bowl and heat for 60 seconds until the butter melts and the ingredients incorporate; let cool slightly. Whisk the eggs into the mixture.

Pour the wet ingredients into the dry ones, and fold to combine. Add in the raspberries and chocolate chips into the batter. Pour the batter into the tin and cook for 30 minutes at 350 F.

Amazing Marshmallows Pie

Ready in about: 10 minutes | Serves: 4

Ingredients

4 graham cracker sheets, snapped in half
8 large marshmallows

8 squares each of dark, milk and white chocolate

Directions

Arrange the cracker halves on a board. Put 2 marshmallows onto half of the graham cracker halves. Place 2 squares of chocolate onto the cracker with the marshmallows. Put the remaining crackers on top to create 4 sandwiches. Wrap each one in the baking paper so it resembles a parcel. Cook in the fryer for 5 minutes at 340 F.

Caramel Apple & Cinnamon Cake

Ready in about: 40 minutes | Serves: 4

Ingredients

1 vanilla box cake
2 apples, peeled, sliced
3 oz butter, melted
½ cup brown sugar

1 tsp cinnamon
½ cup flour
1 cup caramel sauce

Directions

Line a cake tin with baking paper. In a bowl, mix butter, sugar, cinnamon and flour until you obtain a crumbly texture. Prepare the cake mix according to the instructions (no baking). Pour the batter into the tin and arrange the apple slices on top. Spoon the caramel over the apples and add the crumble over the sauce. Cook in the Air fryer for 35 minutes at 360 F; make sure to check it halfway through, so it's not overcooked.

Marshmallows Choco S´mores

Ready in about: 10 minutes | Serves: 4

Ingredients

4 graham cracker sheets, snapped in half
8 large marshmallows

8 squares each of dark, milk and white chocolate

Directions

Arrange the cracker halves on a board. Put 2 marshmallows onto half of the graham cracker halves. Place 2 squares of chocolate onto the cracker with the marshmallows. Put the remaining crackers on top to create 4 sandwiches. Wrap each one in baking paper so it resembles a parcel. Place in your Air fryer and cook for 5 minutes at 340 F.

Delicious Figs with Honey & Mascarpone

Ready in about: 10 minutes | Serves: 4

INGREDIENTS

8 figs
6 oz mascarpone cheese
1 tsp rose water

1 oz butter
3 tbsp honey
2 tbsp toasted almond slices

DIRECTIONS

Preheat the Air fryer to 350 F, open the figs by cutting a cross on top and gently squeezing them. Divide the honey between the figs. Place them on a lined baking sheet and cook for 5 minutes. Combine the mascarpone with the rose water. Place a dollop of the mascarpone onto each fig, top with toasted almonds and serve.

Dark Chocolate & Peanut Butter Fondant

Ready in about: 25 minutes | Serves: 4

Ingredients

¾ cup dark chocolate
½ cup peanut butter, crunchy
2 tbsp butter, diced
¼ cup + ¼ cup sugar

4 eggs, room temperature
⅛ cup flour, sieved
1 tsp salt
¼ cup water

Directions

Make a salted praline to top the chocolate fondant. Add ¼ cup of sugar, 1 tsp of salt and water into a saucepan. Stir and bring it to a boil over low heat on a stove top. Simmer until the desired color is achieved and reduced.

Pour it into a baking tray and leave to cool and harden. Preheat the Air Fryer to 300 F. Place a pot of water over medium heat and place a heatproof bowl over it. Add the chocolate, butter, and peanut butter to the bowl.

Stir continuously until fully melted, combined, and smooth. Remove the bowl from the heat and allow to cool slightly. Add the eggs to the chocolate and whisk. Add the flour and remaining sugar; mix well.

Grease 4 small loaf pans with cooking spray and divide the chocolate mixture between them. Place 2 pans at a time in the basket and cook for 7 minutes. Remove them and serve the fondants with a piece of salted praline.

Dreamy White Chocolate Dessert

Ready in about: 40 minutes | Serves: 2

Ingredients

3 oz white chocolate
4 large egg whites
2 large egg yolks, at room temperature
¼ cup sugar + more for garnishing

1 tbsp melted butter
1 tbsp unmelted butter
¼ tsp vanilla extract
1 ½ tbsp flour

Directions

Coat two 6-oz ramekins with melted butter. Add the sugar and swirl it in the ramekins to coat the butter. Pour out the remaining sugar and keep it. Melt the unmelted butter with the chocolate in a microwave; set aside.

In another bowl, beat the egg yolks vigorously. Add the vanilla and kept sugar; beat to incorporate fully. Add the chocolate mixture and mix well. Add the flour and mix it with no lumps.

Preheat the Air Fryer to 330 F, and whisk the egg whites in another bowl till it holds stiff peaks. Add ⅓ of the egg whites into the chocolate mixture; fold in gently and evenly. Share the mixture into the ramekins with ½ inch space left at the top. Place the ramekins in the fryer basket, close the Air Fryer and cook for 14 minutes.

Dust with the remaining sugar and serve.

Homemade Orange Curd

Ready in about: 30 minutes | Serves: 2

Ingredients

3 tbsp butter
3 tbsp sugar
1 egg

1 egg yolk
¾ orange, juiced

Directions

Add sugar and butter in a medium ramekin and beat evenly. Add egg and yolk slowly while still whisking. the fresh yellow color will be attained. Add the orange juice and mix. Place the bowl in the fryer basket and cook at 250 F for 6 minutes. Increase the temperature again to 320 F and cook for 15 minutes.

Remove the bowl onto a flat surface; use a spoon to check for any lumps and remove. Cover the ramekin with a plastic wrap and refrigerate overnight or serve immediately.

Tasty Choco-Banana Sandwich

Ready in about: 30 minutes | Serves: 2

Ingredients

4 slices of brioche
1 tbsp butter, melted

6 oz milk chocolate, broken into chunks
1 banana, sliced

Directions

Brush the brioche slices with butter. Spread chocolate and banana on 2 brioche slices. Top with the remaining 2 slices to create 2 sandwiches. Arrange the sandwiches into your air fryer and cook for 14 minutes at 400 F, turning once halfway through. Slice in half and serve with vanilla ice cream.

Vanilla Crème Caramel

Ready in about: 60 minutes | Serves: 3

Ingredients

1 cup whipped cream
1 cup milk
2 vanilla pods

10 egg yolks
4 tbsp sugar + extra for topping

Directions

In a pan, add the milk and cream. Cut the vanilla pods open and scrape the seeds into the pan with the vanilla pods also. Place the pan over medium heat on a stove top until almost boiled while stirring regularly. Turn off the heat. Add the egg yolks to a bowl and beat it. Add the sugar and mix well but not too frothy.

Remove the vanilla pods from the milk mixture; pour the mixture onto the eggs mixture while stirring constantly. Let it sit for 25 minutes. Fill 2 to 3 ramekins with the mixture. Place the ramekins in the fryer basket and cook them at 190 F for 50 minutes. Once ready, remove the ramekins and let sit to cool. Sprinkle the remaining sugar over and use a torch to melt the sugar, so it browns at the top.

Orange & Chocolate Fudge with Honey Icing

Ready in about: 55 minutes | Serves: 8

Ingredients

1 cup sugar
7 oz flour
1 tbsp honey
¼ cup milk
1 tsp vanilla extract

1 oz cocoa powder
2 eggs
4 oz butter
1 orange, juice and zest

Icing:

1 oz butter, melted
4 oz powdered sugar
1 tbsp brown sugar

1 tbsp milk
2 tsp honey

Directions

Preheat the Air fryer to 350 F, and in a bowl, mix the dry ingredients for the fudge. Mix the wet ingredients separately; combine the two mixtures gently. Transfer the batter to a prepared cake pan. Cook for 35 minutes. Meanwhile whisk together all icing ingredients. When the cake cools, coat with the icing. Let set before slicing.

Coconut Oat Cookies Filled with White Chocolate

Ready in about: 30 minutes | Serves: 4

Ingredients

5 ½ oz flour
1 tsp vanilla extract
3 oz sugar

½ cup oats
1 small egg, beaten
¼ cup coconut flakes

Filling:

1 oz white chocolate, melted
2 oz butter

4 oz powdered sugar
1 tsp vanilla extract

Directions

Beat all the cookie ingredients, with an electric mixer, except the flour. When smooth, fold in the flour. Drop spoonfuls of the batter onto a prepared cookie sheet. Cook in the Air fryer at 350 F for 18 minutes; then let cool.

Meanwhile, prepare the filling by beating all ingredients together; spread the filling on half of the cookies. Top with the other halves to make cookie sandwiches.

Honeyed White Chocolate Cake

Ready in about: 30 minutes | Serves: 8

Ingredients

6 oz self-rising flour
3 oz brown sugar
2 oz white chocolate chips

1 tbsp honey
1 ½ tbsp milk
4 oz butter

Directions

Preheat the Air fryer to 350 F, and beat the butter and sugar until fluffy. Beat in the honey, milk, and flour. Gently fold in the chocolate chips. Drop spoonfuls of the mixture onto a prepared cookie sheet. Cook for 18 minutes.

Blueberry & Yogurt Cups

Ready in about: 30 minutes | Serves: 10

Ingredients

1 ½ cup flour
½ tsp salt
½ cup sugar
¼ cup vegetable oil
2 tsp vanilla extract

1 cup blueberries
1 egg
2 tsp baking powder
Yogurt, as needed

Directions

Preheat the Air fryer to 350 F, and combine flour, salt and baking powder, in a bowl. In another bowl, add the oil, vanilla extract, and egg. Fill the rest of the bowl with yogurt, and whisk the mixture until fully incorporated.

Combine the wet and dry ingredients; gently fold in the blueberries. Divide the mixture between 10 muffin cups. You may need to work in batches. Cook for 10 minutes.

Creamy Yogurt & Lime Muffins

Ready in about: 30 minutes | Serves: 6

Ingredients

2 eggs plus 1 yolk
Juice and zest of 2 limes
1 cup yogurt

¼ cup superfine sugar
8 oz cream cheese
1 tsp vanilla extract

Directions

Preheat the Air fryer to 330 F, and with a spatula, gently combine the yogurt and cheese. In another bowl, beat together the rest of the ingredients. Gently fold the lime with the cheese mixture. Divide the batter between 6 lined muffin tins. Cook in the Air fryer for 10 minutes.

Easy Cinnamon Snickerdoodle Cookies

Ready in about: 30 minutes | Serves: 6

Ingredients

1 box instant vanilla Jell-O
1 can of Pillsbury Grands Flaky Layers Biscuits

1 ½ cups cinnamon sugar
 melted butter, for brushing

Directions

Preheat the Air fryer to 350 F, and unroll the flaky biscuits; cut them into fourths. Roll each ¼ into a ball. Arrange the balls on a lined baking sheet, and cook in the air fryer for 7 minutes, or until golden.

Meanwhile, prepare the Jell-O following the package's instructions. Using an injector, inject some of the vanilla pudding into each ball. Brush the balls with melted butter and then coat them with cinnamon sugar.

Foolproof Cherry Pie

Ready in about: 30 minutes | Serves: 8

Ingredients

2 store-bought pie crusts
21 oz cherry pie filling

1 egg yolk
1 tbsp milk

Directions

Preheat the Air fryer to 310 F, and place one pie crust in a pie pan; poke holes into the crust. Cook for 5 minutes.

Spread the pie filling over. Cut the other pie crust into strips and arrange the pie-style over the baked crust.

Whisk milk and egg yolk, and brush the mixture over the pie. Return the pie to the fryer and cook for 15 minutes.

Vanilla & Chocolate Chip Cookies

Ready in about: 15 minutes | Serves: 5

Ingredients

¾ cup flour
¼ tsp baking soda
¾ tsp salt
⅓ cup brown sugar
¼ cup unsalted butter, softened

2 tbsp white sugar
1 egg yolk
½ tbsp vanilla extract
½ cup chocolate chips

Directions

Preheat air fryer to 350 F. Line the basket or rack with foil. Whisk flour, baking soda, and salt together in a small bowl. Combine brown sugar, butter, and white sugar in a separate bowl.

Add egg yolk and vanilla extract and whisk until well-combined. Stir flour mixture into butter mixture until dough is just combined; gently fold in chocolate chips. Scoop dough by the spoonfuls and roll into balls; place onto the foil-lined air fryer basket, 2 inches apart.

Cook dough in the air fryer until cookies start getting crispy, 5 to 6 minutes. Transfer foil and cookies to wire racks or a plate, and let cool completely. Repeat with remaining dough.

Banana Fritters

Ready in about: 6 minutes | Serves: 6

INGREDIENTS

6 bananas
4 large eggs, beaten
1 cup breadcrumbs

1 cup bread flour
1 cup oil

DIRECTIONS

Peel the bananas and cut them into pieces of less than 1-inch each. In a bowl, mix the beaten eggs with the bread flour and the oil. Dredge the banana first into the flour, then dip in the beaten eggs, and finally in the crumbs. Line the banana pieces in the Air Fryer and cook them for 10 minutes at 350° F, shaking once halfway through. Serve with vanilla ice cream.

Pineapple Chocolate Cake

Ready in about: 50 minutes | Serves: 4

Ingredients

2 oz dark chocolate, grated
8 oz self-rising flour
4 oz butter
7 oz pineapple chunks

½ cup pineapple juice
1 egg
2 tbsp milk
½ cup sugar

Directions

Preheat the Air fryer to 390 F, place the butter and flour into a bowl, and rub the mixture with your fingers until crumbed. Stir in pineapple, sugar, chocolate, and juice. Beat eggs and milk separately, and then add to the batter.

Transfer the batter to a previously prepared (greased or lined) cake pan, and cook for 40 minutes. Let cool for at least 10 minutes before serving.

Grandma's Buttermilk Biscuits

Ready in about: 25 minutes | Serves: 4

Ingredients

1 ¼ cups flour, plus some for dusting
½ tsp baking soda
½ cup cake flour
¾ tsp salt

½ tsp baking powder
4 tbsp butter, chopped
1 tsp sugar
¾ cup buttermilk

Directions

Preheat the Air fryer to 400 F and combine all dry ingredients, in a bowl. Place the chopped butter in the bowl, and rub it into the flour mixture, until crumbed. Stir in the buttermilk.

Flour a flat and dry surface and roll out until half-inch thick. Cut out 10 rounds with a small cookie cutter. Arrange the biscuits on a lined baking sheet. Cook for 8 minutes.

Homemade Doughnuts

Ready in about: 25 minutes | Serves: 4

Ingredients

8 oz self-rising flour
1 tsp baking powder
½ cup milk

2 ½ tbsp butter
1 egg
2 oz brown sugar

Directions

Preheat the Air fryer to 350 F, and beat the butter with the sugar, until smooth. Beat in eggs, and milk. In a bowl, combine the flour with the baking powder. Gently fold the flour into the butter mixture.

Form donut shapes and cut off the center with cookie cutters. Arrange on a lined baking sheet and cook in the fryer for 15 minutes. Serve with whipped cream or icing.

Glazed Lemon Cupcakes

Ready in about: 30 minutes | Serves: 6

Ingredients

1 cup flour
½ cup sugar
1 small egg
1 tsp lemon zest
¾ tsp baking powder

¼ tsp baking soda
½ tsp salt
2 tbsp vegetable oil
½ cup milk
½ tsp vanilla extract

Glaze:
½ cup powdered sugar

2 tsp lemon juice

Directions

Preheat the Air fryer to 350 F, and combine all dry muffin ingredients, in a bowl. In another bowl, whisk together the wet ingredients. Gently combine the two mixtures. Divide the batter between 6 greased muffin tins.

Place the muffin tins in the Air fryer and cook for 12 to 14 minutes. Meanwhile, whisk the powdered sugar with the lemon juice. Spread the glaze over the muffins.

Dark Chocolate Lava Cakes

Ready in about: 20 minutes | Serves: 4

Ingredients

3 ½ oz butter, melted
3 ½ tbsp sugar
1 ½ tbsp self-rising flour

3 ½ oz dark chocolate, melted
2 eggs

Directions

Grease 4 ramekins with butter. Preheat the Air fryer to 375 F and beat the eggs and sugar until frothy. Stir in the butter and chocolate; gently fold in the flour. Divide the mixture between the ramekins and bake in the Air fryer for 10 minutes. Let cool for 2 minutes before turning the lava cakes upside down onto serving plates.

Summer Citrus Sponge Cake

Ready in about: 50 minutes | Serves: 6

Ingredients

9 oz sugar
9 oz self-rising flour
9 oz butter
3 eggs

1 tsp baking powder
1 tsp vanilla extract
zest of 1 orange

Frosting:

4 egg whites
Juice of 1 orange
1 tsp orange food coloring

zest of 1 orange
7 oz superfine sugar

Directions

Preheat the Air fryer to 160 F and place all cake ingredients, in a bowl and beat with an electric mixer. Transfer half of the batter into a prepared cake pan; bake for 15 minutes. Repeat the process for the other half of the batter.

Meanwhile, prepare the frosting by beating all frosting ingredients together. Spread the frosting mixture on top of one cake. Top with the other cake.

Perfect Chocolate Soufflé

Ready in about: 25 minutes | Serves: 2

Ingredients

2 eggs, whites and yolks separated
¼ cup butter, melted
2 tbsp flour

3 tbsp sugar
3 oz chocolate, melted
½ tsp vanilla extract

Directions

Beat the yolks along with the sugar and vanilla extract; stir in butter, chocolate, and flour. Preheat the Air fryer to 330 F and whisk the whites until a stiff peak forms. Working in batches, gently combine the egg whites with the chocolate mixture. Divide the batter between two greased ramekins. Cook for 14 minutes.

Sesame Banana Dessert

Ready in about: 15 minutes | Serves: 5

Ingredients

1 ½ cups flour
5 bananas, sliced
1 tsp salt
3 tbsp sesame seeds

1 cup water
2 eggs, beaten
1 tsp baking powder
½ tbsp sugar

Directions

Preheat the Air fryer to 340 F, in a bowl, mix salt, sesame seeds, flour, baking powder, eggs, sugar, and water.

Coat sliced bananas with the flour mixture; place the prepared slices in the Air fryer basket; cook for 8 minutes.

Effortless Apple Pie

Ready in about: 30 minutes | Serves: 9

Ingredients

4 apples, diced
2 oz butter, melted
2 oz sugar
1 oz brown sugar

2 tsp cinnamon
1 egg, beaten
3 large puff pastry sheets
¼ tsp salt

Directions

Whisk white sugar, brown sugar, cinnamon, salt, and butter, together. Place the apples in a baking dish and coat them with the mixture. Place the baking dish in the Air fryer, and cook for 10 minutes at 350 F.

Meanwhile, roll out the pastry on a floured flat surface, and cut each sheet into 6 equal pieces. Divide the apple filling between the pieces. Brush the edges of the pastry squares with the egg.

Fold them and seal the edges with a fork. Place on a lined baking sheet and cook in the fryer at 350 F for 8 minutes. Flip over, increase the temperature to 390 F, and cook for 2 more minutes.

Triple Berry Lemon Crumble

Ready in about: 30 minutes | Serves: 6

Ingredients

12 oz fresh strawberries
7 oz fresh raspberries
5 oz fresh blueberries
5 tbsp cold butter
2 tbsp lemon juice

1 cup flour
½ cup sugar
1 tbsp water
A pinch of salt

Directions

Gently mass the berries, but make sure there are chunks left. Mix with the lemon juice and 2 tbsp. of the sugar.

Place the berry mixture at the bottom of a prepared round cake. Combine the flour with the salt and sugar, in a bowl. Add the water and rub the butter with your fingers until the mixture becomes crumbled.

Arrange the crisp batter over the berries. Cook in the Air fryer at 390 F for 20 minutes. Serve chilled.

French Apple Cake

Ready in about: 25 minutes | Serves: 9

Ingredients

2 ¾ oz flour
5 tbsp sugar
1 ¼ oz butter

3 tbsp cinnamon
2 whole apple, sliced

Directions

Preheat the Air fryer to 360 F and in a bowl, mix 3 tbsp sugar, butter and flour; form pastry using the batter. Roll out the pastry on a floured surface and transfer it to the fryer's basket. Arrange the apple slices atop.

Cover apples with sugar and cinnamon; cook for 20 minutes. Sprinkle with powdered sugar and mint, to serve.

Honey Hazelnut Apples

Ready in about: 13 minutes | Serves: 2

Ingredients

4 apples
1 oz butter
2 oz breadcrumbs
Zest of 1 orange

2 tbsp chopped hazelnuts
2 oz mixed seeds
1 tsp cinnamon
2 tbsp honey

Directions

Preheat the Air fryer to 350 F and core the apples. Make sure to also score their skin to prevent from splitting. Combine the remaining ingredients in a bowl; stuff the apples with the mixture and cook for 10 minutes. Serve topped with chopped hazelnuts.

Classic Pecan Pie

Ready in about: 1 hr 10 minutes | Serves: 4

Ingredients

¾ cup maple syrup
2 eggs
½ tsp salt
¼ tsp nutmeg
½ tsp cinnamon
2 tbsp almond butter

2 tbsp brown sugar
½ cup chopped pecans
1 tbsp butter, melted
1 8-inch pie dough
¾ tsp vanilla extract

Directions

Preheat the Air fryer to 370 F, and coat the pecans with the melted butter. Place the pecans in the Air fryer and toast them for 10 minutes. Place the pie crust into an 8-inch round pie pan, and place the pecans over.

Whisk together all remaining ingredients, in a bowl. Pour the maple mixture over the pecans. Set the Air fryer to 320 F and cook the pie for 25 minutes.

Crumble with Blackberries & Apricots

Ready in about: 30 minutes | Serves: 4

Ingredients

2 ½ cups fresh apricots, de-stoned and cubed
1 cup fresh blackberries
½ cup sugar
2 tbsp lemon Juice

1 cup flour
Salt as needed
5 tbsp butter

Directions

Add the apricot cubes to a bowl and mix with lemon juice, 2 tbsp sugar, and blackberries. Scoop the mixture into a greased dish and spread it evenly. In another bowl, mix flour and remaining sugar.

Add 1 tbsp of cold water and butter and keep mixing until you have a crumbly mixture. Preheat the Air fryer to 390 F and place the fruit mixture in the cooking basket. Top with crumb mixture and cook for 20 minutes.

Vanilla Almond Cookies

Ready in about: 145 minutes | Serves: 4

Ingredients

8 egg whites
½ tsp almond extract
1 ⅓ cups sugar
¼ tsp salt

2 tsp lemon juice
1 ½ tsp vanilla extract
Melted dark chocolate to drizzle

Directions

In a mixing bowl, add egg whites, salt, and lemon juice. Beat using an electric mixer until foamy. Slowly add the sugar and continue beating until completely combined; add the almond and vanilla extracts. Beat until stiff peaks form and glossy.

Line a round baking sheet with parchment paper. Fill a piping bag with the meringue mixture and pipe as many mounds on the baking sheet as you can leaving 2-inch spaces between each mound.

Place the baking sheet in the fryer basket and bake at 250 F for 5 minutes. Reduce the temperature to 220 F and bake for 15 more minutes. Then, reduce the temperature once more to 190 F and cook for 15 minutes. Remove the baking sheet and let the meringues cool for 2 hours. Drizzle with the dark chocolate before serving.

Vanilla Brownie Squares

Ready in about: 25 minutes | Serves: 2

Ingredients

1 whole egg, beaten
¼ cup chocolate chips
2 tbsp white sugar
⅓ cup flour

2 tbsp safflower oil
1 tsp vanilla
¼ cup cocoa powder

Directions

Preheat the Air fryer to 320 F and in a bowl, mix the beaten egg, sugar, oil, and vanilla. In another bowl, mix cocoa powder and flour. Add the flour mixture to the vanilla mixture and stir until fully incorporated.

Prepare a baking form for your Air fryer and pour the mixture into the form; sprinkle chocolate chips on top. Add the baking form in the cooking basket and cook for 20 minutes. Cut into squares and chill to serve.

Authentic Raisin Apple Treat

Ready in about: 15 minutes | Serves: 4

Ingredients

4 apples, cored
1 ½ oz almonds

¾ oz raisins
2 tbsp sugar

Directions

Preheat the Air fryer to 360 F and in a bowl, mix sugar, almonds, raisins. Blend the mixture using a hand mixer. Fill cored apples with the almond mixture. Place the prepared apples in your Air Fryer's cooking basket and cook for 10 minutes. Serve with a sprinkle of powdered sugar.

Honey Banana Pastry with Berries

Ready in about: 15 minutes | Serves: 2

Ingredients

3 bananas, sliced
3 tbsp honey

2 puff pastry sheets, cut into thin strips
Fresh berries to serve

Directions

Preheat your Air fryer up to 340 F and place the banana slices into the cooking basket. Cover with the pastry strips and top with honey. Cook for 10 minutes. Serve with fresh berries.

Quick Coffee Cake

Ready in about: 30 minutes | Serves: 2

Ingredients

¼ cup butter
½ tsp instant coffee
1 tbsp black coffee, brewed
1 egg
¼ cup sugar

¼ cup flour
1 tsp cocoa powder
A pinch of salt
Powdered sugar, for icing

Directions

Preheat the Air fryer to 330 F and grease a small ring cake pan. Beat the sugar and egg together in a bowl. Beat in cocoa, instant and black coffee; stir in salt and flour. Transfer the batter to the prepared pan. Cook for 15 minutes.

Gluten-Free Fried Bananas

Ready in about: 15 minutes | Serves: 8

Ingredients

8 bananas
3 tbsp vegetable oil
3 tbsp corn flour

1 egg white
¾ cup breadcrumbs

Directions

Preheat the Air fryer to 350 F, and combine the oil and breadcrumbs, in a small bowl. Coat the bananas with the corn flour first, brush them with egg white, and dip them in the breadcrumb mixture. Arrange on a lined baking sheet and cook for 8 minutes.

Baked Pears with Almonds

Ready in about: 35 minutes | Serves: 2

Ingredients

2 pears, cored, bottom intact
2 tbsp butter, cold

2 tbsp honey
3 tbsp crushed almonds

Directions

In a bowl, mix butter, honey, and almonds. Arrange the pears in the Air fryer. Stuff them with the filling mixture. Cook for 30 minutes at 390 F.

Made in the USA
Columbia, SC
22 December 2019